FAITH

HOPE

& JOBS

The Catholic Church and the Nation-State: Comparative Perspectives
Paul Christopher Manuel, Lawrence C. Reardon, and Clyde Wilcox, Editors

The Christian Right in American Politics: Marching to the Millennium
John C. Green, Mark J. Rozell, and Clyde Wilcox, Editors

Faith, Hope, and Jobs: Welfare-to-Work in Los Angeles
Stephen V. Monsma and J. Christopher Soper

Of Little Faith: The Politics of George W. Bush's Faith-Based Initiatives
Amy E. Black, Douglas L. Koopman, and David K. Ryden

School Board Battles: The Christian Right in Local Politics
Melissa M. Deckman

Uncompromising Positions: God, Sex, and the U.S. House of Representatives
Elizabeth Anne Oldmixon

The Values Campaign? The Christian Right and the 2004 Elections
John C. Green, Mark J. Rozell, and Clyde Wilcox, Editors

FAITH
HOPE
& JOBS

WELFARE-TO-WORK IN LOS ANGELES

STEPHEN V. MONSMA

J. CHRISTOPHER SOPER

Georgetown University Press
Washington, DC

As of January 1, 2007, 13-digit ISBN numbers will replace
the current 10-digit system.
Paperback: 978-1-58901-110-6
Cloth: 978-1-58901-111-3
Georgetown University Press, Washington, D.C.

Library of Congress Cataloging-in-Publication Data
Monsma, Stephen V., 1936–
Faith, hope, and jobs : welfare-to-work in Los Angeles /
Stephen V. Monsma and J. Christopher Soper.
    p. cm. — (Religion and politics series)
Includes bibliographical references and index.
ISBN 1-58901-111-2 (hardcover : alk. paper) —
    ISBN 1-58901-110-4 (pbk. : alk. paper)
1. Welfare recipients—Employment—California—Los Angeles. 2. Public welfare—
Contracting out—California—Los Angeles. 3. Social service—Contracting out—
California—Los Angeles. 4. Public-private sector cooperation—California—
Los Angeles. 5. Church charities—California—Los Angeles. 6. Evaluation research
(Social action programs)—California—Los Angeles. I. Soper, J. Christopher.
II. Title. III. Series: Religion and politics series (Georgetown University)
HV99.L7M66 2006
362.5'840979494—dc22
2006003023

Printed in the United States of America

13 12 11 10 09 08 07 06   9 8 7 6 5 4 3 2
First printing

CONTENTS

List of Illustrations   *vii*
Acknowledgments   *xi*

Introduction   *1*

1   THE EFFECTIVENESS MUDDLE   *7*
Defining Effectiveness   *13*
Clashing Effectiveness Arguments   *18*
The Findings of Previous Research   *21*

2   THE STUDY   *38*
The Five Stages of the Research   *39*
The Seventeen Programs   *48*
The Study Respondents   *55*

3   CLIENT EVALUATIONS OF THEIR PROGRAMS   *67*
Staff Empathy   *69*
Instrumental Evaluations   *76*
Evaluations of Religious Elements in Faith-Based Programs   *80*
Observations   *86*

4   ENABLING OUTCOMES   *93*
Increased Hope and Optimism   *94*
Program Completion   *102*
Social Capital   *107*
Observations   *125*

5   INTERMEDIATE AND ULTIMATE OUTCOMES   *127*
Full- and Part-Time Employment   *128*
Wage Levels   *142*
Economic Self-Sufficiency   *149*
Summary and Observations   *156*

6 OBSERVATIONS AND RECOMMENDATIONS   *164*
Summary Conclusions   *165*
Public Policy Recommendations   *171*
Recommendations for Program Managers   *182*
Recommendations for Researchers   *185*

Appendix A: The Questionnaire Survey   *189*

Appendix B: The Survey Instruments   *193*

Appendix C: The Faith-Based/Segmented versus
Faith-Based/Integrated Distinction   *209*

Notes   *211*

Index   *221*

ILLUSTRATIONS

Tables

2.1 Median Number of Part-Time Employees and Volunteers, by Program Type   44

2.2 Distribution of Completed Interviews at Baseline, Six Months, and Twelve Months, by Program Type   46

2.3 Respondents at Six and Twelve Months, as a Percentage of Baseline Respondents, by Program Type   47

2.4 Key Characteristics of Baseline, Six-Month, and Twelve-Month Respondents   47

2.5 Key Demographic Characteristics, by Program Type, Six-Month Respondents   58

2.6 Religious Involvement at Baseline, by Organization Type, Six-Month Respondents   59

2.7 Percentage of Respondents with Less Than a High School Education, by Program Type, Six-Month Respondents   60

2.8 Total Skills Measure at Baseline, by Program Type, Six-Month Respondents   61

2.9 Life-Situation Barriers at Baseline, by Program Type   63

2.10 Level of Attitudinal Optimism at Baseline, by Program Type, Six-Month Respondents   65

3.1 Perceived Staff Empathy at Six Months, by Program Type   71

3.2 Perceived Staff Empathy, by Religious Involvement and Program Type   73

3.3 Perceived Staff Empathy, by Race and Program Type   74

3.4 Instrumental Evaluations at Six Months, by Program Type   77

3.5 Instrumental Evaluations, by Religious Involvement and Program Type   79

3.6 If the Faith-Based Nature of Their Program Made Respondents More or Less Eager to Participate in It *81*

3.7 Religious Aspects of Faith-Based Programs Recalled by Respondents *82*

3.8 Respondents' Evaluations of the Religious Aspects of Their Program *83*

3.9 Percentage of Respondents Giving the Most Positive Evaluation of the Religious Aspects of Their Program *85*

3.10 Classification of Positive Comments in Response to Two Open-Ended Questions *88*

3.11 Classification of Negative Comments in Response to Three Open-Ended Questions *89*

4.1 Percentage of Respondents Whose Attitudes Were More or Less Optimistic at Six and at Twelve Months Compared with Attitudes at the Baseline, by Program Type *96*

4.2 Percentage of Clients with More Optimistic Attitudes Minus the Percentage of Clients with Less Optimistic Attitudes, Compared with the Baseline, at Six and at Twelve Months, by Program Type *97*

4.3 Optimism at Baseline, by Religious Involvement, Six-Month Respondents *98*

4.4 Changes in Optimism, Baseline to Twelve Months, by Level of Religious Involvement *99*

4.5 Percentage of Respondents More Optimistic, Baseline to Twelve Months, by Religious Involvement and Program Type *100*

4.6 Percentage of Respondents More Optimistic, Baseline to Twelve Months, by Race or Ethnicity and Program Type *101*

4.7 Percentage of Respondents Who Failed to Complete Their Programs, by Program Type *103*

4.8 Percentage of Respondents Who Failed to Complete Their Programs, by Level of Religious Involvement *104*

4.9 Percentage of Respondents Failing to Complete Their Program, by Baseline Religious Involvement and Program Type *105*

4.10 Percentage of Respondents Failing to Complete Their Programs, by Race or Ethnicity and Program Type *106*

4.11   Respondent Contacts with Staff since Leaving Program, by Program Type   *109*

4.12   Perceived Helpfulness of Contacts with Program Staff after Leaving Program, at Six and at Twelve Months, by Program Type   *111*

4.13   Percentage of Respondents Reporting Many or a Few Contacts with Program Staff at Six and at Twelve Months, by Religious Involvement and Program Type   *112*

4.14   Respondent Contacts with Fellow Participants since Leaving Program, by Program Type   *116*

4.15   Respondent Contacts with Fellow Participants, by Level of Religious Involvement and Program Type   *118*

4.16   Church Attendance at Baseline and at Twelve Months, by Program Type, Twelve-Month Respondents   *121*

4.17   Changes in Religious Involvement, by Program Type, Twelve-Month Respondents   *122*

5.1   Employment at Baseline and at Six Months, by Program Type   *130*

5.2   Employment at Baseline and at Twelve Months, by Program Type   *131*

5.3   Determinants of Either Full- or Part-Time Employment at Six and at Twelve Months   *135*

5.4   Determinants of Full-Time Employment at Six and at Twelve Months   *137*

5.5   Percentages of Respondents Who Were Employed at Six or Twelve Months, by Program Type and Religious Involvement   *138*

5.6   Percentages of Respondents Who Were Employed at Six or Twelve Months, by Program Type and Race/Ethnicity   *142*

5.7   Hourly Wages of Employed Respondents, by Program Type   *144*

5.8   Net Changes in Wages at Six and at Twelve Months Compared to Baseline Wages, by Program Type   *146*

5.9   Hourly Wages of Employed Respondents, by Program Type (only those respondents who were employed at the baseline)   *148*

5.10   Percentage of Respondents at Twelve Months Earning Ten Dollars or More an Hour, by Program Type and Race/Ethnicity   *149*

5.11 Percentage of Respondents Receiving TANF at Six and at Twelve Months, by Program Type and Whether or Not Receiving TANF at Baseline *151*

5.12 Determinants of TANF Status at Six and at Twelve Months *155*

5.13 The TANF and Economically Self-Supporting Status of Respondents Who Had Been Receiving TANF at the Baseline, and at Twelve Months, by Religious Involvement *156*

5.14 The TANF and Economically Self-Supporting Status of Respondents Who Had Been Receiving TANF at the Baseline, and at Twelve Months, by Race/Ethnicity *157*

5.15 Summary Assessments of Employment, Wage, and Welfare Outcomes, by Program Type *158*

6.1 Summary Assessments of Respondent Evaluations and Enabling Outcomes, by Program Type *166*

6.2 Summary Assessments of Respondents' Personal Religious Involvement and Race/Ethnicity as They Relate to Program Outcomes *172*

Figures

1.1 Research Examining the Relationship between Religion and Health Outcomes *24*

1.2 Research Examining the Relationship between Religion and Well-Being Outcomes *25*

2.1 Comparison of the Number of Programs and the Number of Full-Time Employees, by Program Type *43*

2.2 Demographic Characteristics of CalWORKS Population and Six-Month Respondents *57*

ACKNOWLEDGMENTS

Studies that are based on field research carry with them many advantages. But they also result in a huge debt of gratitude. First and foremost we wish to thank the many hundreds of participants in the welfare-to-work programs we studied. Without their willingness to answer what must have seemed like countless questions, and to do so on three separate occasions, we could not have even begun, much less completed, this study successfully. Also indispensable were the staff members of the welfare-to-work programs who took the time to fill out our written questionnaire, meet with us, answer our many questions, and welcome us to observe their programs.

We also wish to thank the John Randolph Haynes and Dora Haynes Foundation of Los Angeles for its generous financial support. This study would not have been possible without its assistance. The willingness of its directors to support serious, academic social science research in the Los Angeles area is a major contribution to both Los Angeles and the cause of increasing our knowledge and understanding of complex social phenomena. We also wish to acknowledge and thank both the Smith Richardson Foundation and our home institution, Pepperdine University, for their financial support.

We also wish to acknowledge publicly the splendid work of our associate researcher, Carolyn M. Mounts. She was involved at almost every stage of this project, from playing the major role in the daunting task of assembling the original list of all welfare-to-work programs in the Los Angeles area, to visiting many of the welfare-to-work programs we selected for intensive study, to obtaining the baseline questionnaires from hundreds of clients, to reading the manuscript for this book and making many useful suggestions for its improvement.

A major part of the success of this study is due to the excellent work done by ORC Macro in completing the six-month and twelve-month telephone interviews of the respondents who had completed the baseline questionnaire. We warmly thank its lead person, Leslyn Hall, and its corps of telephone interviewers, who diligently persisted in finding the respondents and used tact and skill in completing the interviews.

We also wish to thank Richard Brown and others at Georgetown University Press for their editorial skill and their exemplary work in producing this book, and also the two anonymous reviewers for their very useful suggestions for revision.

Finally, we wish to thank Pepperdine University and its administration for their encouragement and their flexibility in freeing up time for us to work on this study. In addition, Monsma wishes to thank the Henry Institute for the Study of Christianity and Politics at Calvin College for giving him a place in which he could continue to work on this project once he had retired from Pepperdine University in 2004.

We close with the customary, yet nonetheless sincere, disclaimer: Any errors, omissions, or inappropriate interpretations that may be in this book should be attributed to the authors, not to any of those previously mentioned who helped us along the way.

INTRODUCTION

One of the leading issues on the public policy agenda today is the increasing use of partnerships between government and nongovernmental entities—from houses of worship to for-profit firms; from long-established, secular nonprofits to small, newly created faith-based, nonprofit organizations.

Martha Minow has rightly observed, "Religious, secular nonprofit, and for-profit players operate in each of these [public policy] fields, and government contracts with them."[1] She noted that in the educational field there is a push for vouchers that parents can redeem at secular or religious schools and that schools run by for-profit companies are a viable option in some localities. Similarly, in the criminal justice area, for-profit prisons are cropping up and faith-based groups are actively involved in providing prison programs, halfway houses, and other prison-release support programs. In the health care area, public hospitals are being privatized, and secular nonprofit, religiously based, and for-profit hospitals and nursing homes are all part of the health care mix. In the social welfare field—the field with which we are concerned in this book—there is a long tradition stretching back to colonial days of government working in partnership with nongovernmental entities to provide needed social services.[2] Today large for-profit corporations such as Lockheed Martin IMS and Maximus are providing a variety of social welfare services in many states and communities. As one scholar has reported: "In virtually every area of social welfare policy, the United States is considering, or experimenting with, public–private partnerships to deliver services."[3]

The passage of the 1996 Personal Responsibility and Work Opportunity Reconciliation Act (PRWORA, or simply Welfare Reform) increased the attention being paid to faith-based organizations working in partnership with government to meet the needs of those seeking to move from welfare dependence to economic self-sufficiency. It included a provision that has come to be called charitable choice, which requires states that contract out welfare-related services to allow faith-based organizations (including houses of worship) to compete for those contracts

1

on an equal basis with secular organizations, protects certain religious autonomy rights of the religious groups that receive government money, and aims to preserve the religious freedom rights of the recipients of services from faith-based providers.[4] Between 1997 and 2000 similar language was included in three additional pieces of legislation.[5]

With the presidency of George W. Bush, the emphasis on the use of faith-based and other local community groups to provide essential social services received a huge boost. He created a White House Office of Faith-Based and Community Initiatives and parallel offices in eleven executive departments. He rarely misses an opportunity to promote the "armies of compassion," as he terms them, as a keystone in his philosophy of compassionate conservatism. During his first term of office he gave more than forty speeches explicitly centered on his faith-based initiative.[6] When legislation incorporating key goals of his faith-based initiative foundered in Congress, one group of scholars reported that "President [Bush] has used executive orders, rule changes, managerial realignment in federal agencies, and other prerogatives of his office to aggressively implement the Initiative."[7] A March 2006 report released by the White House Office of Faith-Based and Community Initiatives reported that in fiscal year 2005, 11 percent of almost 20 billion dollars in competitive funding by seven federal agencies went to faith-based organizations.[8] This included 24 percent of 2 billion dollars in Housing and Urban Development (HUD) funding and 7 percent of more than 10 billion dollars of Health and Human Services (HHS) funding. It also reported that the number of grants to faith-based organizations increased by 22 percent from fiscal year 2004 to fiscal year 2005.

This is not, however, merely a Republican or George W. Bush initiative. Democratic president Bill Clinton signed into law four separate pieces of legislation containing charitable choice provisions. And in his 2000 campaign Al Gore declared, "Today I give you this pledge: if you elect me your President the voices of faith-based organizations will be integral to the policies set forth in my Administration."[9] In 2004 John Kerry declared in a campaign appearance, "I know there are some who say that the First Amendment means faith-based organizations can't help government. I think they are wrong. I want to offer support for your efforts, including financial support."[10]

One of the forces driving this movement toward public–private partnerships is the assumption that faith-based, for-profit, and perhaps other nongovernmental entities provide needed social services more efficiently and more effectively than do large government bureaucracies. Claims to this effect are often made. Jim Towey, former head of the Bush administration's Office of Faith-Based and Community Initiatives, cited the following example in a 2002 speech:

> I went to the Bowery Mission in New York City, a homeless shelter that has been on the Lower East Side for 122 years. It has lots of caring volunteers, lots of community connections. The work they do is impressive. Under its nine-month program the recidivism rate is 7 percent. The City of New York has 12,000 shelter beds; some of the city-run shelters are over a thousand beds each. Think about the quality of life in those kind of facilities. They look like little more than prisons. And the recidivism rate back into the shelter system is 90 percent.[11]

The story of the Ten Point Coalition in Boston has often been told. It consists of a group of forty churches that were brought together in 1992 by the Reverends Jeffrey Brown, Ray Hammond, and Eugene Rivers, after the murder rate among young African American men seemed to be spiraling out of control.[12] The coalition brought together the resources of the churches and the Boston police department. The Boston homicide rate dropped by an astounding 80 percent.

In spite of anecdotal faith-based success stories and several case studies that demonstrate considerable success of faith-based efforts, an examination of the field of comparative studies of program effectiveness very quickly reveals the lack of careful, empirical studies. Scholar after scholar has had to acknowledge that what is known about the comparative success of faith-based versus other types of social service programs is very, very thin. Byron Johnson, for example, reported, "Our extensive search of the literature yielded only 25 studies that assessed in some manner the efficacy of faith-based interventions."[13] Johnson also reports that he contacted "the largest and most recognized" faith-based organizations to inquire about any research they or others had conducted on their effectiveness, and found that

> the Salvation Army, Lutheran Services in America (LSA), Catholic Charities, Association of Gospel Rescue Missions, Habitat for Humanity, and United Jewish Communities identified no subsequent research documenting the

extent of the effectiveness of their respective programs. After contacting these organizations, it was disheartening to learn that both the Salvation Army, which received $275 million in government contracts in year 2000, and LSA, which received between $2 billion and $3 billion last year from government, produced no quantitative findings on program effectiveness by which the public might hold them accountable.[14]

Two other scholars made a similar point and added the important observation that the belief that religious providers are more effective than their secular counterparts "is a belief that has never been tested—indeed, there is comparatively little research on the efficacy of social welfare programs in general."[15] The lack of research on the effectiveness of faith-based social service programs is only part of a larger lack of research on the comparative effectiveness of different types of social service programs, whether government run, for-profit, secular nonprofit, or religious nonprofit in nature. After reviewing the record of for-profit firms in the social services area, Mark Carl Rom concluded, "There is, still, little research explicitly comparing the effectiveness of public versus private welfare services delivery."[16] Similarly, referring to the nonprofit sector generally, two researchers concluded, "Very little research has directly addressed questions of organizational effectiveness in the nonprofit arena."[17]

This book is an attempt to begin filling that research gap. It presents a study of the effectiveness of seventeen welfare-to-work programs in Los Angeles County, grouped into five categories for comparative purposes. Government, for-profit, nonprofit, and two types of faith-based programs are included. Our goal was to throw additional light on the question many are asking of whether faith-based social service programs have better outcomes than does government or any other category of program. Similarly, we sought to explore the same question for for-profit programs, which some have put forward as being especially cost-effective, but which have been especially controversial in the welfare field in Los Angeles County. We believe, however, that if our study only sought answers to the very basic question of which category of program as a whole is more or less effective, it would be woefully incomplete. Our experience as social science researchers indicates that we would be very unlikely to find that a certain type of program—whether faith based, government run, for-profit, or nonprofit—is generally effective or ineffective across the board. In the social science field at least, the real world is rarely that simple and unidimensional. One is much more likely to find that individual programs within an overall category vary in effectiveness and that some programs or categories of programs are especially effective in providing certain services or in working with certain types of clients, and ineffective in providing other services or in working with other types of clients.

Thus our motivation in exploring the issue of the comparative effectiveness of different types of welfare-to-work programs in Los Angeles was to cast further light on three basic questions. Our first question was whether or not certain types of welfare-to-work programs seem to provide selected types of services in a particularly effective manner. From the beginning of our study we believed it highly unlikely that any one category of program would do everything poorly and other categories would do everything well. Common sense and experience indicated that it was more likely that some programs and some categories of programs would do some things well and others not as well. For effective public policy it is important to find out what programs do what well or poorly. Our second basic question was whether or not certain types of welfare-to-work programs seem to provide services to selected types of clients in a particularly effective manner. Some might do better with clients facing multiple barriers to finding employment, while others would do better with those who face only one or two challenges. Some might do better with clients of a certain ethnic or racial background. Some might do better with deeply religious clients, while others might do better with those who are less religious. In the complex world of human services, with a wide range of clients facing a wide range of needs, it would be surprising if one type of program would be best for all types of clients.

Finally, we hope to give added insight to the issue of the difficulties and possibilities of effectiveness research. There is a reason for the dearth of research on the effectiveness of different types of programs; namely, it is extremely difficult research to conduct and is marked by a host of pitfalls. We discuss these challenges in detail in the next chapter. We are convinced, however, that just as it is hard to learn how to dive without ever diving into a swimming pool, so it is hard to learn how to do comparative effectiveness research without performing the research—with the best theories, concepts, and tools that one at that time can muster to the cause. We believe the only way the social science and public policy research communities will learn how to engage in comparative effectiveness research is by diving in and doing it, learning from our mistakes, improving our research measures, and developing our theories and concepts. We hope that this book and the research reported here will be a part of such an effort.

1

THE EFFECTIVENESS MUDDLE

Almost every study of the effectiveness of nonprofit organizations, whether secular or faith based in nature, begins with a statement concerning the difficulty of doing good effectiveness research. The opening words of a thoughtful article by Daniel Forbes are typical: "Organizational effectiveness is both a powerful and problematic concept. It is powerful in the sense that it represents a useful tool for critically evaluating and enhancing the work of organizations; it is problematic in the sense that it can mean different things to different people and there exist many alternative ways of measuring organizational effectiveness."[1] Even more succinctly, Robert Wuthnow and his colleagues have written that "the question of service agency effectiveness is more complicated than is sometimes recognized."[2] Indeed it is. In this chapter we outline four particularly troublesome features of comparative effectiveness research and conclude by stating why we nevertheless think it is important to engage in and report on the research presented in this book.

Effectiveness research is a challenge, first, because *effectiveness can be defined in a host of ways.* There is no one obvious, agreed upon definition of effectiveness. We devote the next section of this chapter to a discussion of the concept of effectiveness and how we have operationalized it for this study. Here it is only important to note that effectiveness is a multidimensional concept and thus that there are multiple ways of viewing effectiveness.[3] It can be defined in terms of outputs, that is, in terms of the products produced or activities engaged in by an organization. Or it can be defined in terms of outcomes, that is, hoped for or desired results. Others have defined effectiveness by the extent to which an organization achieves the goals it has set for itself; yet others emphasize the goals or expectations that society as a whole has for the organization. Overlaid on these and other conceptualizations of effectiveness is the concept of cost-benefit analysis. Here one takes into account the monetary costs it takes to produce each unit of results. This gets one close to the concept of efficiency, a close cousin of effectiveness. In brief, the first challenge facing persons engaging in effectiveness research is to be clear on the meaning they are attaching to effectiveness.

The next challenge is determining *how to measure effectiveness*, however one has defined it. This too presents many challenges. Official data, whether gathered by the government or by nonprofit or other organizations, may be incomplete, inaccurate, and selective. Or it simply may not be in a form that will answer the questions the researcher has posed. Interviewing clients of the services being studied has many decided advantages, but it poses the problem of what to do about persons who may be hard to reach or who refuse to be interviewed. Those who are making use of social services may move about often and may be suspicious of official-sounding contacts. Even when they can be interviewed, how much credence should be attached to their evaluations of the services they have received? Some believe they are likely to be in a poor position to judge the effectiveness of the services they have received; others believe they, as recipients or consumers of the services, are in the best possible position to judge the effectiveness of what is being delivered. Interviewing the administration and staff of the organization whose effectiveness one is seeking to determine has advantages but also disadvantages. There is always the very human tendency to make oneself and one's organization look good. Another basic methodological question is whether one should look at the results only for clients who have completed the social services program under study, or also for those who dropped out of the program before completing it. If researchers only look at persons who have completed a program, they might be considering only persons with the initiative and perseverance to succeed even without the program. If, alternatively, they include persons who dropped out of a particular program without completing it, they may be unfairly biasing the results by including in a study of program results persons who never went through the full program.

In short, the potential problems and challenges in gathering data are legion. All researchers experience this, but in measuring data related to the effectiveness of social service agencies the problems seem to be especially formidable. An added danger is, as Paul DiMaggio has written, that "readily measurable indicators will tend to drive out less easily measurable ones."[4] Especially in the social services field, where many important outcomes may consist of intangible attitudes or skills, there is the very real danger that researchers will measure the easily measurable, not what is necessarily the most important. When this is done, premature conclusions may be reached concerning the effectiveness or ineffectiveness of a particular agency or type of agency.

A third, and perhaps the most difficult challenge of all, is taking into account the fact that *the programs one is seeking to compare may have different types of clients to begin with.* One of the seventeen programs that is included in the study reported here is a faith-based program created specifically—quoting from a handout describing the program—for "hard to place welfare recipients of Los Angeles, ex-offenders or individuals who have exhausted, or are approaching their time limits for receiving case assistance. . . . In addition, ——— participants also may include those who have characteristics associated with long-term welfare dependence such as school drop-out, teenage pregnancy, poor work history or other significant barriers to self-sufficiency."[5] To compare the outcomes of such a program with those of one primarily working with persons who are high school graduates, have no history of drug abuse and no criminal record, and are only recently on welfare would clearly be comparing dissimilar programs. The latter could have higher overall success rates than the one working with welfare recipients that face many barriers, but in terms of making an actual difference in the lives of persons, it might have less of an impact and thus might be less effective than the one working with more challenging clients.

It is, however, very difficult to overcome this challenge. One potential way to surmount it is to randomly assign clients to the various programs. Two researchers have written, "The ideal study design would involve randomly assigning individuals into training programs and observing their outcomes over an extended period of time post training."[6] In this way one could be assured that no program or type of program is starting out with a predominance of clients either especially easy or especially challenging to work with.

There are, however, both practical and theoretical problems in using random assignment as a means to control for different programs having different types of client with which to work. Practically, it is usually impossible to engage in random assignment of clients to different program types. This is especially true when it comes to faith-based programs, because persons under charitable choice, and presumably under the First Amendment, may not be required to take part in a faith-based program if they would prefer a secular alternative. There is the added practical problem that, even if random assignment could be followed, the clients would soon figure out what sort of a program they are in, and this knowledge could affect the outcomes. Government and for-profit programs, for example, might carry a negative stigma in some persons' minds, and that in itself might reduce the chances of those persons experiencing a positive outcome. An effectiveness researcher faces a much more difficult situation than does a drug company doing a double-blind study in order to test the effectiveness of a new drug.

There are also theoretical problems in the random assignment model. It has a hidden assumption; namely, that different types of pro-grams are or should be equally effective with all types of persons. It is a one-size-fits-all assumption. This needs to be challenged. In terms of assignment to a faith-based versus a secular program, think of two persons, one for whom religion has played an important part in her life since childhood and one who is very antagonistic toward religion. The former is still actively involved in a church and thinks of herself as a child of a loving God. The latter has bad memories of a harsh, condemn-ing religion, has no use for religion in any form, and has sworn never to darken the doors of a church again. It takes no great insight to real-ize that a deeply faith-oriented drug treatment program, for example, is much more likely to achieve positive results with the first person than the second and that a thoroughly secular program is more likely to achieve positive results with the second person than the first. To take another example, randomly assigning Latino clients to two different so-cial service programs, one of which is staffed predominantly by Latinos and one of which is staffed predominantly by "Anglos," just assumes that the ethnic or racial makeup of a program's staff is irrelevant. This flies in the face of common sense.

In brief, factors such as the neighborhood in which a program is located, the ethnic or racial makeup of a program's staff, the religious or secular nature of a program, and past acquaintance with a program and its staff may affect the outcomes experienced by the persons taking part in it. Yet those who call for research studies to involve the random assignment of persons to programs implicitly seem to assume that any program should be equally effective with any person. In the social sci-ences, when dealing with drug treatment, employment and training, ex-offender reentry, literacy, and other highly personal programs that involve counseling and a building of relationships between staff and client, one would create an artificial situation by practicing random assignment, even when legally it could be done.

There are two ways to deal with the problem of nonrandom assignment of persons to different programs that one wishes to compare. One way is to come up with a list of key, relevant characteristics, find out how many of the persons in the programs one is comparing possess each of those characteristics, and then statistically control for those characteristics. Then one is comparing program outcomes among groups of persons who share the same key characteristics. But this is not a foolproof solution. It depends, of course, on the researcher's knowing ahead of time what the key characteristics that are relevant to the success or failure of persons in the programs being compared are. It is easy to miss key characteristics. This approach needs to have many clients included in one's study in order to have sufficiently large numbers of persons in the various subcategories in order to conduct the statistical tests with any degree of confidence in the results. For example, if one is comparing recidivism rates among ex-offenders who have gone through three different types of reentry programs to the recidivism rate of ex-offenders who have gone through no reentry program, one might want to break down the information on the persons in the four different categories by race, age, nature of their original offense, educational level, and previous incarceration record. One thus might want to compare African Americans in the different programs who possess a high school education, are under twenty-five years of age, had a nonviolent offense, and had no previous record of incarceration. Unless one begins with thousands of ex-offenders—which may not be practicable—one soon ends up comparing ten persons in one program with fifteen in another. With such small numbers one is very unlikely to generate statistically significant results. But if one avoids this problem by combining many of the categories we used in our example, one is ignoring what intuitively one feels are important variables that could affect the outcomes of the different types of programs.

A second, similar approach is to create a matched group of persons who share key characteristics with the persons who went through the programs one is comparing, but did not take part in any of the programs. Then one can use this matched group as a baseline against which one compares the outcomes of the several programs. But again one is faced with the problem of determining what the key characteristics are. As one group of scholars has noted, "Identifying valid comparison groups can be tricky. . . . The comparison group's members need to be sufficiently similar to the clients in order to ensure a valid comparison."[7]

These are perennial problems when seeking to determine cause and effect. The fundamental, yet difficult-to-answer question is what is causing what result? Martha Greenway summarized the problem well when she wrote, "The ultimate purpose of the nonprofit human service sector is to improve the condition of people. But people are affected by an infinite array of experiences, opportunities, organizations, and other people. Even the synergistic effect of these combinations of factors change as individuals move through time and across geographic boundaries. To specifically identify the contribution of any particular organization, or sector of organizations, toward measurable improvement in the lives of individuals is tricky business indeed."[8]

A fourth challenge that is faced by persons researching the comparative effectiveness of different types of social service programs is *the lack of guiding theory*. As Paul DiMaggio has noted, "In order to make any confident statements about the effectiveness of an organization or set of organizations, we need what social scientists call a 'causal model.'"[9] Such a model, or theory of causal relationships, is helpful—perhaps even essential—in guiding research, framing the questions for which research seeks answers, and generating hypotheses to be tested. Yet there has been very little systematic theoretical thinking about the comparative effectiveness of different types of human service programs. In the absence of systematic theoretical thinking, researchers are left to fall back on their commonsense hunches, speculations, and all too often, their unconsciously held biases.

In light of these formidable challenges to researching the comparative effectiveness of different types of social service programs, why have we plunged into the task of comparing the effectiveness of government, nonprofit, for-profit, and faith-based welfare-to-work programs in Los Angeles County? Perhaps we should plead temporary insanity! However, we believe there is another defense: that in research, as in many worthwhile but difficult endeavors, it is important to do what one can with what resources and abilities one has available, even while wishing one could do a more complete job. We believe it is important to begin the process of researching different types of welfare-to-work and other social service programs, because it is in doing so that one can first frame the research questions that need to be addressed. Asking the right questions is often the most important and most difficult part of research. One can begin the research by reading and contemplation, but at some point one needs to go out into the field and apply the best insights and concepts—the best framing of the questions—that one can at that time. Often it is only in doing so that one can learn what questions have been properly framed, what questions need reframing, and what questions were missed completely. We also believe that as the arduous task of collecting data is begun additional insights and hypotheses for further testing will be revealed. Some questions may even be tentatively answered.

This study of necessity is exploratory, not definitive, in nature. But exploratory studies have their purposes. They test the waters, find out which research methods do and do not work, generate hypotheses, and suggest some tentative answers to key questions. These are the goals of the study we report here. Before moving into the study itself, however, we need to define more precisely the concept of effectiveness as we use it in this study, explore what theoretical insights are available, and consider those few empirical studies of comparative program effectiveness that exist.

Defining Effectiveness

As noted earlier, in this book we report on a study of the comparative effectiveness of seventeen Los Angeles welfare-to-work programs, grouped into five categories: government, for-profit, nonprofit/secular, and faith-based, with the faith-based programs further divided into those that explicitly integrate religious elements into their programming (faith-based/integrated) and those that do not (faith-based/segmented). Our first task is to define effectiveness, which, as previously noted, is multidimensional in nature and subject to a wide variety of conceptualizations. In this section we initially eliminate two concepts of effectiveness with which we do not deal in this study and then move ahead to present our conceptualization of effectiveness.

First, we need to distinguish between agency or organizational effectiveness and program effectiveness. It is the latter with which this study is concerned. Most of the seventeen welfare-to-work programs in our study were run by organizations that also ran some other and often many other programs. Two of the government-run programs, for example, were run by community colleges, and one of the faith-based programs was run by a community development corporation that managed many other projects. In such cases we focused on the effectiveness of the welfare-to-work programs, not the overall effectiveness of the community colleges or the community development corporation. Also, we did not attempt to conceive of effectiveness in relationship to the costs of the various programs. We did not engage in a cost-benefit analysis—or the related study of the efficiency—of the individual programs of the five types of programs. Such an exercise no doubt would have been interesting and helpful, but we did not do so in order to establish some boundaries for the study. Finding out the exact expenditures of a certain program, as distinguished from other activities and programs of an entity, is in many cases a challenging accounting exercise, and one we did not have the resources to engage in.

After making these two exclusions, we were still far from having a practical, working conceptualization of effectiveness. To move in that direction it is helpful to distinguish between outputs and outcomes of a program.[10] Outputs consist of the various products or activities of a program—such as the number of clients served, classes held, and referrals made. Outcomes, on the other hand, consist of the results of the outputs. A study of outcomes seeks to answer the question of the success of a program in achieving certain program goals or objectives. One group of researchers has defined outcomes simply as "the consequences or results achieved."[11] Martha Greenway defines outcomes similarly: "Program outcomes are the results that accrue to participants in an individual program."[12] In this study we define effectiveness in terms of outcomes, not outputs.

Conceptualizing effectiveness in terms of program outcomes still leaves a wide, not fully specified field of study. Outcomes can take many different forms. As Greenway has also written, "There are an infinite number of possible outcome measures in human services, some of which are shorter term, others of which are longer term."[13] In our study of welfare-to-work program outcomes, we have divided the outcomes studied into three categories: ultimate, intermediate, and enabling. The ultimate outcome in the case of welfare-to-work programs is assisting persons who are economically dependent on government-sponsored welfare assistance to the point where they are employed, economically self-sufficient, and no longer in need of welfare assistance.

In the complex world of welfare-to-work, it would be a mistake to focus exclusively on this ultimate outcome, however. Doing so would ignore crucial intermediate and enabling outcomes. Intermediate outcomes can also be considered partial outcomes. They consist of movement, or steps, toward the ultimate outcome of economic self-sufficiency. It is rare for someone who is unemployed and barely surviving on welfare assistance suddenly to obtain a job of sufficient wage levels and with enough benefits that he or she is no longer in need of any cash assistance or supportive services. Normally a person will move from unemployment to either part-time employment or a minimum wage job with no benefits. He or she will still be in need of various supportive services, such as child care or transportation, and perhaps continued cash assistance. Then, hopefully, the part-time job will turn into a full-time job or the minimum wage job into a higher paying job. Benefits and wages adequate to fully support the person and his or her family may come even later. As is often said to persons enrolled in welfare-to-work programs: "Get a job, get a better job, get a career." Thus it is essential to include in welfare-to-work program outcomes intermediate outcomes that are markers on the way toward full economic self-sufficiency.

There are also enabling outcomes. These are outcomes that make it possible or more likely for a person to gain success in a particular field. In the welfare-to-work field, enabling outcomes can be essential for the intermediate and ultimate outcomes for which welfare recipients and society are looking. There are four types of enabling outcomes that are especially important for welfare-to-work clients to acquire: basic language and educational attainments, vocational skills, attitudinal and behavioral changes, and social capital. Taking each of these in turn, language and educational attainments include learning English for non-English speakers, improving reading and writing skills for those with literacy difficulties, and earning a high school equivalency certificate (GED). None of these are ultimate outcomes, nor are they even intermediate outcomes in the sense of their constituting partial economic success. But they are important markers toward a person's being able to "get a job, get a better job, get a career." A similar point can be made regarding vocational skills. As one learns computer keyboarding, truck driving, the basics of nursing care, or a host of other marketable skills, one is better situated to move ahead economically. They are thus enabling outcomes.

The third type of enabling outcome consists of attitudinal and behavioral changes. If persons on welfare have very low self-esteem and are discouraged to the point of despairing of ever being able to forge a better life, if they have had almost no positive, productively employed role models in their lives, or if they have not mastered appropriate workplace behavior, they are unlikely to feel able to go out into a highly competitive job market and succeed in moving themselves ahead. Thus welfare-to-work programs are achieving positive enabling outcomes when their clients master such behavioral traits as promptness and anger management, or when their clients achieve such attitudinal changes as increases in self-esteem, a sense of hope for the future, and positive attitudes toward work. Some argue that among enabling outcomes the attitudinal and behavioral changes are the most important and most difficult of all to achieve. One study in Memphis, for example, found that

> employers are seeking entry-level employees who are motivated, understand appropriate behaviors for the workplace, can balance their family responsibilities with workplace obligations, and are reliable and on time. The development of soft skills and competencies include communication, thinking and cognitive abilities, conflict resolution, anger management, interpersonal and teamwork skills, habits of punctuality and regular attendance, physical appearance and dress, and a strong work ethic. Such skills are often deemed more important than technical skills training, which can be provided on the job or at the place of employment.[14]

Closely related to enabling outcomes of an attitudinal character are social capital outcomes, the fourth and final type of enabling outcome. Robert Putnam has made a useful distinction between two types of social capital: bridging capital and bonding capital.[15] The latter consists of ties to family, ethnic, religious, or other in-groups of which one is a member. Bonding capital emphasizes exclusive ties that identify one as a member of an in-group, with the supports and expectations that go with being a member of the in-group. Bridging capital consists of ties to broader groups in the community. It reaches across divisions and groups in society and ties one into communities and groups other than one's own. Most persons have a reservoir of social capital of both types on which they can draw when in need: extended families, friends, business contacts, and more. Thus when child care arrangements fall through at the last minute, one usually has a friend, neighbor, or family member on whom one can call. When looking for work, one has potentially helpful contacts at church, among friends and neighbors, and former work associates. But many persons who are receiving welfare are socially isolated. They may be alienated or living long distances from family, have few friends or neighbors who have contacts that can help, and have no former work associates on whom to call. Their lives are bound up with their children and the daily struggles to survive. If a welfare-to-work program can weave a person into a network of persons who can offer help and support—material and emotional—one's social capital has been increased, and the program has achieved the enabling outcome of increasing social capital.

In short, programs' success, as defined as their clients' attaining a wide variety of skills, appropriate attitudes, and support systems, should be considered enabling outcomes. These are neither ultimate nor intermediate outcomes, but they are outcomes that will enable—or at the least will make more likely—the attainment of ultimate and intermediate outcomes. Thus they are markers along the way to ultimate and intermediate outcomes.

In summary, we conceptualize welfare-to-work programs' effectiveness in terms of their successful contribution to their clients' ultimate, intermediate, and enabling outcomes. Our study design does not allow us fully to assess the seventeen programs' contributions to all of these types of outcomes—and especially to all four types of enabling outcomes—but we present in this study at least some measures of all three types of outcomes. In doing so we self-consciously avoided the temptation to focus exclusively, or even primarily, on the ultimate outcome of clients' successfully transitioning to full-time employment at sufficient wages that they leave the welfare rolls. We did so for two reasons. One is that we are convinced welfare-to-work programs' effectiveness is conceptualized most accurately and realistically as being multidimensional in nature. The various types of outcomes discussed in this section are in fact all positive program outcomes. To focus on one or two and to ignore the others would be to distort reality. Also, accurately measuring any one outcome is a tricky business indeed, as more that one scholar has noted. We believe we have measured various outcomes as accurately as we can and more fully and accurately than earlier studies have, but this study remains an exploratory one. Until confirmed by other researchers in other settings, any one outcome measure must be treated as tentative in nature. This is another reason why we believe it is important for us to consider, weigh, and measure a variety of outcomes. We have more confidence in the accuracy of the various outcome measures taken together, and the overall picture they form, than we do in any one measure taken by itself.

Clashing Effectiveness Arguments

As noted earlier, very little theoretical thinking has been done in the area of constructing models of comparative program effectiveness, and thus there is little on which this section of the chapter can draw. However, many key arguments have been made for and against the effectiveness of the various types of human service programs, and of welfare-to-work programs in particular. We briefly consider these arguments here, as they underlie most of the questions we examine in this study. This of necessity will be an exploration in assumptions, biases, and projections rather than in systematically derived theoretical models. We have relied on news media reports, popular essays and books, and, to a much lesser degree, more scholarly essays and books. In deciding how to organize our study and what data to gather and report, we have been largely guided by the clashing arguments and assumptions we outline here. In this section we consider the cases that have been made for and against the effectiveness of government, for-profit, secular nonprofit, and faith-based human service programs.[16]

Government Human Service Programs

The case is more often made against than for government-run human service programs. The charge is that they are large, inflexible, impersonal, and uncaring. Civil service and other public sector rules and processes, as well as public labor unions with additional work rules and processes, create a situation in which it is hard to experiment with new approaches, shift quickly to meet changing needs, or eliminate unproductive employees. Also the claim is that recipients of government services are treated as mere numbers by professional bureaucrats who are more interested in quitting time—when they escape from an impoverished neighborhood to a more affluent area of the city—than they are in helping those in need. An earlier study by one of the authors of this volume indicates that this stereotypic view of government social service agencies may need some reworking in the welfare-to-work area. He found evidence that even government-run programs were generally staffed by persons who exhibited a genuine concern for and interest in the persons with whom they were working.[17] In this current study we found that none of the welfare-to-work programs in Los Angeles County were being provided directly by the large, bureaucratic Los Angeles County Department of Public Social Services but by a host of contractors. Thus the government welfare-to-work providers included in our study were entities such as local community colleges and the Los Angeles Unified School District, which operated out of neighborhood offices. The case can be made that even government human service programs may be run by caring persons out of neighborhood locations.

For-Profit Firms

The chief argument made in favor of the use of for-profit firms to provide human services is that the profit motive is a force constantly working to improve efficiency. Also, for-profit organizations are more flexible due to the absence of such factors as civil service rules and employee unions that, it is claimed, create inflexibility in government programs. Thus for-profit firms, so the argument goes, are freer to experiment with new ways of organizing the work flow and work assignments. They are also freer to hire and fire based on merit and to offer financial incentives to especially effective workers. Conversely, the case is made that for-profit firms are likely to put profits ahead of the welfare of the clients they are charged with helping. Every dollar they spend on client services is one dollar less in profits. These firms are pressured, so the argument goes, to minimize the services being provided in the push to increase profits. Also, many large companies, such as Lockheed Martin and Maximus, are active in providing welfare-to-work services. If government agencies are large and impersonal, there is no reason to believe large corporations such as these will be any less so. Alternatively, the same study conducted by one of the present authors cited earlier also showed that most for-profit welfare-to-work staff members cared deeply about their clients. In addition, the profit motive, it has been argued, is a good means to ensure that an organization will produce. If it does not run a successful, effective welfare-to-work program, it will lose its government contract and be out of business.

Secular Nonprofit Organizations

Nonprofit organizations, many have argued, possess the great advantages of being driven by altruistic concerns and having an ability to attract volunteers and private donations and to give personalized, caring services. They are freed from the bottom line and thus can focus first and foremost on the needs of the people whom they are serving. Furthermore, some have argued that nonprofit organizations have deeper roots in the neighborhoods they serve then either large government bureaucracies or for-profit corporations. Thus it is easier to develop ongoing contacts between staff and clients, thereby building social capital. Others have argued that this is an overly idealistic picture. In fact, they argue, many nonprofits are as large, professionalized, and bureaucratized as are government agencies. Most of their funding comes from the government, not donations.[18] Some have charged that government programs often continue to pour money into these programs, even in the absence of persuasive evidence that they are effective in what they are doing: Comfortable, long-term relationships and bureaucratic inertia have taken over. There is also evidence that counters some of these arguments, especially in the fact that even many large nonprofit organizations operate out of decentralized, neighborhood offices.

Faith-Based Organizations (FBOs)

Faith-based nonprofit organizations are seen by some as possessing the strengths of nonprofit organizations at their best, with the added advantage of a spiritual dimension. They are small and localized, with many ties to the communities they serve. They are able to attract many volunteers and private donations. In addition, their religious dimension enables them to deal with whole persons, including their attitudes and values relevant to the human services being offered. If human beings are indeed—so it is argued—physical, emotional, and spiritual creatures, it is important that programs seeking to help persons to overcome often seemingly overwhelming difficulties be able to address all these facets, and not merely some of them. Others have argued, however, that FBOs are so small and inexperienced that they do not have the capacity to serve more than a handful of persons, especially with assistance that goes beyond emergency services such as food and clothing. They simply do not have the organizational skills, size, and expertise needed to address the complex, multifaceted barriers that welfare-to-work clients typically face. Others contend that faith-based organizations are no more likely than government providers to deliver services in a more personal way.[19] Also, many fear that persons will be made to feel unwelcome or at least uncomfortable if they do not share the religious emphasis or tone present in a faith-based program. There may be church-state conflicts and problems if government funds faith-based programs, especially if religious teaching or proselytization is a part of the services being rendered.

The arguments and assumptions briefly outlined in this section formed much of the basis for this study. The outcomes on which we decided to focus and the data we collected in large part were guided by these sorts of conflicting arguments that have been made. That is why we felt it essential that at the outset we lay out these arguments that have played a role—even if usually a background role—in shaping this study.

The Findings of Previous Research

What systematic studies there have been of human service organization effectiveness usually focus on the effectiveness of individual human service organizations or compare the effectiveness of organizations marked by different management styles or treatment modalities. The United Way, government, and grant-making foundations have all in recent years emphasized program outcomes in the nonprofit programs they fund.[20] This has given rise to a number of studies of program outcomes and attempts to link these outcomes to such factors as management style, organizational culture, and governing board characteristics. Melissa Stone and Susan Cutcher-Gershenfeld have listed ten studies of nonprofit effectiveness published between 1982 and 1996.[21] All seek to measure effectiveness empirically and then relate that effectiveness to such organizational characteristics as the relationship of the nonprofits' boards to the organizations' executive staff and the management style of the nonprofits' leaders.

There are also a fairly large number of studies of the outcome effectiveness of human service organizations pursuing different approaches or treatment models. Here one finds, for example, studies comparing the outcomes of residential drug treatment programs with programs based on outpatient care and counseling. Or one can find studies that compare the results of "work first" approaches to welfare-to-work that seek to place persons into jobs—any job—as soon as possible with programs that emphasize longer-term job skills or vocational training. An instance of this is a study of Los Angeles County welfare-to-work programs that marshals evidence in support of the conclusion that "work first" approaches have less positive employment and wage outcomes than do education and training programs.[22] It also found that persons who had been approved for participation in programs in which they themselves had requested to take part experienced more positive outcomes than those who had been placed in programs not of their choosing.

What these types of effectiveness studies do not do, however, is to compare the effectiveness of human service programs that are run or sponsored by different types of organizations, such as for-profit versus nonprofit organizations, faith-based versus secular organizations, or large nonprofit versus small community-based organizations. It is only in very recent years—no doubt prompted by the current media and public policy interest in faith-based solutions to persistent social ills—that a few studies comparing the effectiveness of human service programs sponsored by different types of organizations have begun to emerge. All have focused on the faith-based versus secular distinction. Because of this and the fact that the comparative effectiveness of faith-based versus secular welfare-to-work programs is a primary, even if not the sole, focus of this study, we focus in this section on the effectiveness of faith-based human service programs compared with their secular counterparts, although we also examine two studies that compare the effectiveness of for-profit and nonprofit health care services.

It is helpful to begin with a distinction that Byron Johnson has made between organic religion and intentional religion. The former can also be called personal religion and consists of "religious practices and involvements" of individuals.[23] It represents "the influence or impact of religion practiced over time, such as children who were raised and nurtured in religious homes."[24] Studies of organic religion seek to answer the question of whether or not individuals who are personally religiously observant are more likely to exhibit certain socially positive characteristics, such as lower crime rates, greater psychological health, and better physical health. In contrast to organic religion and its attendant studies is what Johnson terms intentional religion. "Intentional religion is the exposure to religion one receives at a particular time in life for a particular purpose."[25] Studies of intentional religion seek to answer the question of whether persons taking part in human service programs that have a religious component are more likely to achieve certain program goals than are persons taking part in similar or parallel human service programs, but without a religious component.

Following a comprehensive study of hundreds of published research studies, Johnson uniformly found that organic religion was positively and significantly associated with a host of desirable social characteristics. The results are summarized in figure 1.1. As Johnson concludes:

> In sum, a review of the research on religious practices and health outcomes indicates that, in general, higher levels of religious involvement are associated with: reduced hypertension, longer survival, less depression, lower level of drug and alcohol use and abuse, less promiscuous sexual behaviors, reduced likelihood of suicide, lower rates of delinquency among youth, and reduced criminal activity among adults. . . . [T]his substantial body of empirical evidence demonstrates a very clear picture—those who are most involved in religious activities tend to fare better with respect to important and yet diverse outcome factors.[26]

Johnson also examined studies that focused on persons' organic or personal religious involvements and their sense of personal well-being or traits associated with possessing mental health. Figure 1.2 reveals what he found. Johnson writes, "To summarize, a review of the research on religious practices and various measures of well-being reveals that, in general, higher levels of religious involvement are associated with increased levels of: well-being, hope, purpose, meaning in life, and educational attainment."[27]

Findings such as these do not, of course, speak directly to the issue of whether faith-based human service programs are more effective than their secular counterparts, but they do speak indirectly to this issue. If religion has a positive impact on a person's physical and mental health, and if it has a positive effect on his or her social behavior—such as reducing drug and alcohol abuse and delinquent behavior—there is reason to believe that human service programs with a religious component might

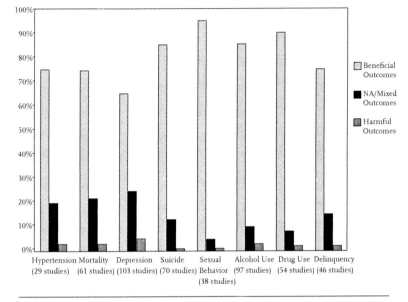

Figure 1.1

Research Examining the Relationship between Religion and Health Outcomes:
Eight Fields of Study (total of 498 studies reviewed)

Source: Byron R. Johnson, *Objective Hope: Assessing the Effectiveness of Faith-Based Organizations: A Review of the Literature* (Philadelphia: Center for Research on Religion and Urban Civil Society, University of Pennsylvania, 2002), 11.

have an additional facet that will result in more positive outcomes. This is particularly true in the case of welfare-to-work programs and the well-being studies surveyed by Johnson. Educational attainment, healthy self-esteem, and a sense of hope or optimism (in contrast to a sense of hopelessness, a sense that life will never be better) would all seem to be associated with being able to obtain employment and move off welfare. If persons who are religious are more likely to possess these qualities than persons who are irreligious, one could suppose there is something in religion that generates feelings of self-esteem, hope, and a desire for education (or a perseverance that leads to educational success). If this indeed is the case, it may be that faith-based programs will be better able to generate such feelings than can secular programs.

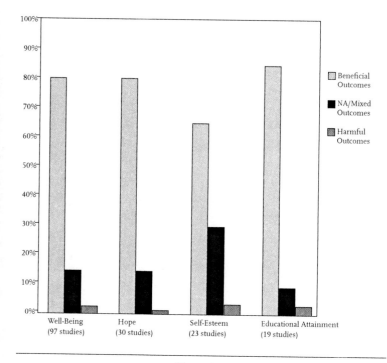

Figure 1.2

Research Examining the Relationship between Religion and Well-Being Outcomes:
Four Fields of Study (total of 171 studies reviewed)

Source: Byron R. Johnson, *Objective Hope: Assessing the Effectiveness of Faith-Based Organizations: A Review of the Literature* (Philadelphia: Center for Research on Religion and Urban Civil Society, University of Pennsylvania, 2002), 11.

These findings also raise the question of the interplay between organic, personal religion, and the religious or secular nature of a human service program, a question we raised earlier in the context of the random assignment of persons to programs. If an individual is already deeply religious and then becomes involved in a faith-based human service program, that program may be able to bring out and build upon the benefits of religion that are already there in latent form. That same person might fare less well in a secular program, because it would not be appealing to and building upon the faith elements already important in that person's life. By the same reasoning, one could project that a person for whom religion plays only a peripheral role in his or her life would not respond positively—and might even respond negatively—to the religious elements in a faith-based program and would respond more positively to a secular program and the nonreligiously based appeals it would make. The entire topic of the interplay between individual clients' own religious commitments and the religious or secular nature of the human service programs in which they take part remains unexplored, but it is potentially a rich area of research.

This leaves the question of what previous studies that focus on the effectiveness of faith-based programs in changing client attitudes or behaviors and thereby client levels of success have shown in regard to the effectiveness of intentional religion. Unfortunately, as one approaches more directly the topic with which this study is concerned, the number of existing, systematic studies dwindles dramatically. As Johnson and others noted earlier have pointed out, such studies are few and far between. Johnson, after his comprehensive review of the literature, found twenty-five such studies, and even some of these were case studies rather than true systematic, empirical studies. "Of these 25 studies, eight were case studies, six were descriptive studies, and 11 were multivariate studies."[28] Of these latter eleven studies, six dealt with the use of churches for certain health interventions, such as interventions aimed at increasing screening for breast cancer, weight loss, or lowering blood pressure. Four of the eleven studies dealt with faith-based in-prison programs, and one dealt with Teen Challenge, a faith-based drug treatment program. All used control groups or random assignment. Of these eleven studies, ten showed significantly improved results by the faith-based interventions, and one showed no significant difference.[29]

There are eight empirical studies, or series of studies, that are especially relevant to our study, and we will examine each of them more closely. One of these was included in Johnson's eleven multivariate studies and four were not—three because they came out after the Johnson survey of the literature and one because Johnson apparently did not consider it to fall within the purview of his literature search.

First we will consider a series of studies that compare the educational outcomes of children attending religiously based, largely Catholic, K–12 schools with those of children attending traditional public schools. Studies of the effectiveness of faith-based K–12 schools are usually assumed not to be relevant to a consideration of the effectiveness of faith-based human service programs, but we believe they are highly relevant. Inner-city K–12 schools with many students from minority and poverty-level families face challenges and opportunities very similar to those faced by human service agencies. Unstable family situations, racial discrimination, language problems for non-English speakers, health issues, discouragement and feelings of hopelessness, lack of motivation, and basic survival issues such as adequate food and clothing, utility cutoffs, and physical safety are challenges that both students attending K–12 inner-city schools and clients of antipoverty human service agencies all too often face. Thus we begin our consideration of empirical studies of the comparative effectiveness of faith-based and government programs with a review of several key studies that compared the educational outcomes of students attending faith-based inner-city K–12 schools with those attending inner-city public schools.

The first such studies were conducted by James Coleman and his associates in the late 1970s and early 1980s. These studies included thousands of students in public and private high schools. In brief, Coleman and his associates found that the Catholic schools were more effective than their public school counterparts in reducing the educational gap between students coming from dissimilar backgrounds. They summarize: "The achievement of blacks is closer to that of whites, and the achievement of Hispanics is closer to that of non-Hispanics in Catholic schools than in public schools."[30] Another one of the Coleman reports focused on students from disadvantaged backgrounds: "The achievement growth benefits of Catholic school attendance are especially strong for students who are in one way or another disadvantaged: lower socioeconomic status, black or Hispanic."[31] Recently two scholars have reported, "Subsequent studies have tended to reaffirm Hoffer, Greeley, and Coleman's findings."[32]

A more recent study compared test scores of children who attended private schools under privately funded voucher programs in New York City, Washington, D.C., and Dayton, Ohio, with children who had applied for the voucher program but had not been selected. In all three cases there had been more applicants for the vouchers than there were vouchers available, and a lottery was used to determine who would receive the vouchers. Thus the principle of random assignment was used to determine who went to the private schools and who remained in the public schools. The researchers found that African American students did significantly better after both one and two years in the private schools than did their counterparts who remained in the public schools, but the non–African American students did not do significantly better.[33] Most of the private schools were religious schools, with a plurality in each of the three cities being Catholic schools and most of the remaining schools being Protestant.[34]

In summary, this series of school studies indicates that faith-based schools tend to have positive educational outcomes for disadvantaged youths, and especially African American youths. It thereby raises the possibility that intentionally faith-based programs may have especially beneficial effects among minority, disadvantaged groups.

Another study compared the outcome effectiveness of Teen Challenge and an Alcoholics Anonymous (AA) short-term inpatient program.[35] Aaron Bicknese conducted pre- and post-telephone interviews with graduates of the three largest Teen Challenge programs (in Pennsylvania, Missouri, and California). Bicknese started out with 150 graduates of the Teen Challenge program, was able to obtain consent forms from 70 persons who were available for interviewing, and in fact completed telephone interviews with 59 of them. His comparison group consisted of 118 persons who had taken part in AA short-term inpatient programs and for whom data had been gathered by the research firm New Standards, for the Ramsey Clinic in St. Paul, Minnesota. He explored four outcomes: freedom from addictive substances, improved full-time employment outcomes, the elimination of criminality, and the reduction of precipitants of drug use (such as depression and cravings). He found that Teen Challenge clients, when compared to all of the AA clients, were significantly more likely not to suffer drug use relapses, but when compared to only the AA clients who continued to attend AA meetings on a regular basis, the differences with Teen Challenge clients did not reach statistical significance.[36] However, he found that in terms of needing to return for further treatment, the Teen Challenge clients fared significantly better than the AA clients, even when compared to those who continued to attend AA meetings. On the employment measure he also found the Teen Challenge clients faring significantly better: "Teen Challenge graduates were found to have worked full time on an average of 5 ½ months out of the last six prior to the interview, while STI [short-term inpatient AA program] respondents had worked about 2 ¹/₃ of the previous six months: and nearly 90% of Teen Challenge respondents held a full time job, as opposed to about 41% of the comparison group. (Both differences were significant at p = 0.0001.)"[37]

In regard to criminality, Bicknese found that 7 percent of the Teen Challenge clients had experienced arrest, and 17 percent of the AA clients had, but he warned against attaching too much significance to this finding due to some methodological problems.[38] He measured four precursors of drug use, and Teen Challenge clients fared significantly better on two of them and only marginally better for the other two.[39]

What can one conclude from the Bicknese study? First, it adds credence to the proposition that faith-based human services may indeed lead to more positive outcomes than do their secular counterparts. Bicknese found that by some outcome measures the heavily faith-oriented Teen Challenge program had significantly more positive outcomes, and by no measures did the largely secular AA program have more positive outcomes. Second, the study warns against expecting a simplistic, one-dimensional outcome in which the faith-based program outcomes by all measures and by overwhelming margins are more effective. The real world rarely is like that, and Bicknese did not find this to be the case in his study.

A third study it is helpful to consider is a 2003 study by Byron Johnson of a faith-based Texas in-prison program called InnerChange Freedom Initiative (IFI).[40] In 1997, under then-governor George W. Bush, IFI was launched in the Carol Vance Unit, a 378-inmate prison in Richmond, Texas. It was run by Prison Fellowship, a Christian organization founded by Charles Colson of Watergate notoriety, who later became a "born again" Christian. It was funded completely by private funds, and prisoners could volunteer to take part in this program. It consisted of concentrated Bible study, life-skills education, and accountability to group members. It made heavy use of volunteers and linked prisoners with mentors and churches, both before and after release from prison. The total program lasted eighteen to twenty-four months. Johnson compared the recidivism rates for the IFI offenders with three groups: a matched group of prisoners that met certain selection criteria but were not part of the IFI program, a group of prisoners who had been screened and found to be eligible to take part in the program but had declined to volunteer for it or had volunteered but had not been selected to participate, and a group of prisoners who had volunteered for the program but did not participate due to their failing to meet one of several criteria.

When the IFI participants were compared demographically with the three control groups they were not found to differ notably in age, type of offense, or risk score assigned by the prison authorities. Johnson writes that "the matched groups look very much like the study group on key factors known to be associated with recidivism."[41] Johnson measured recidivism in terms of both arrests and incarceration.

The study found that after two years those prisoners who had completed the IFI program had significantly lower recidivism rates than any of the three control groups. Seventeen percent of the IFI graduates had been arrested and 8 percent had been incarcerated, while the comparable figures for the match group were 35 percent and 20 percent, those for the group that had been found eligible to participate but did not do so were 35 percent and 22 percent, and those for those prisoners who had volunteered for the program but did not participate were 29 percent and 19 percent.[42] However, over half of the IFI participants did not complete the lengthy program for one reason or another—they were released from prison early, they dropped out of the program, or they were expelled from the program. When one takes not only the IFI graduates but all who participated in the program, the differences between IFI participants and the comparison groups disappear. Thirty-six percent of the IFI participants were arrested within two years of their release, and 24 percent were incarcerated.[43] In fact, those who participated in the program but did not complete it had slightly worse recidivism rates than those who had never participated in the program.

This study reveals that faith-based programs can indeed be effective. Those who completed the program had significantly lower recidivism rates. But it also demonstrates the importance of distinguishing between those who take part in a program and do not complete it and those with the opportunity and commitment to complete a program. In the study of Teen Challenge discussed earlier, Bicknese only looked at program graduates. One is left to wonder what the impact of the program was on persons who started but did not complete the program. One can, of course, question whether it is fair to judge a program by persons who began it but did not complete it. After all, they did not have the full benefit of the program. In fact, some might drop out after only taking part very briefly in it. In such cases, to judge a program on the basis of individuals who barely took part in it seems unfair. But if a program has a high drop-out rate, it also seems unfair only to judge it by those who complete it. This study also demonstrated the sometimes maddeningly unexpected in social science research. One would surely think that if completing a program had a measurable, positive impact, completing part of the program would have *some* positive impact. But here this was not the case. One is led to suspect that either the program was crafted to be a whole experience and that the entire package was needed for any positive effect, or that the program may have had minimal effect and the positive recidivism rates for program completers resulted simply from the program having had the effect of screening out those most likely to be repeat offenders.

Another study relevant to what we report in this book was based on client interviews, conducted in the Lehigh Valley of Pennsylvania by Robert Wuthnow.[44] It involved 2,077 telephone interviews of persons randomly selected who were living in low-income areas. They were asked, among other questions, from what agencies they had sought assistance in the past year, and then they were asked, for each agency from which they had sought assistance, to grade it on a scale from A to F, "in terms of its effectiveness in meeting your need."[45] Wuthnow found that the public welfare department was graded the lowest, the churches the highest, and the secular and faith-based agencies somewhere in between. The "grade point average" was 2.47 for the public welfare department (with an A equaling 4 points and an F equaling 0 points), 3.10 for the secular nonprofit organizations, 3.13 for the faith-based organizations, and 3.59 for the churches. He also noted that the respondents reported turning to different types of agencies for different types of needs, and he concluded that this might explain some of the variation in the grades given the different types of agencies. Also he found that "people seeking financial assistance and employment or job training are the least likely to have felt the assistance they received was effective."[46] Wuthnow's study suggests that from the clients' standpoint government-run programs may indeed be less effective than those run by nongovernmental entities. It also suggests that employment and job-training services may be the most difficult to provide in an effective manner, which should perhaps temper the levels of successful outcomes we should expect to find among our seventeen welfare-to-work programs.

Two additional studies we examine here dealt with employment and training programs in Indiana. It thereby dealt more closely with programs of the type studied in this book than the other studies discussed

in this chapter, but both studies also had some methodological problems. One is a study conducted by Partha Deb and Dana Jones on employment and job training programs in Marion County (Indianapolis)
and Lake County (Gary/Hammond/East Chicago area).[47] It was a part of
a larger study on the implementation of the charitable choice provision
of the 1996 Welfare Reform Act.[48] The researchers used official management reports to determine what programs or agencies were providing
job training services and only considered programs that were receiving government funding. They classified a program as faith based if
it qualified on any one of eight possible faith dimensions (what those
dimensions were was not revealed in the essay). Thus they apparently
included faith-based programs with only a minimal religious character.
They used official reports to obtain demographic information on the
programs' participants and monthly employment data reported by the
counties to the state to determine the employment status of the program participants. From these sources they were able to determine certain demographic characteristics of the individuals in the different programs and whether or not they obtained a job, and for those that found
employment they determined their wage rates, their hours worked, and
whether or not they had health insurance. These latter data constituted
their outcome measures. Apparently only initial job placement was considered and not job retention or advancement over time.

Deb and Jones conclude, "There appears to be no significant difference in placement rates between faith-based and secular providers of
job training services."[49] Using regression analysis they found there was
no statistically significant difference for the faith-based providers in job
placement and hourly wages; they fared neither better nor worse than
their secular counterparts. They found significant negative relationships, however, for the faith-based providers in hours worked per week
and in receiving health insurance coverage.[50] In other words, clients of
faith-based job training programs were as likely as their counterparts
who had taken part in secular programs to find employment, but those
that found employment and were in faith-based programs were likely
to work fewer hours and were less likely to have health insurance benefits than those that found employment and were in secular programs.
This study has the weaknesses of only considering the initial jobs the
clients were able to obtain and not considering longer-term effects of
the programs in which they took part and of using a very broad defini-

tion of what constitutes a faith-based program. But it nevertheless is a signal that faith-based programs may on some outcome measures be as effective as their secular counterparts and on some measures may be less effective. It thereby indicates that it is important to look not only at employment levels when considering job training outcomes but also at such things as wage levels, hours worked, and benefits.

Another study it is useful to examine compared certain perceptions and attitudes of clients before and after they took part in secular and faith-based job training programs.[51] Its findings are based, using written questionnaires, on the responses it obtained from clients taking part in three secular job training programs, one moderately faith-based program, and one strongly faith-based program. All the programs were located in three Indiana counties. The researchers do not report the number of respondents included in their findings. They found, first, that the clients taking part in the three different types of programs did not differ greatly in educational levels or age.[52] The clients in the strongly faith-based program tended to be somewhat more likely to be nonwhite, but surprisingly tended to be much less religious, measured by church attendance, than the clients in the other two types of programs.[53] They also tended to face more barriers to employment than did the clients from the other two types of programs.[54] Most importantly, the researchers then reported their findings in regard to several enabling outcomes, as we have termed them. They found that the clients from the three types of programs did not vary to a notable degree in changes in their feelings of self-confidence from before to after taking part in the programs. They did find, however, that the clients in the strongly faith-based program were more likely to gain in terms of seeing advantages in planning ahead than were the clients in the other two programs.[55] The usefulness of these findings, however, are limited by the very small number of programs studied (one strongly faith-based program and one moderately faith-based program) and the failure of the researchers to reveal how many clients were included in the study.

The final two studies we review include considerations of the relative effectiveness of for-profit and nonprofit programs. They are helpful for our purposes because we included for-profit welfare-to-work programs in our study and compare their outcomes with those of government, secular nonprofit, and faith-based programs. Both of these studies consider the comparative effectiveness of providers in the health care area.

One of these studies, conducted by Mark Ragan, considered the performance of for-profit, government, secular nonprofit, and faith-based nonprofit nursing homes and home health care agencies.[56] Ragan utilized available performance data collected by the Centers for Medicare and Medicaid Services in the Department of Health and Human Services. For nursing homes, he used data on the characteristics of the nursing home patients and the number of inspection deficiencies and formally filed complaints as measures of effectiveness. For home health care providers, he used ten outcome measures, such as the percentage of clients who became better at walking or moving about, the percentage of clients who got better at getting dressed, and the percentage of clients who had to be admitted to a hospital. Thus, for nursing homes, some of the reported patient characteristics were purely descriptive (e.g., "Percent of residents who spend most of their time in bed or in a chair") and others could be considered outcome measures (e.g., "Percent of residents whose ability to move about in and around their room got worse"). The deficiencies the study noted included both outcome measures and what are usually termed outputs, that is, activities or actions taken by the nursing homes under study. The reported deficiencies could range from patients with an excessive number of bedsores (an outcome measure) to fewer nurses on duty than required or inadequate record keeping (output measures). For home health care, the study truly measured outcomes, but the official government records on which it depended relied on the caregivers' own assessment of the outcomes.

Ragan found that in terms of patient characteristics there was no substantial difference among the different types of nursing homes. In terms of deficiencies uncovered by inspections, he found that the for-profit homes had more deficiencies than did the other types of homes. He found that the for-profit homes had an average of 6.5 deficiencies, the government homes 4.8, the secular nonprofit homes 4.7, and the church-related homes 4.4.[57] In terms of deficiencies based on complaints, Ragan found that church-related nursing homes had about 57 percent fewer complaints.[58] Overall he concluded that "the differences between church-related and other non-profit nursing homes were substantially less than the differences between non-profit and other types of nursing homes (which includes both for-profit and government-run nursing homes)."[59] The for-profit and the government nursing homes tended to fair less well than did the nonprofit homes, whether faith-based or not.

In terms of the home health care outcome measures he found, "For seven of the eight measures, outcomes for patients of religiously-affiliated home health agencies were on average better than the average for all other home health agencies. However, the differences were small."[60]

Ragan's study—based on available government-collected performance data—illustrates the value and the limitations of officially gathered numbers. The value of these statistics lies in their accessibility and comprehensive nature. As Ragan himself points out, however, their value is limited by a failure to distinguish clearly between faith-based and secular nonprofit programs, by self-reporting, and by missing information.[61] Nevertheless, this study is particularly helpful in suggesting that for-profit providers may not give as effective care as do nonprofit providers and that faith-based and secular nonprofit providers may not differ greatly in the services they provide.

A final study we considered analyzes the community benefit activities of health maintenance organizations (HMOs).[62] As the authors of this study note, over the past twenty years managed care has moved from a nonprofit domain to one in which nonprofit and for-profit organizations now compete with each other. What has not been systematically analyzed, however, is whether or not the type of health plan ownership affects the community benefit activities pursued by different health plans.

We noted previously that the chief argument for those who advocate the use of for-profit firms in delivering human services is that the profit motive will provide them an incentive to increase their efficiency and flexibility, and thereby their effectiveness. The counter to this argument, as we also noted, is that precisely because they are focused on the bottom line, for-profit firms may provide a lower quality of services. They also may shift their costs and activities away from any unprofitable but socially desirable public benefits that they may provide. Nonprofits, by contrast, are not similarly constrained by the need to make a profit, and we might therefore expect that nonprofits would be better able to provide public goods.[63]

The study used a nationally representative sample of 112 HMOs that were at least two years old and that had a minimum of ten thousand enrollees. The survey collected information about the nature of each HMO's commitment to various community benefits including providing subsidized care, offering services that have benefits beyond the direct recipient of the service, a commitment to medical research, and open access to services, to name a few. It thereby did not focus on outcomes but on provider outputs, that is, on the activities or actions taken by the HMOs under study. In addition, it focused on community benefit outputs, that is, outputs with a broad societal, or public, benefit, as distinguished from outputs of benefit to their individual paying clients.

The study found that although the nonprofit plans exceeded their for-profit counterparts on some community benefit outputs, there was no statistically significant ownership-related difference on other types of public-benefit outputs. For-profit plans actually appeared more active than nonprofit HMOs in one area, that of notifying their enrollees about potential problems with their medical care. The authors of the study conclude that "the findings are clearly mixed."[64] Contrary to what one might expect, nonprofit HMOs did not systematically outperform for-profits in providing public goods.

This study highlights key issues when comparing the behavior of for-profit firms and not-for-profit organizations that are involved in the same activity. They include whether or not an organization's for-profit or nonprofit status affects its behavior, if for-profit organizations are more or less likely than nonprofit organizations to produce public goods, and how the behavior of a nonprofit organization is affected—positively or negatively—by the presence of a for-profit firm active in the same field. These are vital questions that we consider later when we report our own findings on for-profit, government-run, and nonprofit welfare-to-work programs. The study is also significant because it demonstrates that there are ways to assess effectiveness other than outcome measures. In the health care field, effectiveness means more than whether a health plan provides quality care for sick people, as important as this obviously is. The effectiveness of a health care plan may also include such quality measures as its ability to train future doctors, its commitment to providing services for the indigent, and its willingness to notify enrollees about potential problems in their care. The same can be said in the welfare-to-work field. Even as we focus on effectiveness defined in terms of outcomes, we will define outcomes broadly enough to include a wide range of measures beyond the simple outcome of finding full-time employment.

In the title to this chapter we refer to the "effectiveness muddle." By now it should be clear why we do so. Effectiveness—even when defined in terms of program outcomes—is a complex concept that is often misunderstood. There are methodological problems in operationalizing a study that seeks to measure program outcomes from different types of programs in order to compare their relative effectiveness. There are few existing theories or studies to guide us. Nevertheless, public policymakers constantly seek to make decisions based on the presumed relative effectiveness of different types of human services programs. We believe a tentative, exploratory study that seeks to investigate the comparative effectiveness of welfare-to-work programs can prove profitable. Doing so can clarify the relevant concepts, test research strategies, and develop tentative findings that can be tested and refined by other researchers. This is what we seek to do in the following chapters.

2

THE STUDY

As discussed in the previous chapter, there are indeed formidable challenges in systematically studying the comparative outcomes of different types of human service programs. In this chapter we explain how we attempted to meet these challenges and operationalize the basic concepts we developed in the prior chapter. We believe the challenges to be indeed formidable, but not insurmountable.

This study, as stated earlier, focused on welfare-to-work programs in Los Angeles County. We selected this focus for our study, first, because at the time of our study both of us were located in Los Angeles County and it was thus convenient for us to study, but also because in Los Angeles—a very large, diverse urban center with a very large welfare caseload—one finds almost all of the issues and challenges the welfare system is facing today. In fact, Los Angeles accounts "for 8 percent of all U.S. recipients and 14 percent of all U.S. welfare expenditures."[1] Los Angeles certainly has its unique attributes, but there are no markers that would lead one to suspect that what we found here would have only limited bearing on the rest of the nation. In addition, the area of welfare-to-work is one in which Los Angeles is typical of most other large urban areas in that it has relied upon many different types of organizations—governmental and nongovernmental—to provide human services. We were attracted to the area of welfare-to-work because of the continuing large number of welfare caseloads and the pressures of many Temporary Assistance for Needy Families (TANF) recipients reaching the maximum five-year eligibility time limits for receiving cash assistance. This latter element makes it especially urgent for researchers to throw whatever additional light they can on what types of welfare-to-work programs work effectively.

The Five Stages of the Research

The findings reported in this book are based on the study of seventeen welfare-to-work programs and their clients in the Los Angeles area.[2] The research was conducted in five basic stages.

Identifying All Welfare-to-Work Programs in Los Angeles

The first stage was comprised of compiling a list of all the welfare-to-work programs in urban Los Angeles County.[3] We defined a welfare-to-work program as any program providing one or more of the following services to welfare recipients: job search, education/literary, education/ESL (English as a second language), education/GED preparation, education/vocational training, work preparedness, life skills, job placement, job internships or apprenticeships, client assessment, and mentoring. This list of services excluded services that are purely supportive of persons' job attainment efforts, such as child care and transportation. We thereby only included programs that provide training or education in attitudes, values, or skills with a direct relationship to job attainment or advancement.

We compiled the list of welfare-to-work programs by using published directories, formal and informal lists of programs, consultations with knowledgeable community leaders, meetings of collaborative councils of programs, and innumerable phone calls. We identified 511 welfare-to-work programs in urban Los Angeles County. As explained more fully in appendix A, we have reason to believe that our efforts to identify all of the welfare-to-work programs in urban Los Angeles County were highly successful. We no doubt missed a few programs, especially among small, relatively unknown programs, but we are very confident that our initial list of programs was substantially complete.

Using a Mailed Questionnaire to Obtain Basic Program Information

The second stage of our research involved mailing a questionnaire to all of the identified welfare-to-work programs in order to obtain basic information about them. The questionnaires elicited such information as the services provided, size, sponsoring entity, faith-based or secular character, funding sources, number of volunteers, staff characteristics, and contacts with government agencies. (See appendix B for a copy of the questionnaire we sent out.) A total of 211 questionnaires were mailed back to us for a good response rate of slightly over 41 percent. Eleven of the organizations returning questionnaires indicated that they did not provide any welfare-to-work services and thus were eliminated from our analyses. Four of the questionnaires were so incomplete we could not use them, resulting in a total of 196 programs that could be included in our analyses. A comparison of the neighborhood locations of the programs that responded to our questionnaire with the neighborhood locations of all the programs on our original list indicated that the responding programs were similar to the programs on our initial list in terms of location. (See appendix A.) Because geographic location tends to correspond with such characteristics as racial and ethnic makeup and socioeconomic status, this finding increased our confidence that the responding programs were indeed representative of all the welfare-to-work programs on our initial list.

Classifying the Programs

The third stage of our research involved, first, classifying the 196 programs into five categories: government-run, for-profit, nonprofit/secular, faith-based/segmented, and faith-based/integrated programs. The first two categories are self-explanatory; programs were placed in these categories based on their self-identification as a government or a private, for-profit program. The nonprofit programs were placed in the nonprofit/secular category if they self-identified themselves either as "a private, nonprofit program with no religious base or history" or as "a private, nonprofit program that at one time had a religious orientation, but today has evolved into a program that is largely secular in nature." The latter programs were included in the secular category because, even though they had had a religious connection or orientation in their pasts, today they are secular in nature. Programs were placed in one of the faith-based categories if they self-identified themselves as "a private, nonprofit program that continues to have a clear religious base and orientation." The segmented versus integrated distinction was based on the faith-based programs' responses to a question that listed ten potential religiously rooted practices, plus one additional "other" category. (See question 11 of the questionnaire in appendix B.) A scale was developed depending on the number and the nature of the religiously rooted practices in which the programs reported engaging. Those practices that had a more integrative nature—such as "using religious values or motivations to encourage clients to change attitudes or values" and "hiring only staff in agreement with your religious orientation"—were weighed more heavily than less integrative practices—such as "placing religious symbols or pictures in the facility where your program is held" and "using religious values as a guiding motivation for staff in delivering services." (For a complete account of how this scale was constructed, see appendix C.) Those faith-based programs whose religious elements were implicit and in the background we placed into the segmented category, and those whose religious elements were explicit and incorporated into the services they provided were placed in the integrated category. What we are here designating as faith-based/integrated is not the same as what some other researchers have termed "faith-saturated."[4] Faith-saturated programs consist of those where religion permeates virtually every aspect of what they do, while faith-based/integrated programs are ones with religious elements clearly present in the programs, but they do not necessarily permeate every aspect.

Of the 196 useable questionnaires, 86 (44 percent) fell into the government category, 4 (2 percent) in the for-profit category, 79 (40 percent) in the nonprofit/secular category, 17 (9 percent) in the faith-based/segmented category, and 10 (5 percent) in the faith-based/integrated category. In order to understand the research being reported here, it is important to understand that most of the faith-based programs were very small. We determined that the number of full-time staff members is the best measure we had of program size. Other measures, such as the number of clients served and budget size, proved less reliable measures of program size. The problem in using the number of clients served as a measure of program size is that the programs varied greatly in their length and intensity. Some lasted no more than three or four weeks and others for months; some included daylong sessions and even residential services, whereas others consisted of half-day classes or counseling sessions on an "as needed" basis. Thus a program with only a few clients, but which lasted six months or more with around-the-clock residential services might be small in terms of the total number of clients, but large in terms of the services delivered. We also obtained budget information from the various programs, but it became apparent to us that this question was interpreted by some organizations to be asking for the annual budget for the entire organization, and others answered in terms of only the specific welfare-to-work program. (We intended for them to answer in terms of the latter.) In addition, 40 of the 196 responding programs (20 percent) did not provide budget figures at all, which made the use of budget figures to calculate program size further problematic. Thus we concluded that the number of full-time employees was by far the best measure of program size.

Figure 2.1 compares the proportion of the five program types with the proportion of the full-time, paid staff members employed by each of the five program types. When considering the number of full-time employees, one can clearly see that the faith-based programs were very small. Less than 2 percent of the full-time welfare-to-work employees came from the two types of faith-based programs taken together. At least two-thirds of both the segmented and integrated programs had three or fewer full-time employees. The other three types of programs, and especially the government-run programs, were much larger. The government programs made up 44 percent of all the welfare-to-work programs in our study but provided 71 percent of the welfare-to-work full-time employees. The secular nonprofit programs also play a large role in the provision of Los Angeles welfare-to-work services. They employ almost one-fourth of all of the full-time welfare-to-work employees.

It could, however, be argued that the faith-based programs are actually larger than what their numbers of full-time employees would suggest, because they may have many more part-time employees and volunteers than do the other types of programs. Table 2.1 shows the median number of part-time employees and volunteers for each program type. We used the median of part-time employees and volunteers, rather than the mean, because a very small number of programs reported very large numbers of part-time employees or volunteers. Therefore using the median gave us a more accurate picture of the overall use of part-time employees and volunteers for each program type than using the mean would have done. When we took the number of part-time employees into account, the size advantage of the government programs over the faith-based programs actually increased. The median government programs had an average of four part-time employees, compared to only one for the faith-based programs. The faith-based programs did, however, have many more volunteers than the other types of program. The median faith-based/segmented program had twenty volunteers a month, and

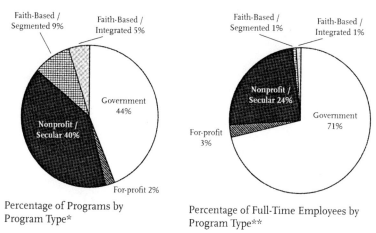

Faith-Based / Segmented 9%
Faith-Based / Integrated 5%
Government 44%
Nonprofit / Secular 40%
For-profit 2%

Percentage of Programs by Program Type*

Faith-Based / Segmented 1%
Faith-Based / Integrated 1%
Nonprofit / Secular 24%
Government 71%
For-profit 3%

Percentage of Full-Time Employees by Program Type**

Figure 2.1

Comparison of the Number of Programs and the Number of Full-Time Employees, by Program Type

* The percentages are based on the total number of programs in the study (N = 196).

** The percentages are based on the total number of full-time, paid employees working for the programs in the study (N = 5,020).

the median faith-based/integrated program had fifteen. Given the small number of full-time employees at most of the faith-based programs, their use of volunteers is clearly a key component of their overall work force. However, Virginia Hodgkinson and Murray Weitzman have estimated the average number of hours put in per week by volunteers is 4.2 hours per week.[5] If one takes the number of volunteers per program and assumes that each volunteer contributes 4.2 hours per week, one ends up with the median faith-based/segmented program adding the equivalent of a little more than two full-time staff members and the faith-based/integrated adding one and a half staff members. These figures indicate that when one takes volunteers into account the faith-based programs indeed appear larger—their work force about doubles in size. In terms of their overall work force, compared to that of the three other types of programs, however, they still have only about 4 percent of the total welfare-to-work work force in Los Angeles County.

Table 2.1

Median Number of Part-Time Employees and Volunteers, by Program Type

Program Type	Median Number of Part-Time Employees per Program	Median Number of Volunteers per Program
Government	4.0	0.0
For-profit	0.5	0.0
Nonprofit/secular	2.0	2.5
Faith-based/segmented	1.0	20.0
Faith-based/integrated	1.0	15.0

Studying Seventeen Programs Intensively

Out of the 196 responding welfare-to-work programs, we selected seventeen for intensive study. This was the fourth stage of our study. Of these seventeen, four were government programs, two were for-profit programs, three were nonprofit/secular, four were faith-based/segmented, and four were faith-based/integrated. Given the small number of programs with which we were working, we did not attempt to select them at random. Instead, we determined several basic characteristics that tended to mark the programs in each of our five categories, such as size, age, percentage of welfare recipients out of all their clients, and number of services offered. Next, we selected programs that were near the norm for that category of program on those characteristics. Thus we were assured that the programs selected for intensive study were representative of the other programs in that category on these key characteristics. We obtained detailed information about the seventeen selected programs via site visits. All seventeen programs were visited by one of the primary researchers or our professional, full-time associate researcher.[6] These on-site visits involved interviews with key staff members and observations of welfare-to-work classes and activities. We kept extensive notes and recorded and transcribed key interviews.

Obtaining Individual Client Data for the Seventeen Selected Programs

The fifth stage of our research consisted of obtaining individual data from clients participating in the seventeen programs' welfare-to-work activities. Baseline data on the individual clients were obtained by way of a written questionnaire (in English and Spanish versions) that was administered in person by the associate researcher at each of the seventeen sites. Participation by the clients was purely voluntary, and each signed a confidentiality statement. Respondents were told that they would be called back for more information after six months and again after twelve months. Gift cards to Target stores were offered as an incentive for those who decided to take part in the study. A few clients who were approached declined to take part in the study, but almost all elected to take part in it. A total of 436 completed baseline questionnaires were obtained. The baseline questionnaire obtained name and contact information; demographic information such as gender, age, and ethnicity; religious orientation and involvement; language skills; work history; income and welfare dependency information; number of children; and sense of optimism or hope for the future. (See appendix B for a copy of the baseline questionnaire.) In this baseline questionnaire we were primarily seeking information that would give us insight into the respondents' personal life situations and the number and type of barriers they faced in seeking employment.

The questionnaire respondents were interviewed by way of telephone interviews after six months, and those that we reached after six months were again interviewed after an additional six months.[7] A Target gift card was used each time as an incentive for participation. The interviews were conducted in English or Spanish as appropriate. Tables 2.2 and 2.3 reveal the response rates that we obtained for each of the five types of programs. We obtained excellent response rates of 75 percent at six months and 81 percent at twelve months, and the response rates did not vary notably among the five program types. As table 2.2 shows, we clearly oversampled the faith-based programs. As shown by figure 2.1, they—based on the number of full-time employees—represent only about 2 percent of the welfare-to-work efforts in Los Angeles County, yet just over 20 percent of the respondents in our study were from faith-based programs. Similarly, the for-profit programs were overrepresented, and the government and nonprofit/secular programs were underrepresented. This was done purposely in order to have enough respondents in each of the five program types for purposes of analysis. Table 2.2 also demonstrates that the percentage of our six- and twelve-month respondents that came from each of the five program types did not vary greatly from the baseline respondents. This indicates that, although there was some drop-off as we followed up on our baseline respondents six and twelve months later, those we were unable to reach

Table 2.2

Distribution of Completed Interviews at Baseline, Six Months, and Twelve Months, by Program Type

Program Type	Baseline		Six Months		Twelve Months	
	N	%	N	%	N	%
Government	141	32	96	29	75	28
For-profit	113	26	91	28	72	27
Nonprofit/secular	80	18	66	20	61	23
Faith-based/segmented	51	12	36	11	27	10
Faith-based/integrated	51	12	38	12	30	11
Total	436	100	327	100	265	99

were not disproportionately from one or two of the program types. Table 2.3 demonstrates this latter point more clearly by giving for each program type the percentage of its baseline respondents that we successfully interviewed again at six and twelve months. It shows that the response rates varied somewhat but not drastically from one program type to another. The nonprofit/secular program clients had the best response rates and the government and faith-based/segmented program clients the worst. Even among the program types whose clients we had the most trouble tracking, we were able to interview about 70 percent of the baseline clients at six months and over 50 percent at 12 months.

Table 2.4 compares several key characteristics of the baseline respondents with the respondents we were able to reach with our follow-up six- and twelve-month telephone interviews. It demonstrates that, on the key characteristics of gender, race, employment status, and education, the respondents we were able to reach at six and twelve months were very similar to the baseline respondents. This increases our confidence that a lack of information from the persons we were not able to reach in follow-up telephone interviews did not introduce a bias into our data.

The six-month interview schedule used by our telephone interviewers elicited information about the respondents' current employment situation and welfare receipt status, their sense of optimism and hope for the future, and their evaluations of the programs they had been in. (See appendix B for a copy of the interview schedule that we used.) The information about employment, wages, and receipt of welfare was used to measure ultimate and intermediate outcomes, as defined in the previous chapter. We largely used the responses to questions about hope and

Table 2.3

Respondents at Six and Twelve Months, as a Percentage of Baseline Respondents,
by Program Type

Program Type	Number of Baseline Respondents	Percent of Baseline Respondents Interviewed at Six Months	Percent of Baseline Respondents Interviewed at Twelve Months	Percent of Six-Month Respondents Interviewed at Twelve Months
Government	141	68	53	78
For-profit	113	81	64	79
Nonprofit/secular	80	83	76	92
Faith-based/segmented	51	76	53	75
Faith-based/integrated	51	75	59	79
All respondents	436	75	61	81

optimism and evaluations of the programs to measure enabling outcomes. The twelve-month interview schedule was shorter, focusing on the respondents' employment and wage situation and current welfare status. Thus its focus was on ultimate and intermediate outcomes. (The twelve-month interview schedule can also be found in appendix B.)

The original, baseline questionnaires were filled out from late January to mid-March 2002, the six-month telephone interviews were completed from mid-August to early October 2002, and the twelve-month telephone interviews were completed from mid-February to early April 2003. The unemployment rate in the Los Angeles–Long Beach metropolitan area went from 6.8 percent in February 2002, to 7.0 percent in August 2002, to 6.7 percent in February 2003. Thus the employment

Table 2.4

Key Characteristics of Baseline, Six-Month, and Twelve-Month Respondents

Characteristics	Baseline Respondents		Six-Month Respondents		Twelve-Month Respondents	
	%	N	%	N	%	N
Percent female	83	432	84	325	84	263
Percent Latino	49	436	50	327	51	265
Percent African American	29	436	28	327	28	265
Percent unemployed at baseline	65	432	63	324	65	262
Percent less than high school	31	432	29	322	30	260

situation during the time of our study was holding steady, but unemployment was higher than the national average, making it more difficult for clients in the programs to find employment. Under more favorable economic conditions this study might have found more positive outcomes in terms of employment and wage levels, but there is no reason to believe that the relative differences among the five types of programs were affected by the economic conditions.

The Seventeen Programs

Following is a brief description of each of the seventeen programs included in our study. Having some insight into the nature of the programs whose clients we surveyed will prove helpful in interpreting the results of our study. The names of the following programs have all been changed in order to protect the confidentiality of the programs and, most importantly, of the clients.

Government Programs

Responsible Fathers. Responsible Fathers is a program run by Community and Senior Services of Los Angeles County. It is designed to help noncustodial parents who are behind on support payments to become more faithful in financially supporting their children and, more broadly, to encourage them to take a more responsible approach to their role as parents. It is a large program, serving more than a thousand clients annually at multiple locations. A majority of the clients are Latino. Most are males and have been referred by the district attorney's (DA's) office due to their owing back child support. Many, in fact, are required by the D.A. to attend. Most are unemployed or are employed "off-the-books." The program assigns clients to peer support classes that stress improving attitudes, life skills, and basic educational skills (English as a second language [ESL] classes or GED preparation). Once clients are deemed job ready, they are assigned to a counselor from a for-profit company with whom Responsible Fathers has a contract to provide job search and job placement services. The thirteen Responsible Fathers respondents included in our study were drawn from two different peer support classes.

Bay City College. Bay City College is a community college located in a high poverty area. It offers an employment program specifically for

CalWORKs clients (that is, clients of the California Work Opportunity and Responsibility to Kids program, which is the California version of TANF). It is funded through CalWORKs, and most of the clients are referred to the program by the Department of Public Social Services (DPSS). The program largely consists of classes designed to teach certain marketable skills, such as training in child care, nursing assistance, and forklift operation. The program also offers some GED preparation and ESL classes. In addition, there are counselors available to help the clients with assessment and problem solving. Job placement services seemed to be weak. One instructor acknowledged that "they [the clients] have to find jobs on their own." It is a very large program with about three thousand clients passing through the program annually. Of the fifty Bay City College respondents included in our study, twenty-six were drawn from a certified nursing assistant class, ten from a child care training class, seven from a GED preparation class, and seven from an ESL class.

Suburban Community College. Suburban Community College is in an attractive, suburban setting in Los Angeles County. It offers similar programs for CalWORKs (TANF) clients to the ones offered by Bay City College, but it is a smaller program with about one thousand clients annually, which is a third of the size of Bay City College's program. It offers skills training in a number of areas, as well as counseling and personal case-management services. Most students also gain work experience by way of an on-campus work-study program. Most have been referred to the program by the DPSS. The staff members we interviewed impressed us as being among the most capable and best motivated of all staff in the programs included in our study. As was the case with Bay City College, job counseling and job placement seemed not to be as strong as they could have been. Of the twenty-three respondents included in our study from Suburban Community College, thirteen were from a training program in early child care and ten were from several other associate of arts programs. This was a well-funded program with impressive supportive services such as case management and a state-of-the-art child care facility.

Center for Adult Education. The center is run by the Division of Adult and Career Education of the Los Angeles Unified School District. It offers a wide variety of vocational and basic education classes. Some of these classes are specifically designed for CalWORKs (TANF) recipients. Some soft-skills training is also offered (interviewing techniques, personal presentation, job preparedness, etc.). The ten respondents from the Center for Adult Education included in our study were students in a computer keyboarding class.

For-Profit Programs

People-at-Work. People-at-Work is a national, for-profit corporation that has existed for more than twenty years and has provided work-force development services in twenty different states. It holds welfare-to-work contracts with several southern California governmental entities. We studied a large one-stop career center run by People-at-Work in the city of Los Angeles. It provides a resource center, case management, and various training classes and workshops. It makes what appear to be strong job placement and job retention efforts. The culture of the program is hard to capture, yet also real. It seems to consist of two features. First, there is a strong consumer orientation. Clients are referred to as "customers," and there appears to be a genuine effort to meet their needs. Second, there is a sense that due to the controversial nature of using a for-profit firm to provide welfare-oriented services they are under close scrutiny and need to perform at a very high level. As the site director said, "And we do work under, I feel, like a different set of rules [than nonprofits]. We are scrutinized more." Later he added, "We are looked at under a microscope every single day." The thirty-six persons from People-at-Work who took part in our survey were from an office assistant's class in which the actual instruction was provided by the Los Angeles Unified School District under contract to People-at-Work.

Western College. Western College is a vocational college, specializing in training for medical careers. It has several campuses in Los Angeles County. Among other programs, it runs a welfare-to-work program, receiving referrals from several one-stop centers and directly from the county DPSS. About half of the students are paying students and half are welfare-to-work students whose expenses are covered by one or more government programs. It previously had a contract with the Los Angeles County DPSS, but that contract had recently not been renewed at the time of our study. Costs for its welfare-to-work students are typically covered by funds from several sources such as the one-stop centers, Pell grants, and Supplemental Educational Opportunity grants. Western College is a fairly small operation, with a total of eight hundred students. Nevertheless, it has three full-time persons and one half-time person working on job placements for its students. One strategy they pursue with reported success is to place students in internships that later turn into jobs. Of the fifty-five respondents from Western College included in our study, thirty-five were from a medical assistant class and twenty from a dental assistant class.

Nonprofit/Secular Programs

Eastern One-Stop. Eastern One-Stop is a career center run by a nonprofit organization in eastern Los Angeles that has been in existence for more than thirty years. It has contracts under the Work Investment Act and with the Department of Labor to provide employment services for welfare recipients and other low-income persons. It provides such services as assessment, job search, GED classes, and skills training. It closely collaborates with a number of government agencies, such as the DPSS and the Los Angeles Unified School District, and receives all of its funding from governmental sources. The one-stop and other welfare-to-work services are only one type of many community economic development services Eastern One-Stop provides. The thirty-nine respondents included in our study were from a job search class, not from a vocational or job training program, as were most of the respondents from the government-run and for-profit programs.

Opportunity-for-All. Opportunity-for-All is a large nonprofit with offices in a number of cities around the country. It specializes in providing resettlement services to immigrants and refugees and runs job clubs and employment counseling and training classes. Almost all of its funding comes from various government sources, including until recently the Los Angeles County DPSS. Only three respondents were from Opportunity-for-All and they were from a job club class.

Together-We-Win. Together-We-Win is a nonprofit organization in south central Los Angeles that seeks to be a multicultural center. Both staff and clients are predominantly African American. This organization provides case management, child care, life skills, and—through the Los

Angeles Unified School District—training in the use of computers. It is medium sized, with one site and ten employees. It serves about two hundred clients a year. Most of its clients are recruited from the community by a variety of means: word of mouth and contacts with other agencies, churches, neighborhood organizations, and elected officials. It receives partial government funding, but also works hard to maintain its own private sources of funds. The twenty-four respondents included in our study were drawn from an office computer training class.

Faith-Based/Segmented Programs

Ellis Center. Ellis Center is a program of Catholic Charities that at the time of our study was running a Department of Labor welfare-to-work program. It was a small program with about thirty-six clients, all of whom had been receiving TANF or some other form of welfare assistance for three years or more. It primarily provides supportive services so that clients can find and maintain employment. The program works with their clients on such needs as job preparedness skills, child care, and emergency assistance. All ten of the Ellis Center respondents were drawn from its welfare-to-work program.

New Beginnings Center. New Beginnings Center is a legally incorporated nonprofit entity run by a predominantly African American Protestant church in a very economically depressed area. The center is located in the church building. It offers a range of services for welfare recipients and other low-income persons, including a hot meals program, a homeless shelter, computer classes (taught by instructors from the Los Angeles Unified School District), and a program for noncustodial fathers. New Beginnings Center runs a small program, with about forty to fifty clients a year, not counting the much larger number of persons served hot meals. A majority, but not all, of its funding comes from government sources. Of the fifteen New Beginnings Center respondents included in our study, eleven were from two different computer classes and four were from the noncustodial fathers program.

Our Father's House. Our Father's House is run directly by a mainline Protestant church. It grew out of a food bank and has added programs over the years as community needs were identified. It seeks to find immediate work for those in need but also provides skills training in office computers. It is a small program, with one full-time and three part-time employees. It receives a little government funding. The county DPSS refers clients to it, but it also recruits clients by word of mouth and various community contacts. Of the eight Our Father's House respondents included in our study, five came from an office computer class and three from the immediate employment program.

Olsen Center. The Olsen Center is a south central Los Angeles community center sponsored by a mainline Protestant denomination. It has a recreation program (its building contains a gym), a food distribution program, a clothes closet, a seniors program, and ESL and computer classes. It serves a very economically depressed area that is largely African American and Latino. It receives no government funding. The three respondents included in our study were from an ESL class (which was taught by an instructor provided by the Los Angeles Unified School District) for Spanish-speaking persons.

Faith-Based/Integrated

Love and Life Center. Love and Life Center is a residential program for unmarried expectant mothers. It initially grew out of a conservative Protestant church but is now an independent nonprofit entity supported by individuals. It receives no government funding. Most of the women with whom it works are receiving assistance under the CalWORKs (TANF) program. In addition to providing residential care, Love and Life Center provides case management; life skills, health, parenting, and Bible study classes; and personal counseling. It has a program for former residents that seeks to follow-through with them and offers additional help. It largely does referrals to other programs for employment services. It is a small program, with only six mothers or expectant mothers in residence at any one time. But with its efforts to maintain continuing contacts with former residents, it is in touch with and seeking to support more than eighty women at any one time. The sixteen respondents from the Love and Life Center included in our study were all from the residential program and included clients who were in residence at the time or who had recently left the residential portion of the program.

New Skills Center. The New Skills Center is a nonprofit entity sponsored by a church in the west Los Angeles County area. It provides life skills classes, mentoring (by members of the sponsoring church), and computer skills classes. It has a strong emphasis on career planning and career choice. It had received no government funding in the past, but recently received a state grant at the time of our study. It is a small program, with ten to fifteen clients in a class that the center runs twice a year. Its clients are largely recruited by word of mouth and a variety of community contacts. The ten respondents included in our study were all from the current or a just completed class.

Community Skills Center. The Community Skills Center is a program run by a nonprofit community development corporation sponsored by a large, predominantly African American Protestant church in south central Los Angeles. It was a new program at the time of our study and was designed to work with the hardest-to-employ CalWORKs (TANF) recipients. More specifically, it largely works with ex-offenders or persons who are near to exhausting their five-year time limit for receiving cash assistance and have a poor work history. The program largely consists of life skills and job skills classes that take about five weeks to complete. It also provides individualized case management services that include assessment, job placement, and retention services. About ten to fifteen persons are involved in the program at any one time. It is fully funded by government money. All eleven respondents included in our study were currently participants in the program.

New Hope Services. New Hope Services is a program located in southern Los Angeles County. It is an independent nonprofit entity that works closely with a number of churches in its community. It is a very young (one year old at the time of our study), small program, with only one full-time and one part-time employee. It works closely with the sponsoring congregations that refer persons with special needs to them. At the time of our study its main program was a mentoring program where members of the sponsoring congregations were linked with persons in need, almost all of whom were receiving some form of public assistance. It receives no government funds. The four persons included in our study from New Hope Services were all taking part in the mentoring program.

From these descriptions a clear distinction emerges between the faith-based programs on the one hand, and government and for-profit programs on the other. The faith-based programs—and especially the faith-based/integrated programs—tended to emphasize training in life skills and work preparedness, that is, training in such things as attitudes, career aspirations, interviewing skills, personal dress and grooming, workplace expectations, and emotional and physical support. These are often referred to as soft skills.[8] With only one exception (Responsible Fathers), the government and for-profit programs tended to emphasize vocational training and the development of marketable or hard skills.[9] In this area, the three nonprofit/secular programs fell in between the government and for-profit programs, on the one hand, and the faith-based programs, on the other. They offered less vocational training and more soft-skills training than the former, and more vocational training and less soft-skills training than the latter.

It is also important to note the small size and often struggling financial nature of most of the faith-based programs. They had an average of only 4.4 full-time employees, and four of the eight faith-based programs had only one or two full-time employees. Their physical facilities were typically spartan and marked by limited equipment and classroom amenities. Only one of the four faith-based/integrated programs included in our study received any government funding, and although three of the four faith-based/segmented programs received government funding, a majority of their funding came from private sources (an average of 53 percent). The four government programs, in contrast, had an average of forty-two full-time employees, the two for-profit programs had an average of sixty-three employees, and the three nonprofit/secular programs had an average of thirteen full-time employees. Almost all of these programs' funding came from government sources, and often amounted to more than a million dollars. Their physical facilities, while hardly lavish, were much larger than the faith-based programs', and were functional and well equipped.

The Study Respondents

This section of the chapter explores, first, whether or not the clients responding to our study appear to be representative of the welfare population of Los Angeles County as a whole, and second, whether or not the respondents appear to differ from one program category to another. If the respondents in our study differ greatly from the Los Angeles welfare population as a whole, there would be reason to believe that for some reason our study tapped into a biased sample of welfare recipients. This would raise doubts about the extent to which our findings are generalizable to the Los Angeles welfare population as a whole. A second issue is whether some types of programs tend to have clients with atypical demographic and other characteristics, which would indicate that the outcomes we later report for them might simply be a result of the different type of clients with which they were dealing. In order to be confident about the conclusions that we draw in this book, therefore, it is important for us closely to examine certain basic characteristics of the persons we surveyed.

First, however, it is helpful to ask whether or not the seventeen programs included in our study were representative of the welfare-to-work programs in urban Los Angeles County. We believe they are. As mentioned earlier and further documented in appendix A, there is evidence that our initial list of 511 welfare-to-work programs was comprehensive and largely complete. As also demonstrated in appendix A, based on the geographic location of the 211 providers that responded to our mailed questionnaire, there is reason to believe that they are not markedly different from the providers that did not respond. Finally, the seventeen programs selected for inclusion in our study were chosen as representative of the other programs in their program category, based on such characteristics as size, services provided, and ethnic or racial makeup.

Figure 2.2 provides the gender, age, and race or ethnicity for the persons who were included in our six-month survey and, for comparative purposes, persons in Los Angeles County who were receiving CalWORKs (TANF) benefits at about the time of our study.[10] Our survey respondents are nearly identical to the CalWORKs population in their gender, racial or ethnic, and age composition. Women compose 81 percent of the CalWORKs population and 84 percent of our survey respondents. Latinos are the largest racial or ethnic group both in our survey and in the CalWORKs population (50 percent and 48 percent, respectively), followed by African Americans (28 percent and 32 percent, respectively), Caucasians (14 percent in both), and Asian Americans (3 percent and 6 percent, respectively). Finally, the age distribution in our survey is very similar to that of the CalWORKs population. These results increase our confidence that the respondents from the seventeen programs that took part in our survey were in fact representative of the welfare population of Los Angeles County as a whole.

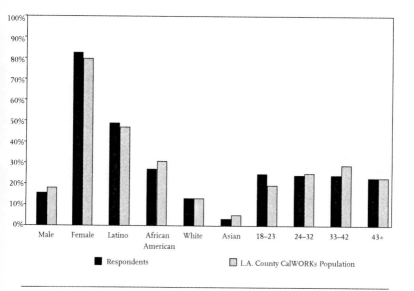

Figure 2.2

Demographic Characteristics of CalWORKs Population and Six-Month Respondents

The results are similar when the clients from the five program types are compared. In no single type of program, for example, were women less than 64 percent of the clients surveyed, although the for-profit and faith-based/integrated programs had a higher proportion of women (95 percent) than the other three program types (see table 2.5). The program types differed in the racial or ethnic composition of their clients. Sixty-six percent of those surveyed from for-profit organizations were Latino, while only 18 percent of the faith-based/integrated clients were Latino. Meanwhile, both of the faith-based program types had a larger proportion of black clients than any of the other types of programs, with the for-profit programs having only 7 percent black clients. The faith-based/integrated programs had a higher percentage of white clients (26 percent) than the other types of programs. Although the figures are not included in table 2.5, the for-profit clients tended to be younger and the nonprofit/secular clients to be older than those of the other programs. More than half (53 percent) of those surveyed from the for-profit organizations were under twenty-four years old, while 47 percent of those from nonprofit/secular groups were over forty-three. In summary, in

Table 2.5

Key Demographic Characteristics, by Program Type, Six-Month Respondents

	Gender			Race/Ethnicity of Respondents					
Program Type	Male	Female	N	Latino	Black	White	Asian	Other	N
	%					%			
Government	18	82	94	46	32	15	3	4	96
For-profit	6	95	91	66	7	21	2	4	91
Nonprofit/secular	21	79	66	55	33	2	3	6	66
Faith-based/segmented	36	64	36	44	47	6	0	3	36
Faith-based/integrated	5	95	38	18	42	26	5	8	38
All respondents	16	84	325	50	28	14	3	5	327

terms of gender, age, and race or ethnicity, the respondents from the five program types tended to be similar, although compared to the other program types more of the for-profit and faith-based/integrated program clients were female, more of the for-profit program clients were Latino and younger, more of the faith-based program clients were black, and more of the nonprofit-secular program clients were older.

Because the level of religious involvement of our respondents might affect their reactions to and how well they would do in faith-based or secular programs, we also asked our respondents about their church attendance. Table 2.6 gives the results. The faith-based/integrated clients were the most likely to report frequent church attendance. Some 63 percent reported at least weekly church attendance (a higher percentage than that for any other program type) and only 21 percent reported rarely attending church (a lower percentage than that for any other program type). The nonprofit/secular and faith-based/segmented clients also reported high levels of religious activity, with more than 50 percent reporting at least weekly church attendance. The government and for-profit clients reported the lowest levels of religious involvement. These differences were statistically significant. We will return to them later as we interpret many of our findings.

It is also important for interpreting our findings to ask whether or not the barriers our respondents faced in seeking employment varied from one program type to another. There is little question that there are barriers that can make it more difficult for a person to find a job. We sorted these obstacles into three large categories: skills barriers, situation-in-life barriers, and attitudinal barriers. We sought to determine

Table 2.6

Religious Involvement at Baseline, by Organization Type, Six-Month Respondents

Program Type	High[a]	Moderate[a]	Low[a]	Total N	%
Government	32%	18%	50%	94	100
For-profit	36%	25%	39%	91	101
Nonprofit/secular	52%	17%	31%	65	100
Faith-based/segmented	53%	19%	28%	36	99
Faith-based/integrated	63%	16%	21%	38	100
All respondents	43%	20%	37%	324	100

$X^2(8) = 19.86, p < .01$

[a] Based on reported level of church attendance at baseline, with high = at least weekly, moderate = a few times a month, and low = a few times a year or never.

if the five program types were drawing clients who were similarly situated in terms of the challenges that they faced in seeking employment. A common criticism of programs that claim a high level of success in moving persons from welfare to work is that those programs have not demonstrated that they have drawn their clients from a representative sample of persons on welfare. "Creaming" the clients with the fewest barriers to employment will predictably lead to higher than average positive outcomes.

First, we considered three potential skills barriers: the lack of a high school education, lack of fluency in English, and the inability to read English well. Many program heads we interviewed for this project suggested that among the most significant skills barriers to a person finding employment is the lack of a high school education. One study of women who left welfare, for example, found that those women with at least a high school education were nearly 40 percent more likely to stay off welfare than those women without a high school education.[11] When we asked the respondents about their educational attainment, nearly one-third (29 percent) reported not having a high school diploma.[12] As table 2.7 shows, however, there are some differences among the different categories of programs. Two program types, for-profit and faith-based/integrated, had somewhat smaller percentages of clients with less than a high school education (19 percent and 22 percent, respectively) than did the other three program types.

Table 2.7

Percentage of Respondents with Less Than a High School Education,
by Program Type, Six-Month Respondents

Program Type	Percentage of Respondents with Less Than a High School Education	N
Government	37	95
For-profit	19	90
Nonprofit/secular	33	66
Faith-based/segmented	35	34
Faith-based/integrated	22	37
All respondents	29	322

In addition to persons who lack a high school education, persons who do not speak English face a major barrier to finding employment. Similarly, persons who do not read English well due either to literacy problems or to English not being their native language face a major employment barrier. We therefore asked respondents in our survey how well they spoke and read English. Eighty percent reported that they read English very well, while 85 percent indicated that they spoke English very well.

Table 2.8 provides the percentages of respondents from each of the five program types who had between zero and three of these particular skills (i.e., had a high school diploma, spoke English well, and read English well). The table shows that a majority of the respondents in our survey (59 percent) had all three of these skills. This population would presumably face the fewest skills barriers to employment. By contrast, only 14 percent of respondents had none or only one of these particular skills, while 27 percent had two of the skills in question.

There are, however, some intriguing differences among the program types. In particular, the for-profit and the faith-based/integrated programs had markedly larger percentages of clients with all three skills (71 percent and 77 percent, respectively) and much lower percentages with only one or none of them (9 percent and 3 percent, respectively). None of the other three program types differed greatly in the percentage of clients facing skills barriers.

In addition to skills obstacles to employment, there are what we call life-situation barriers for persons seeking employment. Sometimes persons looking for a job are not so much limited by a lack of education or language skills but by some factors in their lives that make it difficult

Table 2.8

Total Skills Measure at Baseline, by Program Type, Six-Month Respondents

Program Type	0–1 Skills	2 Skills	3 Skills	Total[a] N	%
		%			
Government	17	33	51	95	101
For-profit	9	20	71	90	100
Nonprofit/secular	23	28	50	66	101
Faith-based/segmented	18	35	47	34	100
Faith-based/integrated	3	20	77	35	100
All respondents	14	27	59	320	100

[a] The percentage of respondents who possessed the following skills at the baseline: a high school diploma or its equivalent, an ability to read English well, and an ability to speak English well.

for them to obtain and keep a job. Our interviews with staff persons involved in welfare-to-work programs led us to conclude that there are at least six significant life-situation obstacles to employment: a history of drug or alcohol abuse, health problems, a crime conviction, being single with two or more children living at home, being unemployed, and finally, a weak work history. Some of these challenges are self-evident. Health problems, for example, might increase the likelihood of a person on welfare being frequently absent from a job and therefore losing it. Being single and having two or more children adds considerable time commitments to parents looking for work, particularly for single mothers, who constitute a disproportionate percentage of persons on welfare.[13] They also face challenges in keeping a job once they find one due to the likelihood of missing work when child care arrangements fall through or when children are ill. Such problems were illustrated when a client who had failed to complete her program replied in response to a question during the six-month telephone interview on why she had left the program: "I left because I had to be at the hospital with my daughter. She was born three months early." Another noted that "the most difficult aspect of the job search is the issue of child care. It is the biggest problem for single parents, and one that could use more help from the government or private industry." Both staff and clients frequently commented about problems related to child care.

A number of the persons we interviewed suggested that being employed—in virtually any job—is the best way for a person on welfare to secure an even better job. Persons with strong work histories are more likely to have the skills and recommendations that are oftentimes necessary for them to secure employment when they do not have a job. Thus we asked persons how long they had held their present or most recent job, how many hours a week they were working (or had worked) at it, and the pay level. Those we classified as having a weak work history were persons who had had their current or most recent job less than three months, worked less than twenty hours a week, and earned less than ten dollars an hour.

We counted a life situation as being a barrier only when the respondent had given information that confirmed she or he faced that barrier to employment. If information was missing or incomplete we counted that respondent as not having that barrier. Thus our measure of life-situation barriers to employment should be viewed as the minimum number of barriers with which the respondents had to contend in finding employment.

As we expected, our respondents varied greatly in the number and nature of the life-situation barriers they faced. Sixty-five percent of those surveyed, for example, were unemployed, and 45 percent had two or more children. By contrast, only 9 percent reported health problems, 6 percent reported a crime conviction in their past, and 2 percent indicated that they had a drug or alcohol problem. The range of possible barriers for each person in our survey was, of course, between zero and six, although no one in our survey reported more than four barriers. Table 2.9 lists the percentages of respondents from each program type with between zero and four of these life-situation obstacles. A significant percentage of the clients we surveyed (37 percent) had at least two of the six life-situation barriers to employment. By contrast, 17 percent had none of these particular obstacles. Because any one of these life situations can make it very difficult for a person to find a job, the high percentage of respondents in our survey who had at least two of them suggests that these clients face formidable barriers in finding steady employment. A person in this category could, by way of example, be a single mother with two or more children living with her at home who is also currently unemployed. Or, alternatively, a person with two such barriers could have both a crime conviction and a weak work history.

Some patterns emerge when the clients of the five program types are compared. The nonprofit/secular and faith-based/integrated programs

Table 2.9

Life-Situation Barriers at Baseline, by Program Type

Program Type	3 to 4 Barriers	2 Barriers	1 Barrier	No Barriers	Total[a]	
					N	%
			%			
Government	6	33	41	20	96	100
For-profit	2	25	56	17	91	100
Nonprofit/secular	9	35	49	8	66	101
Faith-based/segmented	6	28	42	25	36	101
Faith-based/integrated	11	32	42	16	38	101
All respondents	6	31	47	17	327	101

[a] The six life-situation barriers we considered were a history of drug/alcohol abuse, health problems, a crime conviction, being single with two or more children, being unemployed, and a weak work history.

were the most likely to have clients with two or more of these challenges (44 percent and 43 percent, respectively, when one combines those with two barriers and those with three or four barriers), and nonprofit/secular programs also clearly had the lowest proportion of clients with none of these barriers (8 percent). It is worth noting that one of the nonprofit/secular programs, Eastern One-Stop, contributed disproportionately to the number of nonprofit/secular clients with two or more barriers (56 percent of their clients), and one of the faith-based/integrated programs, Community Skills Center, contributed disproportionately to the number of faith-based/integrated clients with two or more barriers (64 percent of their clients). For this measure, at least, it is reasonable to conclude that nonprofit/secular and faith-based/integrated programs had more clients with barriers to employment than did the three other types of programs. Government and faith-based/segmented organizations, on the other hand, were the programs most likely to have clients with no life-situation barriers (20 percent and 25 percent, respectively), while the for-profit programs were the least likely to have clients with at least two of these obstacles (27 percent).

Although we do not have exactly comparable data for the Los Angeles welfare population as a whole in regard to skills and life-situation barriers, from a number of studies it appears that our respondents fit the general mold of welfare recipients who face numerous obstacles to employment. One study, for example, found that 26 percent of the Los

Angeles welfare recipients had been unemployed or on welfare for at least two years and did not have a high school education.[14] This compares to the 29 percent of our respondents who did not have a high school education and 31 percent of our respondents who were facing two life-situation barriers. This same study found that 41 percent of the welfare recipients that had been appraised between 1998 and 2001 had multiple vulnerabilities,[15] compared to 37 percent of our respondents who had two or more life-situation barriers to employment. One cannot speak with certainly, but from what information is available, our respondents seem to be at least roughly similar to the Los Angeles welfare population as a whole in the number of barriers to employment they were facing.

Not only are skills and life situation important factors in a person finding employment, but so too are the attitudes that clients bring with them to the job search. Many program directors and staff with whom we spoke reported that client attitudes of pessimism and a lack of self-confidence are major barriers to employment. To measure these subjective obstacles to employment, we asked respondents in the survey to indicate whether they agreed strongly, agreed, were uncertain, disagreed, or disagreed strongly with the following statements: "Sometimes I get so discouraged it is hard for me to keep going," "No matter how hard I work I doubt I will ever have a really good job," and "I am confident one year from now I will be better off than I am now." We then assigned a numerical value of 1 to 5 for each of the five responses (1 being the most pessimistic response and 5 being the most confident) and created an overall score to measure each client's level of attitudinal optimism. With five possible responses to the three questions, the range of scores for each survey respondent was between 3 and 15. Those whose cumulative scores were from 3 to 8 we labeled as having a very low level of optimism, those with scores of 9 to 10 we considered as having a low level of optimism, those with scores of 11 to 13 we considered as possessing high optimism, and those whose total scores were 14 to 15 we labeled as having a very high level of personal optimism.

Table 2.10 highlights the percentage of respondents for this attitudinal measure for each of the five program types. One interesting result is that our respondents were generally optimistic about their chances of getting ahead. Only 17 percent had a very low level of attitudinal optimism, while 27 percent had a very high level of personal optimism.

Table 2.10

Level of Attitudinal Optimism at Baseline, by Program Type, Six-Month Respondents

Program Type	Very Low	Low	High	Very High	Total[a] N	%
			%			
Government	18	20	34	28	89	100
For-profit	14	14	39	34	89	101
Nonprofit/secular	19	14	42	25	57	100
Faith-based/segmented	21	24	42	12	33	99
Faith-based/integrated	19	25	34	22	32	100
All respondents	17	18	39	27	300	101

[a] Based on three attitudinal questions asked in the questionnaire.

There are some, but not large, differences among the five program types. Compared to every other program type, a smaller percentage of respondents from for-profit groups had very low levels of optimism (14 percent), and a higher proportion were very optimistic (34 percent). By contrast, persons from faith-based/segmented programs were much less hopeful about their prospects, with 21 percent having a low level of attitudinal optimism and only 12 percent being very optimistic. Almost one-half (45 percent and 44 percent, respectively) of the faith-based/ segmented and faith-based/integrated clients fell into either the low or very low levels.

In summary, we can safely conclude that the clients of the seventeen welfare-to-work programs who responded to our original, baseline questionnaire and also to our six-month telephone interview were very similar to the Los Angeles welfare population as a whole in key demographic characteristics and in skills, life-situation, and attitudinal barriers that make finding self-supporting employment a challenge. This fact also adds to our confidence that the seventeen programs we selected for intensive study and their clients who took part in our study are indeed representative of the welfare-to-work programs and their clients in Los Angeles.

In terms of the five categories of programs into which we have divided our seventeen programs, there is no evidence that any one program type has clients facing barriers to employment to a much lesser or greater degree than the other program types. Some program types by some measures admittedly tend to have clients with fewer barriers. For example, the faith-based/integrated programs had a higher proportion of white clients, who tend to have an easier time in the job market than nonwhite job seekers. And for-profit providers had clients with more optimistic, hopeful attitudes. But the faith-based/integrated programs also had more female clients and more clients with less than a high school education, both of which are associated with having a more difficult time in the job market. For-profit firms also had a higher proportion of female clients than did the other program types. Thus one can conclude that no one type of program was—purposefully or inadvertently—composed of clients who were more likely to find employment due to their demographic characteristics or the number of skills, life-situation, or attitudinal barriers to employment with which they had to contend. The nonprofit/secular and the two types of faith-based programs had clients who were more religiously active than did the government and for-profit programs.

In the next three chapters we report our findings. Chapter 3 considers client evaluations of the programs they were in, and chapter 4 considers enabling outcomes. Chapter 5 then presents intermediate and ultimate outcomes. We summarize our findings in chapter 6 and suggest some key public policy observations and implications of our findings.

3

CLIENT EVALUATIONS OF
THEIR PROGRAMS

A crucial but almost universally overlooked factor in measuring program effectiveness is the clients' own evaluations of their experiences while participating in a welfare-to-work program.[1] There are various reasons why it is important to consider clients' perceptions of their programs. First, there is good reason to believe that clients with a positive experience in a program will have greater confidence and motivation as they seek employment, whereas clients who feel negatively about a program will be less motivated to persist in seeking work and overcoming the challenges in keeping a job. A positive experience with a program is not everything for a client finding a job, but it is something in helping to understand why some people find work and others do not. Second, we assume that client opinions are largely accurate reflections of the quality of a program. Thus exploring their opinions is an important first step in understanding the effectiveness of the programs under study. Third, client voices are too often ignored in policy discussions about the success of different kinds of welfare-to-work programs. Such neglect not only fails to appreciate what "consumers" need and want but also reinforces the notion that clients are passive recipients of services rather than individual citizens with values that need to be respected and nurtured. We begin, therefore, with client evaluations of the welfare-to-work programs in which they took part. Understanding their evaluations will help in understanding and interpreting the findings we present in later chapters, whether they relate to enabling, intermediate, or ultimate outcomes.

In order to measure client evaluations of their programs, we asked respondents three sets of questions that called on them to evaluate the program in which they had participated. One set of three questions dealt with the degree to which the program staff had shown a caring, understanding attitude toward them personally. These we considered measures of perceived staff empathy. A second set of two questions dealt with client evaluations of the more practical, instrumental value of their program. Finally, we asked those clients who participated in a faith-based program to assess the religious elements of those programs.

We examined the respondents' evaluations of their welfare-to-work programs, categorizing the evaluations by type of program participated in by the respondents: government, for-profit, nonprofit/secular, faith-based/segmented, and faith-based/integrated. However, in this and subsequent chapters we do not simply consider the ways in which the respondents in different programs differ from each other, but also whether or not they differ by level of personal religious involvement and by race or ethnicity.[2] We did so on the basis that we felt different types of programs might be especially effective or ineffective in working with certain types of clients. In the case of personal religious involvement—intentional religion as we conceptualized it in chapter 1—we felt it reasonable to assume that faith-based programs might be especially effective in working with clients who are themselves religiously active. Faith-based programs would have an additional basis on which to connect with their religiously active clients: establishing rapport, building a sense of community, and making appeals based on shared religious values. Also, we felt religiously inactive clients might not do as well in faith-based programs, because the religious elements in those might not be meaningful to them and might even be experienced as negative.

In regard to race or ethnicity, we had less clear expectations, but some earlier studies, as well as common sense, indicate that some programs might be especially effective in working with certain racial or ethnic groups. As reported in chapter 1, for example, Paul Peterson and William Howell found that a program of educational vouchers raised the educational attainment of African American students but not those of the other students. In addition, as we explained in chapter 2, the faith-based programs tended to emphasize training in soft skills, and government and for-profit programs tended to emphasize training in hard, or vocational, skills. Thus one might suppose that persons of differing ethnic or racial backgrounds might respond more positively to one type of training or the other. At the least, we felt that it was worth exploring the question of whether or not some types of programs were more or less effective with persons from different racial or ethnic backgrounds.

Staff Empathy

In the six-month survey we asked the respondents three questions that dealt with staff empathy: whether or not the people running their program took an interest in them personally, really cared about their problems, and understood them and the situation they were in. (See the six-month interview schedule, questions N2A, N2C, and N2D, in appendix B.) For each statement we asked respondents to indicate if the statement was always true, sometimes true, or never true. These questions directly tested the often-made assertions that for-profit and especially government programs treat their clients in a heavily bureaucratic, uncaring manner and that faith-based and nonprofit programs treat their clients in an especially personal, caring manner.

Overall, a majority of the respondents felt positively about their interactions with the program staff. Fifty-eight percent reported that the staff always took a personal interest in them, 55 percent said that staff always cared about their problems, and 57 percent noted that staff always understood their situation.

There are, however, some differences among the five program types on these measures. The for-profit and the government-run programs consistently did less well on these empathy questions than did the nonprofit/secular and both types of faith-based programs. For example, 71 percent of the clients surveyed from nonprofit/secular programs said that the staff running their program always took a personal interest in them, while only 51 percent of those from government programs reported a similar experience. Moreover, 68 percent of clients from faith-based/integrated programs responded that the people running their program always cared about their problems, while less than half (40 percent) of clients felt the same level of personal support from the staff of the for-profit programs. In addition, one in five respondents from for-profit programs felt that the staff never cared about their problems, which was a higher percentage than any other program type. Finally, nearly two-thirds of respondents from nonprofit/secular and both types of faith-based programs said that the people running their program always understood them and the situation they were in. By contrast, less than half of those surveyed from the for-profit programs (47 percent) and just over half of those from government programs (54 percent) had a similarly positive impression of their programs.

Table 3.1 combines the responses to these three questions to create an overall measure of the perceived staff empathy for clients. We assigned a value of 1 to 3, from the least positive response (never true) to the most positive (always true), for each of the three questions. The range of possible scores for each respondent to the survey therefore was from 3 to 9. We considered that those whose scores ranged from 3 to 4 had a low assessment of their program, those with a score of 5 to 6 had a medium assessment, and those with a score of 7 to 9 had a high assessment of their program. As the table indicates, for-profit groups were the least effective program type on this personal empathy scale. Of the five program types, they had the lowest percentage of clients ranking their programs at the high level of staff empathy and the highest percentage ranking them at the low level. Fifty-six percent of all respondents fell into the high ranking category, but only 46 percent of those in for-profit programs did so. Moreover, nearly one-fourth (23 percent) of respondents from for-profit programs rated their program staff negatively, which was significantly above the figure for any other type of program. The nonprofit/secular and faith-based programs, by contrast, did particularly well on this empathy measurement. It is also worth noting that the clients in government-run programs, although ranking their programs' staffs less positively than did the clients of the nonprofit and faith-based programs, ranked their programs' staffs about as positively as did all of the respondents taken together. Their clients' evaluations did not lend support to the popular impression that government social service programs are especially uncaring and overly bureaucratic.

Client comments in their interviews reinforce the difference that a positive experience with program staff can make for a person looking for a job. When asked to name the part of the program that was most helpful to him, a respondent from a government-run program commented on "the dedication of the people teaching the group to help you, to encourage you to get a job, and to use the skills that you have." Some of the sense of warmth and caring that was present in one of the faith-based/integrated programs is clearly reflected in a client who said of the staff in her program: "It was a Christian program; it was encouraging. It helped get me back on my feet and on the right track. It helped turn me into the mature woman that I am now. They helped a lot." By contrast, when asked what about her program was not helpful, a client of a for-profit program complained: "Teachers didn't take time; they were rude

Table 3.1

Perceived Staff Empathy at Six Months, by Program Type

Program Type	High[a]	Medium[a]	Low[a]	Total N	Total %
		%			
Government	51	40	9	76	100
For-profit	46	32	23	88	101
Nonprofit/secular	66	24	10	59	100
Faith-based/segmented	66	25	9	32	100
Faith-based/integrated	66	20	14	35	100
All respondents	56	30	14	290	100

$\chi^2(8) = 15.90, p < .05.$

[a] Based on clients' responses to questions asking about whether their program staff were interested in them personally, cared about their problems, and understood them and their situation.

and discriminated against Mexicans and Blacks." Another for-profit client reported: "They should go a little further. The teacher wasn't fair; people got diplomas that shouldn't have." These latter quotations were the exception, even for the for-profit programs, but they illustrate the sort of negative reactions some of the for-profit clients related.

This leaves the question of how our respondents' own personal religious involvements related to their perception of staff empathy. Here and elsewhere when we consider the relationship between our respondents' personal religious involvement and their evaluations of the programs they were in and the outcomes they experienced, we consider three separate questions. The first one is whether or not religiously active respondents tended to report more positive experiences or outcomes than did the religiously inactive respondents. Based on earlier research, we felt that religiously active persons, no matter what type of program they were in, might have more positive experiences than religiously inactive persons. This would fit with Byron Johnson's findings reported in chapter 1 that most studies of the relationship between religiosity and desirable social characteristics have found that religiously active persons tend to be marked by positive social characteristics. We also asked two further questions: whether or not the religiously active clients of faith-based programs were likely to have more positive experiences than were the religiously inactive clients of faith-based programs, and whether or not religiously active clients were more likely to have more positive experiences at faith-based programs than at secular programs. Common sense suggests that persons who are themselves religiously involved might relate better to faith-based programs and thus would evaluate them more positively and experience more positive outcomes than persons who are not religiously involved.

It should be noted that when we present findings broken down by levels of religious involvement and race or ethnicity caution is in order, as our findings are often based on very small numbers. We seek to avoid attaching too much weight to these findings. Nevertheless, we present them because of what they suggest, not because they necessarily establish a valid, reliable pattern. In doing so we suggest what in fact may be the case and point the way to potentially productive areas for further research.

Therefore we first determined whether or not the level of personal religious involvement made a difference in how our respondents perceived the empathy of their program's staff. We found that those respondents who were themselves highly or moderately religiously active (that is, attended church weekly or at least a few times a month) ranked their programs' staff higher in empathy than did those who were religiously inactive (that is, never attended church or did so only a few times a year). Sixty percent of the highly religiously active and 63 percent of the moderately religiously active respondents rated their programs' staff as being high in empathy, but only 47 percent of the religiously inactive respondents did so. (See table 3.2.) This may be due to the religiously involved having a more positive outlook that leads them to perceive program staff in a positive light, or it may be due to something in the religiously involved clients' makeup that causes the programs' staff in fact to show more understanding of them. Whatever the cause, it comes into play for the moderately and highly active respondents alike.

Second—in line with our next two questions—we asked whether or not clients of faith-based programs who were themselves religiously involved perceived their program's staff as being more empathic than did clients who were not personally religious. We found this tended to be the case among the faith-based/integrated clients but not the faith-based/segmented clients. Seventy-seven percent of the highly religiously active clients of faith-based/integrated programs fell into the high category in perceived staff empathy, while only 38 percent of their religiously inactive clients did so. (See table 3.2.) Also, 77 percent is a higher percent-

Table 3.2

Perceived Staff Empathy, by Religious Involvement and Program Type

Program Type	High Religious Involvement[a]		Moderate Religious Involvement[a]		Low Religious Involvement[a]	
	Percent High in Staff Empathy[b]	N	Percent High in Staff Empathy[b]	N	Percent High in Staff Empathy[b]	N
Government	55	22	75	12	43	40
For-profit	49	33	46	22	42	33
Nonprofit/secular	66	29	73	11	61	18
Faith-based/segmented	59	17	86	7	63	8
Faith-based/integrated	77	22	60	5	38	8
All respondents	60	123	63	57	47	107

[a] Based on reported level of church attendance at the baseline, with high = at least weekly, moderate = a few times a month, and low = a few times a year or never.

[b] Based on the clients' responses to the same three questions on which table 3.1 is based.

age than we found for religiously active clients in the other programs types. In short, the religiously active clients of faith-based/integrated programs ranked higher in perceived staff empathy than both the clients of faith-based/integrated programs who were not religiously active and the religiously active clients of the other types of programs. This suggests that the staff of explicitly religious programs may have a natural, effective basis for understanding their religiously active clients and forging a positive, caring relationship with them. For whatever reason, there seemed to be an especially good fit between religiously active clients and the workers at faith-based/integrated programs.

Another question we explored was whether or not the programs' clients' perception of staff empathy varied by the racial or ethnic background of the clients. One might suppose that minority clients might be less self-confident or assertive, leading to fewer personal contacts with program staff or receiving less attention and less sympathetic attention than white clients. Table 3.3 tests this presupposition. It shows that overall the black clients saw their programs' staffs as being more empathetic toward them than did either whites or Latinos. Sixty-seven percent of the black respondents fell into the high category in perceived staff empathy, compared to 58 percent and 51 percent, respectively, for

Table 3.3

Perceived Staff Empathy, by Race and Program Type

	White		Black		Latino	
Program Type	Percent High in Staff Empathy[a]	N	Percent High in Staff Empathy[a]	N	Percent High in Staff Empathy[a]	N
Government	70	10	58	26	42	33
For-profit	42	19	50	6	50	58
Nonprofit/secular	100	1	94	16	51	35
Faith-based/segmented	100	1	64	14	69	16
Faith-based/integrated	67	9	64	14	57	7
All respondents	58	40	67	51	51	149

[a] Based on the clients' responses to the same three questions on which table 3.1 is based.

the white and the Latino respondents. The major differences in how clients evaluated the different program staffs' sense of empathy was in the government programs, where the whites tended to see the staffs as especially empathic and the black and Latino clients saw them as being much less so, and the nonprofit/secular staffs, where the blacks saw them as being especially empathic.[3] The staffs of the two types of faith-programs tended to be seen as being empathic, and with no sharp differences from one racial group to another.

Generally, the extent to which the program clients from different racial groups differed from each other in perceiving their program staffs' empathy was outweighed by the similarities. There were some differences by race or ethnicity, but with only two exceptions those differences were not large. The two exceptions are the nonprofit/secular programs, whose black clients rated them especially positively, and the government programs, whose white clients ranked them very positively but whose black and Latino clients ranked them less positively.

Our findings run counter to the idea that welfare programs are so bureaucratic and depersonalized that they demonstrate little or no interest in clients or their particular situation in life. All five program types were reasonably effective in creating a caring, understanding atmosphere, although the nonprofit/secular and both types of faith-based programs were especially effective in doing so.

Even the often supposedly highly bureaucratic, uncaring government-run programs had a majority of clients ranking the programs very positively in terms of staff empathy, and they tied with the faith-based/ segmented programs in having the fewest clients ranking the program staff negatively. It may be that many persons' impressions of government-run welfare programs have been determined by welfare offices that primarily take applications for welfare benefits and determine eligibility. They tend to be very large, with long lines and lengthy waiting times. Their physical appearances are often depressingly dreary. But in Los Angeles County—as is often the case throughout the nation—welfare-to-work services are usually not provided directly by the county Department of Public Social Services but by a variety of public and private agencies. Thus, as noted in chapter 2, the four government programs included in this study consisted not of large, impersonal "welfare offices," but of two community colleges, an adult education center run by the Los Angeles Unified School District, and a localized county program especially for noncustodial parents. None fit the stereotype of a "government welfare program."

There are two possible explanations for the higher rankings the staffs of the nonprofit/secular and faith-based programs received as compared to the government and especially the for-profit program staffs. One is that the nonprofit and faith-based programs attracted staff persons who were in fact more empathetic and caring. Perhaps such programs are more likely than their government-run and for-profit counterparts to emphasize the program mission in their hiring choices and thereby attract persons who are especially sensitive and caring toward the clients they serve. This is what has often been alleged, and our data indicate that this in fact may be the case. But there is another explanation as well. It goes back to the fact noted earlier that most of the for-profit and government programs emphasized hard skills, or vocational, training and the nonprofit and faith-based programs had a greater emphasis on soft-skills training. When working with clients on issues such as personal problems, attitudes, and values, the nonprofit and faith-based staff members would tend to come across as caring and concerned on a personal level, while the for-profit and government staffs, emphasizing training in vocational skills, may come across as being less concerned and understanding on a personal level.

The facts that the personally religious clients saw the faith-based/integrated programs as being empathic, that the black clients saw the nonprofit/secular programs as being empathic, and that the Latino clients perceived the government programs as being less empathic is our first indication that some program types may work better with some types of clients and that all program types do not do equally well or equally poorly with all types of clients. We will see this pattern more often.

The level of staff empathy perceived by the clients of a program is important because building empathetic bridges to clients would seem to be an essential first step in reaching out to them. It is difficult—if not impossible—for a staff member to motivate, encourage, and teach persons if they do not feel he or she cares about or understands them. Our findings indicate that it is the secular nonprofit and faith-based programs that were most effective in building these empathetic bridges and that the faith-based/integrated programs were especially effective in doing so with religiously active clients.

Instrumental Evaluations

In addition to asking clients to evaluate the empathy of their program's staff, we also asked respondents to evaluate the more instrumental value of their programs. It is one thing if program staff are caring and understanding people; it is quite another to determine if they are also perceived as being helpful in a practical, instrumental sense. To measure this factor, we asked the respondents if the following statement was always true, sometimes true, or never true: "The people running or teaching in [name of the program] were knowledgeable about how to help me." In addition, we asked respondents if they thought that their program was very helpful, somewhat helpful, or not at all helpful to them. (See questions N2B and N3 in the six-month telephone survey found in appendix B.) We assigned a value of 1 to 3 for each of the three possible responses to the two questions, with 1 being the most positive response and 3 the least positive response. This resulted in a range of scores from 2 to 6. We considered those who scored a 2 as being high in instrumental evaluation of their programs, those who scored a 3 as being medium in instrumental evaluation, and those who scored 4 to 6 as low in instrumental evaluation (see table 3.4).

Overall, clients believed that the programs and the program staff were instrumentally very helpful to them. Exactly one-half judged their programs very positively in terms of their helpfulness and their staffs' knowledgeableness, and another 29 percent fell into the medium cat-

Table 3.4

Instrumental Evaluations at Six Months, by Program Type

Program Type	High[a]	Medium[a]	Low[a]	Total N	%
		%			
Government	59	25	16	75	100
For-profit	42	30	28	88	100
Nonprofit/secular	54	31	15	59	100
Faith-based/segmented	41	44	15	34	100
Faith-based/integrated	50	16	34	38	100
All respondents	50	29	22	294	101

$\chi^2(8) = 15.99$, $p < .05$

[a] Based on clients' responses to questions asking about their program staff's knowledgeableness in helping them and the general helpfulness of their program, with high equaling 2, medium equaling 3, and low equaling 4–6 on a scale of 2 to 6.

egory; only 22 percent judged their programs negatively. This means that 79 percent of the respondents gave either the most positive response to both questions or the most positive response to one of them and the moderately positive response to the other one. One pattern that emerges when the program types are compared is that the government programs—which did not score especially high on the empathy measurements—did better than any other program type on our instrumental scale, with nearly 60 percent of the clients having a very high evaluation of the government program in which they had participated. Respondents often expressed with enthusiasm their appreciation for what they were taught. One client from a government program said, "Every class taught what it was supposed to. Each teacher informed us a little more than they had to." A client from another government program reported, "We were going to on-the-job training, and that really helped a lot because we were learning how to deal with the kids. The program was really good."

The nonprofit/secular programs also did very well in client instrumental evaluations. One client from a nonprofit/secular program noted the effectiveness of the instructor in his program: "Well, I've had computers and I've taken classes before, but with this instructor, ———, he is an excellent instructor. I think he could teach a rock to use a computer!" The faith-based groups that scored very high on the empathy scale, by contrast, did not do as well on the instrumental scale.

Faith-based/integrated programs, for example, scored among the highest on the three personal empathy questions, and although one-half of their clients ranked them high in instrumental value, they also had the most clients among the five program types scoring low. The for-profit programs did somewhat better than they did on the empathy measures, but—along with the faith-based/integrated programs—lagged behind the other three program types.

Table 3.5 reports the respondents' evaluations of their programs' instrumental effectiveness by program type and religious involvement. One pattern worth noting is that respondents who were highly or moderately religiously active—as determined by those who attended church at least a few times a month—generally tended to rank their programs as being more effective than those who were not religiously active. This was true for all of the respondents taken together and for four of the five program types, with the faith-based/segmented programs being the lone exception. As with our empathy measure, religiously involved respondents tended to evaluate their programs more positively than did the religiously uninvolved respondents, and this was the case whether the respondents were highly or moderately involved. This was particularly the case with the faith-based/integrated clients. If one combines those who attended church at least weekly with those who attended a few times a month, some 60 percent of their religiously active clients ranked high in their instrumental evaluations, while only 13 percent of their religiously uninvolved clients did so—a 47 percentage point difference and a much larger one than for any other program type. However, the religiously active clients of the government and nonprofit/secular programs rated their programs as effective as or even more effective than the religiously active clients of the faith-based/integrated programs rated their programs. Seventy-one percent of the highly and moderately religiously involved government clients, taken together, evaluated their programs in a highly positive manner, and 58 percent of nonprofit/secular clients did so. One can conclude that religiously active clients at faith-based/integrated programs reacted more positively to the instrumental effectiveness of their programs than did religiously inactive clients at those same programs, but religiously active clients did not react more positively to their programs if they were in an integrally faith-based program than if they were in a government or secular nonprofit program.

Table 3.5

Instrumental Evaluations, by Religious Involvement and Program Type

Program Type	High Religious Involvement[a]		Moderate Religious Involvement[a]		Low Religious Involvement[a]	
	Percent High Instrumental Evaluation[b]	N	Percent High Instrumental Evaluation[b]	N	Percent High Instrumental Evaluation[b]	N
Government	68	22	75	12	46	39
For-profit	41	32	57	23	33	33
Nonprofit/secular	59	29	55	11	44	18
Faith-based/segmented	47	19	14	7	50	8
Faith-based/integrated	58	24	67	6	13	8
All respondents	54	126	56	59	40	106

[a] Based on reported level of church attendance at the baseline, with high = at least weekly, moderate = a few times a month, and low = a few times a year or never.

[b] Based on the clients' responses to the same two questions on which table 3.4 is based.

In terms of race and ethnicity, there were no major differences among the five program types, although the nonprofit/secular programs tended to be ranked high by blacks and the government programs were ranked high by Latinos (75 percent of the blacks attending nonprofit/secular programs fell into the high category, and 58 percent of the Latinos attending government programs fell into the high category). This finding in regard to Latinos and government programs is somewhat surprising because, as previously mentioned, Latinos did not view their government-run programs very positively in the empathetic measure. It helps demonstrate that our empathic and instrumental measures were indeed tapping into different perceptions and that clients do not always perceive the two as corresponding measures.

The high rankings given the government programs by their clients on instrumental effectiveness is further demonstration that the image of incompetent, wasteful government welfare-to-work programs—at least in Los Angeles County—is in need of some reworking. The government program clients tended to rank them very positively on this measure, and they did especially well among clients from a Latino background, whose ethnicity can make competing in the job market more challenging. We also found evidence that religiously involved respondents tended to rate their programs more positively on instrumental values. This may be due to religiously involved persons' being likely to perceive a program as effective due to a generally more positive outlook on life, or they may be more open to instruction and learning, thereby viewing their programs more positively. The fact that religiously involved clients in faith-based/ integrated programs viewed their programs much more positively than did clients who were not religiously involved strengthens the case that explicitly religious programs may be very helpful to those who themselves are religious, but less so to those who are not.

Evaluations of Religious Elements in Faith-Based Programs

Many questions have been raised about the nature of faith-based social service programs to which some have been looking to play a larger role in the provision of needed social services. Some of these questions are beginning to be answered.[4] A key perspective that almost all studies have thus far missed, however, is that of the clients who are the ones making use of the services being provided. Therefore, we asked the respondents in the twelve-month survey who had participated in a faith-based program their reactions to the religious elements of their programs.[5]

The first question we asked was whether, in deciding to take part in a faith-based welfare-to-work program, its religious character made them more or less eager to take part in it, or whether it made no difference. (See question S1A of the twelve-month telephone survey in appendix B.) We also gave them the option of indicating that they did not know it was faith-based at the time they chose to take part in it. Table 3.6 gives the results. The first notable pattern in the findings here is that only four out of the forty-four persons surveyed (9 percent) indicated that they did not know the program was faith based at the time they decided to take part in it. Some civil libertarians have understandably feared that some clients of social services might end up in faith-based programs without even realizing it at the time of their enrollment. Our study indicates that those fears appear to be misplaced. Over 90 percent of our respondents who entered a faith-based program knew they were entering a faith-based program.

It is also revealing to note that nearly two-thirds of our respondents reported that the religious aspects of their program made them more

Table 3.6

If the Faith-Based Nature of Their Program Made Respondents
More or Less Eager to Participate in It

Program Type	More Eager[a]	Did Not Make a Difference[a]	Less Eager[a]	Did Not Know Was Faith-Based[a]	Total N	Total %
			%			
Faith-based/segmented	68	21	0	11	19	100
Faith-based/integrated	60	24	8	8	25	100
All faith-based respondents	64	23	5	9	44	101

[a] The exact question was "In deciding to take part in this program did the fact that it had a religious or faith-based aspect to it: Make you more eager to take part in it? Make you less eager to take part in it? Have no effect on your desire to take part in it? Or didn't you know that it had religious or faith-based aspects to it when deciding to take part?" See question S1A of the twelve-month interview schedule in appendix B.

eager to participate in it. Only a handful (two out of forty-four, or 5 percent) saw the religious aspect of the program as a negative. This finding supports those who have argued that there is a demand for faith-based programs and that the clients of social services should be able to have a choice between secular and religious programs. Unfortunately, we did not ask the clients of secular programs if they would have preferred to receive their services from a faith-based provider, but it is clear that the majority of our respondents who were in a faith-based welfare-to-work program saw the religious nature of the program as a plus in deciding to take part in it. Therefore having more faith-based programs might make it easier to find persons disposed to participate in welfare-to-work programs.

Somewhat surprisingly, religious involvement, as measured by church attendance, did not seem to affect the respondents' attitudes toward deciding to participate in a faith-based program. Whether one attended church at least once a week, a few times a month, or a few times a year or never, about 60 to 70 percent saw the religious nature of the faith-based programs as an added advantage in deciding to take part in it. It is also interesting that none of the respondents who infrequently attended church reported that they were not aware of the religious nature of the faith-based program when they decided to participate in it. We also found that race did not affect the respondents' attitudes toward taking part in a faith-based program. Regardless of race, most respondents

Table 3.7

Religious Aspects of Faith-Based Programs Recalled by Respondents

Religious Aspects of Programs	Number Recalling This Aspect
An emphasis on not giving up, having faith, God will help	6
Bible study, prayer, devotions	5
An emphasis on accepting other religions, religious differences	4
Being helpful, listening, caring	2
Generally religious, staff believed in God	2
Proselytizing, accepting Jesus	1
Clergy, nuns present	1

reported that they were more eager to participate in a faith-based program because of its religious nature.

We next asked the respondents in an open-ended question to recall some of the religious aspects of their faith-based program. Twenty-one respondents mentioned some specific religious aspect of the program they could recall twelve months after they had been in it. As table 3.7 shows, the most frequently mentioned religious aspect was an emphasis on not giving up, having faith, and believing that God will help them. This was closely followed by Bible study, prayer, or some other devotional activity and by an emphasis on accepting persons of different religions. The often-feared use of social service programs as recruiting tools for one's church or religious beliefs was mentioned by only one person.

This leaves the question of the respondents' evaluations of the faith-based programs they were in. We asked the respondents whether or not they enjoyed the religious aspects of their program, felt they were a waste of time, or made them feel uncomfortable. (See questions S1C2, S1C3, and S1C4 of the twelve-month telephone survey in appendix B.) Table 3.8 gives the respondents' answers to these three items, with the faith-based/integrated and faith-based/segmented respondents combined due to their small numbers. On every measure, respondents rated the specifically religious elements of their program very positively. Nearly three-fourths (72 percent) reported that it was "always true" that they enjoyed the religious parts of their programs, while only 6 percent said that it was "never true." Eighty-eight percent responded that it was "never true" that the religious aspects of their program were a waste of

Table 3.8

Respondents' Evaluations of the Religious Aspects of Their Program

				Total	
Program Type	Always[a]	Sometimes[a]	Never[a]	N	%
If enjoyed religious aspects	72	22	6	32	100
If religious aspects a waste of time	9	3	88	32	100
If religious aspects made feel uncomfortable	6	13	81	32	100

[a] See the twelve-month interview schedule in appendix B for the exact wording of the questions (questions SC2, SC3, and SC4). The respondents from faith-based/segmented and faith-based/integrated programs are combined here.

time, and only 9 percent said that those religious elements were always a waste of time. Nor did the religious aspects of their program make clients feel uncomfortable. Only 6 percent said that they were always made uncomfortable by the religious aspects of their program, while 81 percent said it was never true that those elements made them feel uncomfortable.

The specific comments made by many respondents illustrate their highly positive reactions to the religions elements in their programs. A respondent from a faith-based/integrated program said, "After the group meeting we would pray. They would pray for people who need special prayer. Bible study. It was just a lot of praying when needed, you know, and it helped a lot. Prayer does help." A respondent from a faith-based/integrated program succinctly described the religious aspects of her program this way: "Listening, helping you, just being there." The respondent from a faith-based/integrated program spoke movingly of the love and acceptance she found in her program: "They behaved like Christ. They were gentle, kind, giving, did not discriminate. They gave me a mentor; they taught me spiritually."

Although we did not include them in table 3.8 due to the small numbers involved, it is worth noting that there were some differences in the responses of clients from faith-based/segmented and faith-based/integrated programs. There was a tendency for clients from the segmented programs—which are less overtly religious—to express slightly stronger reservations about the religious aspects of their program. Twenty percent of those clients (two out of ten), for example, reported that the religious aspects of their program were "always" a waste of time, compared to only 5 percent (one out of twenty-two) of those from faith-based/integrated programs. Similarly, two out of the ten faith-based/segmented clients reported that they were always or sometimes made to feel uncomfortable with the religious aspects of their program, compared to three out of twenty-two respondents from the faith-based integrated programs.

It is somewhat ironic that clients from faith-based/segmented programs—where religion is more behind the scenes—would have expressed greater disaffection with the religious aspects of their program than clients from faith-based/integrated programs, where religion is an up-front and central aspect of the program. Segmented programs might invite more of this criticism precisely because the religious features of their programs are not as manifest in how the organizations present themselves and their programs. Faith-based/integrated programs, by contrast, are rarely unclear about the importance of the religious aspects of their programs. Clients therefore may be less surprised or disappointed with those religious elements in the latter than the former program type. These minor differences aside, overall the clients from faith-based programs—segmented and integrated alike—reported that they enjoyed the religious nature of their welfare-to-work programs and reported very few problems.

Somewhat surprisingly, those who were themselves religiously involved did not rank the religious aspects of their programs any more positively than did those who were not involved. Eighty-one percent of those who attended church regularly responded very positively to the religious aspects of their program on all three of the measures in table 3.8 or responded very positively to two of them and moderately positive to one of them. But of the nonregular attendees (i.e., those who attended a few times a year or never), 83 percent ranked their program equally positively. In short, the religious aspects of the programs were generally appreciated, even by those who themselves were not religiously active.

In terms of race, however, there were some differences. The number of respondents for whom we had racial data, who had attended a faith-based program, and for whom we had evaluations of the religious aspects of their programs was very small, and thus these findings must be treated as tentative at best. Yet we decided to present them here because they illustrate how the effectiveness of faith-based programs may vary

Table 3.9

Percentage of Respondents Giving the Most Positive Evaluation of the
Religious Aspects of Their Program

Respondent Characteristic	Always Enjoyed[a]		Never a Waste[a]		Never Uncomfortable[a]	
	%	N	%	N	%	N
White	50	10	80	10	60	10
Black	73	11	91	11	91	11
Latino	88	8	88	8	88	8

[a] See the twelve-month interview schedule in appendix B for the exact wording of the
questions (items SC2, SC3, and SC4). The respondents from faith-based/segmented
and faith-based/integrated programs are combined here.

by the ethnic or racial background of their clients. The black and Latino
respondents attending faith-based programs reported more positive reactions to the religious elements than did the white respondents (see table 3.9). The more positive reactions by blacks and Latinos to faith-based
programs may reflect the generally more religiously oriented nature of
the black and Latino cultures in the United States.[6]

Finally, we also asked the more practical question of whether or not
the respondents felt their programs' religious aspects helped in their efforts to prepare for a good job. (See question S1C1 in the twelve-month
telephone survey in appendix B.) In response, the faith-based clients
linked the religious aspects of their programs with the successful pursuit of more instrumental goals. Nearly two-thirds (63 percent) said it
was "always true" that the religious aspects of their program helped
in their efforts to improve themselves and get a good job, while only
9 percent said that this statement was "never true." The faith-based/
integrated and faith-based/segmented programs did not differ on this
score.

In terms of individual respondent differences we found that 69 percent of the respondents who were themselves religiously involved—
those who attended church a few times a month or more—reported
that the religious aspects of their faith-based programs "always" helped
them to improve themselves and to get a good job, while only 33 percent of the respondents who were not religiously involved did so. This
was even truer among the respondents who had attended faith-based/

integrated programs. In terms of ethnicity, the Latino respondents were more likely to report that they always found the religious aspects of their programs helpful (at 75 percent) than did the black (at 45 percent) or the white (at 60 percent) respondents.

In summary, we found that the clients of faith-based programs were overwhelmingly positive about the faith-based elements in their programs. The positive reactions overshadowed any differences between clients of segmented or integrated programs and any differences among clients of varying levels of religious involvement or of different racial or ethnic backgrounds.

Observations

The findings reported in this chapter suggest several things about welfare-to-work programs. First, the data do not support the criticism that welfare-to-work programs are inherently uncaring and coldly professional in their dealings with clients. An impressive percentage of clients responded positively that staff showed a personal interest in them, that they understood the problems they faced, and that they cared about them. The programs are also doing a good job on our instrumental measurements; as a rule, the clients we surveyed felt that the staff in their particular program was knowledgeable about what they needed and that the program was helpful to them. Finally, clients from faith-based programs responded very positively to the religious aspects of their program. Based on client responses, the faith-based welfare-to-work programs we studied appear to be effective and in keeping with client desires.

Some interesting differences emerged among the clients of the five program types. As we have noted, clients from the secular nonprofit and faith-based groups rated their programs significantly better than did the clients from the government and for-profit programs on our empathy questions, while government programs were rated more positively on instrumental measures. What implications can we draw from this? We think it is likely that programs have different self-understandings about how they can be most successful in working with clients. As we noted in chapter 2, five of the six government and for-profit programs emphasized vocational training and the development of marketable skills, so-called hard skills over so-called soft skills, that is, attitudes, work preparedness, relationships, and general living skills. The latter were emphasized by most of the eight faith-based programs included in our study. Government and for-profit providers seemed to understand their purpose primarily in terms of providing clients with marketable skills for the workplace, while the faith-based programs seemed to see their primary purpose in terms of providing clients with the values, attitudes, and lifestyle practices that will enable them to compete successfully in the job market.

It is worth noting that client evaluations roughly track the different natures of the program types. The programs that emphasize soft skills are the ones whose clients tend to rank them high in staff empathy but tend to rank them lower in instrumental evaluations. Meanwhile, those program types that emphasize the hard skills are the ones whose clients tend to rank them highly in instrumental evaluations but lower in staff empathy.

These program differences are reflected in tables 3.10 and 3.11. Table 3.10 summarizes the findings of an analysis of the clients' positive answers to two open-ended questions, one of which asked about what was helpful about their programs and one of which asked generally about any ideas or suggestions they had concerning the program they had been in. (See questions N3AP and N9P of the six-month telephone survey in appendix B.) Table 3.10 shows how frequently the respondents mentioned various positive aspects of their programs in response to these questions. What is most illuminating for our purposes is that the government and for-profit clients most frequently mentioned their appreciation for training in hard, or job, skills, the very type of training that, we saw in chapter 2, these two types of programs tended to emphasize. Meanwhile, the faith-based/integrated clients most often mentioned either training in soft skills or a helpful, empathic staff, the very type of emphasis that, we saw in chapter 2, these programs tended to have. Similarly, table 3.11 reports an analysis of the responses to three open-ended questions that elicited negative or critical responses from the clients. One asked what features of their program they did not like or were not helpful to them, one asked how they felt the programs could have been improved, and one asked generally about any ideas or suggestions they had concerning the program they had been in.[7] (See questions N3BP, N3CP, and N9P of the six-month telephone survey in appendix B.) Here it is important to note that the faith-based/integrated

Table 3.10

Classification of Positive Comments in Response to Two Open-Ended Questions

Organization Type	Hard Skills, Job Training[a]	Soft Skills, Attitudes[a]	Concrete Help, e.g., Child Care, Transport.[a]	Help Finding a Job[a]	Empathic, Helpful Staff[a]	Generally Helpful, Basic Skills[a]	Misc.[a]	Total Comments N	Total Comments %
			%						
Government	38	14	5	6	7	25	6	85	101
For-profit	55	4	0	9	12	15	5	101	100
Nonprofit/secular	24	10	8	31	3	19	5	59	100
Faith-based/segmented	12	25	6	2	13	33	10	52	101
Faith-based/integrated	12	26	12	9	24	12	6	34	101
All respondents	34	13	5	11	11	21	6	331	101

[a]The questions were "What was it about the program that was helpful to you?" and "Are there any comments, ideas, or suggestions you want to share with the people at Pepperdine or the program you participated in?" [Only positive responses were included in this analysis.] See questions N3A and N9P in the six-month interview schedule in appendix B.

Table 3.11

Classification of Negative Comments in Response to Three Open-Ended Questions

Organization Type	Not Enough or Right Type of Skills, Job Training[a]	Teachers Not Fair, Lacked Concern, Not Effective[a]	Not Enough Help Finding Jobs[a]	Lack of Organization, Poor Equipment, Supplies[a]	Program or Classes Too Short, Not Enough Time[a]	Too Few Teachers, Not Enough Individual Help[a]	Misc.[a]	Total Comments N	%
				%					
Government	2	30	5	9	2	16	36	44	100
For-profit	11	17	12	15	15	9	23	102	102
Nonprofit/secular	6	9	45	6	6	3	24	33	99
Faith-based/segmented	7	19	19	7	7	0	41	27	100
Faith-based/integrated	25	16	6	6	3	0	44	32	100
Total	10	18	15	11	9	7	30	238	100

[a] The questions were "Why do you think the program wasn't helpful? What in particular did you not like about it? How do you think it [the program] could have been improved? Are there any comments, ideas, or suggestions you want to share with the people at Pepperdine or the program you participated in?" [Only negative responses were included in this analysis.] See questions N3BP, N3C, and N9P in the six-month interview schedule in appendix B.

clients most frequently cited the lack of appropriate or helpful training in job skills (25 percent of all negative comments). The government program clients most often cited problems or unhappiness with the staff who were teaching in their programs (30 percent).

These findings demonstrate that the different emphases of the different program types tended, in a rough manner, to be reflected in their clients' positive or negative comments on their programs. Those programs that emphasized marketable skills—the government and for-profit programs—tended to receive many positive and very few negative comments on job training, but received more negative and fewer positive comments on "softer" aspects of their programs such as soft-skills training and concerned, empathetic teachers who gave individual help. Meanwhile, especially the faith-based/integrated programs—which emphasized soft-skills training and not job-skills training—received many positive comments in regard to staff empathy and soft-skills training and more negative comments on the lack of job skills training. The faith-based/segmented programs tended to come out strong in terms of soft-skills training and general helpfulness, which would also seem to reflect their emphasis on soft-skills training. The nonprofit/secular clients, curiously enough, most often mention under their positive comments help in finding jobs, and under their negative comments not enough help in finding jobs. This may reflect their mixture between hard- and soft-skills emphases, thereby raising certain expectations without fully satisfying them. In short, one can say that from the clients' perspective, the different program types were largely successful in what they set out to do.

This is not to suggest that government and for-profit programs are uncaring—our findings do not support that conclusion—but only that this is not a primary focus of their programs and thus it was not seen by their clients as a strength. They are focused, instead, on the instrumental skills that clients will need to find a job. Nonprofit and faith-based programs, by contrast, oftentimes have a mission that encourages staff to think more holistically about clients' social, attitudinal, and spiritual needs. While faith-based and nonprofit/secular programs are neither indifferent to nor unsuccessful at providing clients with the instrumental skills that they will need in the workplace—our findings do not support this conclusion—they seem to be more sensitive to clients' personal needs. This was especially the case with the faith-based/integrated programs. The mission statement of one of these providers included in our study reflects this attitude: "We envision a warm place of refuge and holistic restoration for pregnant women and their children. This is a place of reconciliation where people from all traditions and viewpoints can come together to act justly affirming that the lives of women and their unborn children are highly valued. We see a place where the active love of Christ is tangible, offering women and their children a new chance at life."

There also were some—but limited—differences in the evaluations of their programs by respondents of differing levels of religious involvement, as well as ethnic or racial background. Most notably, on our empathy measure, the faith-based/integrated clients who were religiously active rated their programs very highly—more highly than similarly active clients from any other program type—and the religiously inactive clients rated their programs less positively than the religiously inactive clients of any other program type. This suggests that while intensely faith-based programs may be very effective with clients who are themselves religiously active, they may be less effective among those who are not religiously active. This conclusion is reinforced by the fact that on our instrumental measures, the religiously active faith-based/integrated clients also rated their programs very positively, but their religiously inactive clients rated their programs much less positively (less so than any other program type). However, when asked explicitly about the religious aspects of their faith-based programs, the clients of both types of faith-based programs tended to rate their programs positively, whether or not they were religiously involved themselves. We conclude from this that the integrally faith-based programs may be especially well suited for those who themselves are religiously active, but may be less well suited for those who are not religiously active, even though the religiously inactive in faith-based programs generally do not object to the religious elements in them. We will consider this in greater detail in later chapters.

We also found that the faith-based programs may hold special appeal to minority clients. This was particularly clear in their responses to the questions that explicitly asked about the religious elements in the faith-based programs. Plus, the nonprofit/secular programs were seen by black respondents as being especially empathetic in nature.

What we conclude is that there is merit in a welfare-to-work policy that is fluid enough to allow different programs to provide different needs for different clients. Our findings thus far argue against a "one size fits all" approach. Some clients may already have in place the attitudes and sense of self-confidence that they need to succeed, but they lack a particular skill for employment. For them, a program that focuses largely on skills training may be most appropriate. For other clients, however, the biggest obstacle to employment may be that they may lack the self-confidence or other attitudes necessary to go out and persevere in looking for work. For them, a program that emphasizes certain attitudes or values and responds to certain personal needs may be more helpful than one that simply trains them with a vocational skill. Yet others may need both, and for them a combination of programs may be best. Also, those who are themselves deeply religious may especially benefit from an integrally faith-based program. Similarly, there is some evidence that black and perhaps Latino clients may respond more positively to a faith-based program. We will explore these issues more fully in subsequent chapters.

4

ENABLING OUTCOMES

"Throughout my life, from twelve years old to thirty years old, I had been homeless off-and-on, but [now] I have had a place to live, I have a car, I have child care, I have completed my probation and remained sober. I am healthy emotionally."

"Because I felt like I wanted to quit [the welfare-to-work program] sometimes, but the teachers and the students say don't quit, keep going. They encourage me. They help me a lot with the things in my life and also with program things I didn't understand."

"It raised my self-esteem."

These three comments—made, in order, by participants in a faith-based/integrated, a for-profit, and a government program—illustrate what we consider enabling outcomes. They do not refer to what chapter 1 conceptualized as ultimate or even intermediate outcomes; they do not refer to jobs found or wage increases attained. Instead, they refer to positive outcomes that make finding jobs and attaining increased wages more likely: solutions to transportation, child care, and sobriety issues; an encouraging support system in the form of teachers and fellow students; and increased self-esteem. They illustrate enabling outcomes.

This chapter compares the enabling outcomes experienced by the clients from the five different program types. In chapter 1 we identified four enabling outcomes that are especially relevant in the welfare-to-work field: basic language and educational attainments, vocational or job skills, attitudinal changes, and social capital. We were unable to develop measures for all four of these types of enabling outcomes. There are, however, three outcomes that we used to assess the effectiveness of the five types of programs in helping their clients to achieve enabling outcomes: an increase in a sense of hope and optimism for the future, program completion, and growth in social capital. This chapter considers each of these three outcomes in turn, explaining why we consider them to be enabling outcomes and presenting our findings.

Increased Hope and Optimism

A major barrier to many welfare recipients' ability to achieve gainful employment consists of mental attitudes of hopelessness and despair. A defeatist mindset that becomes a self-fulfilling prophecy is too often the result of seemingly overwhelming problems and past experiences of failure or rejection—at school, in previous jobs, and even in family relationships. A caseworker for a government-run agency put it well: "As far as the problems our clients face, it runs the gamut from gangs, drugs, pregnancy, and not having anyone to help them. When people in Malibu have problems, they have skills and resources to handle the situation. People around here have never learned the skills to manage their problems." Rarely experiencing success and facing multiple problems in their lives can very easily lead persons on welfare to conclude pessimistically that there is no chance for them to find a job and establish a healthy, productive life. Finding a job—which typically involves many rejections before experiencing success—arranging for appropriate transportation, clothing, and often child care, and working with supervisors who may be less than understanding and accommodating is not a task for the fainthearted. It takes perseverance and commitment. In short, vital in efforts to find a job and to persist in an often initially low-paying job is a client's inner strength and sense of personal hope that will help her or him to persevere through difficult circumstances, rather than surrendering to a sense of despair and hopelessness. Thus a very important positive outcome that is an enabler toward economic self-sufficiency is a higher level of optimism and confidence in the future.

The baseline questionnaire asked all of the respondents to indicate whether they agreed strongly, agreed, were uncertain, disagreed, or disagreed strongly with the following three statements: "Sometimes I get so discouraged it is hard for me to keep going," "No matter how hard I work I doubt I will ever have a really good job," and "I am confident one year from now I will be better off than I am now." (See questions 13a, 13b, and 13c in the baseline questionnaire in appendix B.) Table 2.10 in chapter 2 highlights the percentage of respondents who fell into four levels of attitudinal optimism at the baseline. As seen there our respondents generally were surprisingly optimistic about their chances of getting ahead. Only 17 percent had a very low level of attitudinal optimism, while 66 percent had either a high or a very high level of personal optimism. The for-profit clients tended to be somewhat more optimistic and the faith-based clients somewhat less optimistic at the baseline.

In order to assess the impact that the different types of programs had on their clients' levels of attitudinal optimism, we presented these same three items to the respondents after six months and again after twelve months. As we did at the baseline, we assigned scores from 1 to 5 for clients' responses—with 1 representing the most pessimistic attitude and 5 the most optimistic attitude—and then calculated a score for each respondent ranging from 3 to 15. We did this based on the baseline questionnaire as well as on the six-month and twelve-month interviews. This enabled us to determine for each respondent whether he or she moved toward greater or lesser optimism, or whether his or her level of optimism remained stable. If a respondent's attitude did not change at all or by only 1 point, either plus or minus, we considered his or her attitude not to have changed.

Table 4.1 reveals the results. At six months all of the respondents taken together demonstrated almost no net gain in attitudinal optimism. Twenty-seven percent were more optimistic than they had been 6 months earlier, 48 percent had the same level of optimism, and 25 percent were less optimistic. At twelve months there had been a slight gain in optimism, with 32 percent being more optimistic and 25 percent less optimistic. Clearly, the enabling outcome of increased hope and a lessening of despair is not an easy one to come by.

The for-profit and faith-based/integrated providers had a slight edge over the other types of providers, although the differences among the five program types were not statistically significant. What differences there were can be more clearly seen in table 4.2, which subtracts the percentage of clients with lower levels of optimism from the percentage of clients with higher levels of optimism for each program type. At six months the faith-based/integrated programs were doing the best, and at twelve months the for-profit programs were doing the best. The government programs also did well at the time of the twelve-month interviews, and the faith-based/integrated programs were not far behind. The faith-based/segmented programs were clearly the least effective on this measure.

Table 4.1

Percentage of Respondents Whose Attitudes Were More or Less Optimistic at Six and at Twelve Months Compared with Attitudes at the Baseline, by Program Type

	At Six Months				At Twelve Months			
Program Type	% More Optimistic[a]	% Same Level of Optimism[a]	% Less Optimistic[a]	N	% More Optimistic[a]	% Same Level of Optimism[a]	% Less Optimistic[a]	N
Government	29	42	29	89	33	44	23	69
For-profit	25	56	19	88	30	53	17	70
Nonprofit/secular	30	44	26	57	33	33	33	51
Faith-based/segmented	21	46	33	33	30	35	35	23
Faith-based/integrated	28	53	19	32	32	44	24	25
All respondents	27	48	25	299	32	43	25	238

$X^2(8) = 6.37$, $p = .61$ $\qquad\qquad$ $X^2(8) = 7.37$, $p = .50$

[a] These figures are based on the responses to the three items testing for attitudinal optimism. They were obtained by assigning scores ranging from 1 to 5—with 1 as the least optimistic response and 5 as the most optimistic—and then calculating each respondent's score at the baseline and at six and twelve months. We next compared the baseline score with the six- and twelve-month scores for each respondent. Those who scored more than 1 point higher were considered to have gained in optimism, those who scored more than 1 point lower were considered to have lost in optimism, and those who scored the same or only 1 point more or less were considered to have stayed the same in level of optimism. The above percentages are those of respondents from each program type who evidenced more, the same, or less optimism.

Table 4.2

Percentage of Clients with More Optimistic Attitudes Minus the Percentage of Clients with Less Optimistic Attitudes, Compared with the Baseline, at Six and at Twelve Months, by Program Type

	Percentage of Clients with More Optimistic Attitudes Minus the Percentage of Clients with Less Optimistic Attitudes, at 6 Months[a]	Percentage of Clients with More Optimistic Attitudes Minus the Percentage of Clients with Less Optimistic Attitudes, at 12 Months[a]
Government	0	+10
For-profit	+6	+13
Nonprofit/secular	+4	0
Faith-based/segmented	−12	−5
Faith-based/integrated	+9	+8
All respondents	+2	+7

[a] More precisely, the percentage of clients with more optimistic attitudes at six and at twelve months compared with their attitudes at the baseline, minus the percentage of clients with less optimistic attitudes compared with their attitudes at the baseline.

That the faith-based/integrated programs did almost as well as the for-profit programs in increasing clients' attitudinal optimism is remarkable because—as we will see in the next chapter—the for-profit clients had in fact fared better in improving their employment situations and in leaving the TANF program than had the faith-based/integrated clients. Increased optimism among the for-profit clients can be explained because many of them had found jobs and had successfully gotten off of TANF. Clients from faith-based/integrated programs were less likely to have found work at six or twelve months, yet their increases in personal optimism were almost on par with the clients from for-profit programs, many of whom had found jobs. It may be that explicit, positive references to religious themes and ideas play a more important role than is often assumed in achieving the enabling outcome of raising clients' sense of hope and optimism.[1] As the client from a faith-based/integrated program that we quoted in chapter 2 said, "It was a Christian program, it was encouraging, it helped me get back on my feet and on the right track. It helped turn me into the mature woman that I now am. It helped me a lot." The "help" highlighted by this client was not in finding a job, but in helping her to change her attitudes and perspectives on life.

Table 4.3

Optimism at Baseline, by Religious Involvement, Six-Month Respondents

Religious Involvement[a]	Very High Optimism[b]	High Optimism[b]	Low Optimism[b]	Very Low Optimism[b]	Total %	N
			%			
High	24	36	21	20	101	121
Moderate	20	46	20	15	101	61
Low	33	36	15	16	100	116
All respondents	27	38	18	17	100	298

[a] Based on reported level of church attendance at baseline, with high = at least weekly, moderate = a few times a month, and low = a few times a year or never.

[b] Based on responses to questions 13a to 13c in the baseline questionnaire, with a score of 1 to 5 assigned each respondent for each question and the responses totaled for a score of 3 to 15 for each respondent. Those scoring 3 to 8 were considered to be very low in optimism, 9 to 10 to be low in optimism, 11 to 13 to be high in optimism, and 14 to 15 to be very high in optimism.

While not the ultimate outcome of finding employment, this enabling outcome would, nonetheless, be an aid in her pursuit of work.

This leaves the question of the respondents' own personal religious involvements and how they affected their experiences in welfare-to-work programs and their subsequent outcomes. As in the process outlined in chapter 3, we explored three separate questions in regard to personal religion and program outcomes. The first question is whether or not religiously active respondents tended to fare better in terms of outcomes than did the religiously inactive respondents—in this case, whether or not they experienced greater increases in hope and optimism than did the religiously inactive clients. One might suppose that the more religiously active respondents would experience a greater increase in optimism than would the less religiously active. They are more likely than their less religiously involved counterparts to be integrated into support groups in their religious congregations, and they might have inner spiritual resources on which to draw, giving them more hope for the future. In chapter 3 we indeed found that the religiously active respondents tended to evaluate their programs more positively in terms of staff empathy and instrumental effectiveness than the religiously inactive respondents.

However, we found almost no relationships between our respondents' personal religious involvement and positive outcomes in terms

Table 4.4

Religious Involvement[a]	More Optimism[b]	Same Optimism[b]	Less Optimism[b]	Total	
				%	N
		%			
High	32	42	26	100	65
Moderate	30	47	23	100	70
Low	35	38	27	100	74
All respondents	33	42	25	100	209

Changes in Optimism, Baseline to Twelve Months, by Level of Religious Involvement

$X^2(4) = 1.31$, $p = .86$

[a] Religious involvement was based on reported church attendance at the baseline and at the twelve-month interviews. High = attendance once a week or more at both the baseline and twelve months; Moderate = attendance once a week or more at the baseline or at twelve months and lower church attendance at the other point, or attendance a few times a month at both the baseline and twelve months; Low = attendance a few times a year or never at both the baseline and twelve months or attendance a few times a month at the baseline or at twelve months and attendance a few times a year or never at the other point.

[b] The changes in levels of optimism were calculated the same way as they were in table 4.1.

of hope and optimism for the future. Table 4.3, first of all, shows that at the baseline those respondents who were active religiously, as measured by church attendance, did not have more optimism or hope than those who were not religiously active. In fact, there was a trend in the opposite direction. Of those who were highly involved religiously, 24 percent were highly optimistic compared to 33 percent of those who were uninvolved religiously. And of those who were religiously active, 41 percent were low or very low in optimism, while of those who were not active religiously, 31 percent were low or very low in optimism.

This leads to the question of the relationship between religious involvement and changes in optimism. Perhaps those who were religiously involved would be more likely to experience increases in optimism. But this did not turn out to be the case either. Table 4.4 shows that there is no discernable pattern of the religiously involved persons experiencing a greater increase in optimism than did those who were not religiously involved. From the baseline to the twelve-month survey, those who were low in religious involvement were as likely to experience an increase in optimism as were those who were very active religiously.

We next asked two further questions: whether or not the religiously active clients of faith-based programs were likely to experience greater

Table 4.5

Percentage of Respondents More Optimistic, Baseline to Twelve Months, by
Religious Involvement and Program Type

Program Type	High Religious Involvement[a]		Moderate Religious Involvement[a]		Low Religious Involvement[a]	
	Percent More Optimistic[b]	N	Percent More Optimistic[b]	N	Percent More Optimistic[b]	N
Government	41	17	21	14	35	26
For-profit	25	16	32	22	38	21
Nonprofit/secular	33	15	44	16	31	16
Faith-based/segmented	40	10	0	8	50	4
Faith-based/integrated	14	7	40	10	29	7
All respondents	32	65	30	70	35	74

[a] The level of religious involvement was measured the same way as it was in table 4.4.

[b] The changes in attitudinal optimism were measured the same way as they were in table 4.1.

increases in optimism than were the religiously inactive clients of faith-based programs, and whether or not religiously active clients were more likely to experience increases in optimism at faith-based programs than at secular programs. Table 4.5 explores these questions. The numbers in the individual cells are small, and thus the observed patterns must be taken with much caution, but the information in the table has several interesting, suggestive results.[2] Contrary to what we expected to find, there was no clear pattern of the religiously active clients in faith-based programs having a greater increase in their optimism than the religiously inactive clients in those same programs. Those respondents who were low in religious involvement and attended either a faith-based/ segmented or faith-based/integrated program actually experienced a greater increase in optimism than did those clients who were high in religious involvement, the exact opposite of what we had expected. The numbers here are so small that these results should be taken as no more than suggestive of what may be the case, but they do raise an important caution flag in assuming that religiously active clients will do better in a faith-based program. On the other hand, they also suggest that clients may experience positive outcomes in a faith-based program even if they themselves are not religiously active. It may be that the messages

Table 4.6

Percentage of Respondents More Optimistic, Baseline to Twelve Months, by Race or Ethnicity and Program Type

Program Type	Whites		Blacks		Latinos	
	Percent More Optimistic[a]	N	Percent More Optimistic[a]	N	Percent More Optimistic[a]	N
Government	30	10	25	24	41	29
For-profit	40	15	33	6	25	44
Nonprofit/secular	0	1	39	13	29	34
Faith-based/segmented	0	1	30	10	36	11
Faith-based/integrated	50	8	22	9	17	6
All respondents	37	35	29	62	31	124

[a] The changes in attitudinal optimism were measured the same way as they were in table 4.1.

of hope and purpose rooted in religious values experienced in faith-based programs were something new for the nonreligious clients and they responded positively to them, while the religiously involved clients had already heard such messages and thus did not experience the same positive response.

Table 4.5 also shows that those clients who were highly involved religiously did not tend to do better at faith-based rather than at secular programs. In fact, highly religious clients of government-run, for-profit, or nonprofit/secular programs tended to experience as great or a greater increase in optimism than did the highly religious clients of faith-based programs. Again, this is contrary to our expectations. In short, by several measures we found that personal, organic religion was not related to the respondents' level of hope and optimism for the future.

When we tested for changes in levels of optimism by race and ethnicity, we found some modest differences. (See table 4.6.) Overall, more white respondents experienced gains in optimism (37 percent) than did either blacks or Latinos (29 percent and 31 percent, respectively). This may reflect subtle or overt patterns of discrimination still present in society and a larger number of other challenges that black and Latino respondents may face, resulting in more of them experiencing frustrations and disappointments. In terms of differences by program type, whites tended to experience somewhat greater increases in optimism at for-profit and faith-based/integrated programs, blacks at nonprofit/secular programs, and Latinos at government and faith-based/segmented programs. In chapter 3 we found that blacks who attended nonprofit/secular programs rated them very positively in terms of staff empathy, as did Latinos who attended faith-based/segmented programs. The perceived staff empathy may help explain the increases in optimism experienced by blacks at nonprofit/secular programs and Latinos at faith-based/segmented programs. Running counter to this observation, however, are Latinos in government programs, who did not rate their programs positively in terms of staff empathy, yet gained in optimism.

In summary, we found the government, for-profit, and faith-based/integrated programs to be the most effective types of programs in terms of the enabling outcome of increased client optimism and hope for the future. The religiously active clients were not found to experience a greater increase in optimism than did the religiously inactive clients, and this held true whether they were in a faith-based or a secular program. White respondents tended to experience greater increases in optimism than did minority respondents, although blacks at nonprofit/secular programs and Latinos at faith-based/segmented and government programs also did well in this outcome measure.

Program Completion

Completion of a welfare-to-work program can itself be considered an enabling outcome. For many persons struggling to survive on welfare, completing a program in itself is a major achievement. Doing so is evidence of a participant's ability to set a goal and then persist in achieving it. This involves many of the same skills or resources one needs to succeed in the work place: solving child care and transportation challenges, learning to keep a schedule, struggling to pay overdue bills, and persevering in a commitment once made. Many welfare-to-work programs we visited had elaborate "graduation" ceremonies to mark the end of a program, with members of clients' families in attendance and recognition and praise heaped on those who had completed the program. Thus the simple fact of completing a program may appropriately be considered an enabling outcome; it certainly is evidence of the presence of key attitudes and skills that are enabling outcomes. It should be kept in mind, as we noted in chapter 2, that the seventeen programs we

Table 4.7

Percentage of Respondents Who Failed to Complete Their Programs,
by Program Type

Program Type	Percent Who Did Not Complete Program[a]	N
Government	19	96
For-profit	8	91
Nonprofit/secular	40	66
Faith-based/segmented	39	36
Faith-based/integrated	14	36
All respondents	22	325

$X^2(4) = 31.70, p < .001$

[a] That is, the percent of clients who at the baseline were in a welfare-to-work program, but at six months reported that for some reason they did not complete it and left early. The vast majority of those who did not fall into this category had successfully completed the program, although a few were still in the program at six months.

studied varied in length and intensity. Thus completing some programs involved more effort than completing other programs. Nevertheless, we felt that success in taking on and achieving a goal—whether major or modest—constitutes a significant enabling outcome.

Table 4.7 shows that, by this measure, the for-profit and faith-based/integrated programs were the most effective, with only 8 percent and 14 percent, respectively, of their clients dropping out before completing their programs, and the nonprofit/secular and faith-based/segmented were the worst, with about 40 percent of their clients not completing their programs.[3] The government programs were close to the for-profit and faith-based/integrated programs in terms of effectiveness by this measure.

Again, it is helpful to ask concerning the interaction of religious involvement with the ability or inability of respondents to complete the welfare-to-work program that they had begun. Table 4.8 shows the percentages of the clients who did not complete the programs they had begun, divided by their level of religious involvement. The respondents who ranked high or moderate on religious involvement (20 percent and 14 percent, respectively) were less likely to leave their programs before completing them than were those who ranked low on religious involvement (28 percent). If one combines these figures with those of high and moderate levels of religious involvement (i.e., those who reported at-

Table 4.8

Percentage of Respondents Who Failed to Complete Their Programs, by Level of Religious Involvement

Religious Involvement[a]	Percent Who Did Not Complete Program	N
High	20	138
Moderate	14	64
Low	28	120
All respondents	22	322

$X^2(2) = 4.73, p = .09$

[a] Religious involvement was based on information gathered in the baseline questionnaire. The high, moderate, and low categories were based on the same divisions we used in table 4.3.

tending church at least a few times a month), one finds that only 18 percent failed to complete their programs, compared to 28 percent of the religiously inactive. These patterns approach, but do not reach, statistical significance. This may be an indication, as expected, that those with religious resources on which to call—both inner resources of will and determination and outer resources in the form of a support group—tend to be empowered to stick with their programs and complete them. The fact that those with a moderate level of religious involvement (those who attended church a few times a month) had the lowest noncompletion rate of the three groups may indicate that some connection with a religious congregation is enough for these positive effects to be felt, and a higher level of religious activity does not result in more positive effects. This is the same pattern we reported in chapter 3 in regard to the respondents' evaluations of their programs' staffs' sense of empathy. The increase in higher rates of perceiving empathic staffs came between the respondents ranking moderate and low in religious involvements, not between the respondents ranking high and moderate in religious involvement.

This leads to the question of whether or not those who were in a faith-based program and were religiously active were more likely to complete it than their fellow clients who were not religiously active. Table 4.9 throws light on this question. The faith-based/segmented programs showed the expected pattern: 32 percent of their highly religious clients and 60 percent of their religiously inactive clients did not complete

Table 4.9

Percentage of Respondents Failing to Complete Their Program,
by Baseline Religious Involvement and Program Type

Program Type	High Religious Involvement[a]		Moderate Religious Involvement[a]		Low Religious Involvement[a]	
	Percent Who Did Not Complete Programs	N	Percent Who Did Not Complete Programs	N	Percent Who Did Not Complete Programs	N
Government	10	30	6	17	30	47
For-profit	9	33	9	23	6	35
Nonprofit/secular	33	33	36	11	55	20
Faith-based/segmented	32	19	29	7	60	10
Faith-based/integrated	22	23	0	6	0	8
All respondents	20	138	14	64	28	120

[a] The level of religious involvement was measured the same way as in table 4.3.

their programs. This pattern, however, did not hold among the faith-based/integrated clients. Twenty-two percent of them who were highly active religiously failed to complete their programs, while none of the moderately active or nonactive clients did so. Again, caution must be used in interpreting these findings due to the small number of clients involved. But it suggests the surprising finding that, on this measure, faith-based/integrated programs may be at least as effective in working with nonreligious clients as they are in working with religious clients.

When we asked if the religiously active clients did better at faith-based programs than they did at secular programs, we found that fewer faith-based/integrated respondents who were highly religious failed to complete their programs than did the nonprofit/secular respondents who were highly religious (22 percent versus 33 percent). But then the findings become mixed. The religiously active respondents in government and for-profit programs had the strongest records of all in completing their programs (only 9 percent and 10 percent, respectively, failed to do so). As with a sense of hope and optimism, what religious resources a client brings to a program seems to have a greater effect on whether or not she or he will complete it than the religious or secular

Table 4.10

Percentage of Respondents Failing to Complete Their Programs,
by Race or Ethnicity and Program Type

Program Type	Whites		Blacks		Latinos	
	Percent Who Did Not Complete Programs	N	Percent Who Did Not Complete Programs	N	Percent Who Did Not Complete Programs	N
Government	0	14	16	31	27	44
For-profit	0	19	50	6	5	60
Nonprofit/secular	100	1	27	22	49	35
Faith-based/segmented	50	2	47	17	25	16
Faith-based/integrated	30	10	6	16	0	6
All respondents	11	46	25	92	22	161

nature of the program itself. Or, in the terms we introduced in chapter 1, personal, organic religion proved to be more important than intentional religion.

When we explored clients' failure to complete their programs by race and ethnicity, some interesting patterns emerged. (See table 4.10.) First, black and Latino clients had much higher dropout rates (25 percent and 22 percent) than did white clients (11 percent). This helps demonstrate the greater obstacles minority clients face in seeking economic independence. Table 4.7 showed that the for-profit and faith-based/integrated programs fared the best in their clients' not dropping out of their programs. Table 4.10 shows that the faith-based/integrated programs did especially well among black and Latino clients, with only a handful not completing their programs. It may be that the explicit references to religious themes resonate particularly well among minority clients, who tend to be more religious than the population as a whole. For-profit programs did not do well among black clients, but with only six black clients enrolled in for-profit programs, their 50 percent dropout rate should not be given too much weight. They did extremely well among Latino clients, with a dropout rate of only 5 percent. Why this is the case remains a puzzle. The nonprofit/secular and faith-based/segmented programs, who did poorly by this measure overall, did poorly across the different racial and ethnic groups.

In summary, as with the optimism measure, the for-profit and faith-based/integrated programs proved to be the most effective as measured by the low numbers of their clients' failing to complete their programs, with the government programs also doing well. This enabling outcome measure was also similar to the optimism measure in that the clients' own religious involvement was more clearly related to completing the programs they began than was the religious or secular nature of the programs themselves. The faith-based/integrated programs seemed to be especially effective in working with black and Latino clients and the for-profit programs in working with Latino clients.

Social Capital

The third enabling outcome we sought to measure was the creation of social capital that could help clients to overcome obstacles and deal successfully with challenges or crises as they arise. This is the most complex of the three enabling outcomes we sought to measure, but also potentially the most important one. In chapter 1 we noted that there are two types of social capital: bridging and bonding. Bridging social capital refers to ties to groups and persons outside of one's immediate social, ethnic, or neighborhood setting. Bonding social capital refers to ties to groups or persons within one's own social, ethnic, or neighborhood setting. As noted in chapter 1, a number of studies have held that a person's social capital of both the bonding and bridging types is just as important for their successful engagement in society as the vocational or job skills that they have.[4] When asked to assess the most significant obstacle clients face in finding a job, program staff frequently commented to us in interviews that their clients lack the social connections and networks necessary to succeed in the world of work. In describing his own experience with hiring welfare-to-work recipients, a customer service representative for a for-profit program offered this typical assessment: "We hired two welfare-to-work participants and it was a nightmare. So, we know what employers face when they employ a welfare-to-work participant. All of their problems were outside of the employment area. One attempted suicide. The other had her visa expiring and she constantly had to go to court. They were great workers while they were here, but they weren't always here. If they had a support system they would more likely have achieved their goals. The support system they had was not healthy." Even when employees are hard-working and good at what they do—as was the case for the two workers in this case—the absence of a support system, a form of social capital, created tremendous barriers to their keeping their jobs. A key way to assess program effectiveness, therefore, is to measure whether or not the programs are providing clients with the social capital that they will need to make their way successfully in the world of paid employment. Here we examine three sources of social capital that welfare-to-work programs may enable their clients to acquire.

Social Capital: Contact with Staff

Because social capital includes a network of community support, we asked respondents in our six- and twelve-month surveys to describe how much contact they had with program staff once their program had ended. Programs that were able or willing to remain in touch with clients months after the formal part of the welfare-to-work program ended would themselves become a part of their clients' bridging social capital.

Table 4.11 indicates that a majority of the clients (77 percent at six months and 82 percent at twelve months) had either only a few or no contacts with staff since leaving their program, while a much smaller proportion (23 percent at six months and 17 percent at twelve months) had many contacts. At six months the only type of program that seemed very involved with their clients after the programs had been completed were the faith-based/integrated ones. Nearly half (47 percent) of all the respondents from these programs indicated that they had many contacts with program staff six months after the baseline survey, a proportion almost twice as high as any other program type. These differences were statistically significant. The faith-based/integrated programs were unable to sustain this high level of contact for another six months, however. At twelve months only 20 percent reported many contacts, a figure actually slightly lower than that of the government programs (although a high 40 percent of the government program clients reported no contacts at all). More of the faith-based/integrated clients, however, reported either many or a few contacts (77 percent) than did the clients of any other type of program. The faith-based/integrated programs at twelve months still led the other types of programs in having at least some staff contacts with former clients, but their statistically significant advantage over the other program types had disappeared.

Table 4.11

Respondent Contacts with Staff since Leaving Program, by Program Type

Program Type	At Six Months					At Twelve Months				
	Many Contacts	A Few Contacts	No Contacts	N	Total %	Many Contacts	A Few Contacts	No Contacts	N	Total %
	%					%				
Government	24	28	49	76	101	23	37	40	75	100
For-Profit	13	56	32	88	101	11	50	39	72	100
Nonprofit/secular	27	37	36	59	100	18	51	31	61	100
Faith-based/segmented	11	40	49	35	100	15	41	44	27	100
Faith-based/integrated	47	34	18	38	99	20	57	23	30	100
All respondents	23	40	37	296	100	17	46	36	265	99

$\chi^2(8) = 33.71$, $p < .001$ $\chi^2(8) = 8.48$, $p = .39$

This leaves the question of whether or not clients perceived any benefit from the contact that they had with program staff after their program had ended. As table 4.12 shows, most clients who reported contacts with program staff at both the six- and twelve-month interviews indicated that this contact had always been helpful to them (54 percent and 50 percent, respectively). Only about 10 percent of those with some contact with their program said that the contact had never been helpful to them. Interestingly, clients from government programs at six months were the most likely to respond that those contacts had been helpful (72 percent), the highest of the five types of programs. By twelve months this had shrunk to 58 percent, but this was still the highest among the five program types. As we noted earlier, a high percentage of clients from faith-based/integrated programs indicated that they had contact with program staff at both six and twelve months, and a majority of them reported that the contact had been helpful (57 percent at six months and 52 percent at twelve months). While there are fiscal and practical difficulties in program staff keeping close ties with clients months after a program has ended, the data suggest that clients perceive a clear benefit when they are able to maintain personal and professional contacts with program staff. This tends to confirm our original observation that social capital in the form of continuing contact with program staff after the conclusion of a welfare-to-work program is a useful enabling outcome. The faith-based/integrated programs were the most effective in terms of this outcome.

We found evidence that being religiously involved tends to increase the likelihood of a client maintaining contact with their programs' staff. As seen in table 4.13, of those with low religious involvement, about half reported at six months either many or a few contacts with program staff, but about 70 percent of those with moderate or high religious involvement reported contacts with program staff. The difference was not as great at twelve months, but here also more of those who were religiously active reported staff contacts (64 percent) than those who were religiously inactive (58 percent). In the case of the clients of all five program types at both six and twelve months, those with high religious involvement were more likely to report contact with program staff than were those with low religious involvement. The pattern is consistent. It may be that attending church regularly helps persons develop the social skills and self-confidence that encouraged them to maintain contact

Table 4.12

Perceived Helpfulness of Contacts with Program Staff after Leaving Program, at Six and at Twelve Months, by Program Type

Program Type	At Six Months					At Twelve Months				
	Always Helpful	Sometimes Helpful	Never Helpful	N	Total %	Always Helpful	Sometimes Helpful	Never Helpful	N	Total %
	%					%				
Government	72	26	3	39	101	58	38	4	45	100
For-Profit	40	45	15	60	100	44	35	21	43	100
Nonprofit/secular	55	40	5	38	100	48	41	11	42	100
Faith-based/segmented	50	44	6	18	100	50	43	7	14	100
Faith-based/integrated	57	27	16	30	100	52	35	13	23	100
All respondents	54	37	10	185	101	50	38	12	167	100

Table 4.13

Percentage of Respondents Reporting Many or a Few Contacts with Program Staff at Six and at Twelve Months, by Religious Involvement and Program Type

| | At Six Months | | | | | | At Twelve Months | | | | | |
| | High Religious Involvement[a] | | Moderate Religious Involvement[a] | | Low Religious Involvement[a] | | High Religious Involvement[b] | | Moderate Religious Involvement[b] | | Low Religious Involvement[b] | |
Program Type	Percent with Many or a Few Contacts	N	Percent with Many or a Few Contacts	N	Percent with Many or a Few Contacts	N	Percent with Many or a Few Contacts	N	Percent with Many or a Few Contacts	N	Percent with Many or a Few Contacts	N
Government	59	22	75	12	40	40	55	20	73	15	54	28
For-profit	79	33	61	23	63	32	71	17	44	23	62	21
Nonprofit/secular	66	29	73	11	56	18	70	23	65	17	63	16
Faith-based/segmented	53	19	57	7	44	9	46	13	89	9	25	4
Faith-based/integrated	88	24	83	6	63	8	80	10	73	11	75	8
All respondents	70	127	68	59	51	107	64	83	64	75	58	77

[a] As reported at the baseline, with the level of religious involvement measured the same way as in table 4.3.

[b] A combination of religious involvement at the baseline and at twelve months, determined by the same means used in table 4.4.

with program staff, or it may be that those who attend church regularly are the types of persons who already have the social skills and self-confidence that led to their maintaining contact with their programs' staffs. Whatever the reason, the expected pattern of those who were religiously involved tending to be marked by more social capital in the form of ongoing contacts with program staff was in evidence. It is also noteworthy that, as found several times earlier, the highly and moderately religiously active respondents did not differ greatly in their contacts with program staff. It was those marked by low religious involvement that had lower levels of contact.

Further, at six months we found that the religiously active clients who attended a faith-based/integrated program were more likely to have contacts with their staff members than their fellow program members who were low in religious involvement. Almost 90 percent of the religiously active clients who attended a faith-based/integrated program reported at six months having some contact with program staff. This percentage is clearly higher than that of the nonreligious persons who attended a faith-based/integrated program (88 percent versus 63 percent). At twelve months the pattern had not changed but had weakened considerably. Those who ranked high in religious involvement and attended a faith-based/integrated program were still more likely to have maintained contacts with program staff, but by a much smaller margin than at six months. This shrinking of the differences between the religiously active and inactive faith-based/integrated clients occurred both because those with high religious involvement reported fewer contacts and because the religiously inactive reported more contacts.[5] It is nevertheless important to note that, at both six and twelve months among clients of faith-based/integrated programs with low religious involvement, with only one exception a higher percentage were still in touch with program staff than were clients of any other type of program who were also low in religious involvement. (The one exception was that for for-profit programs at six months, where 63 percent of the nonreligious clients of both the for-profit and faith-based/integrated programs reported some contacts with their programs staffs.) This again suggests, somewhat surprisingly, that most of the religiously inactive persons taking part in faith-based/integrated programs were experiencing positive outcomes.

Table 4.13 also shows that clients high in personal religious involvement tended to do better in terms of staff contacts when they attended faith-based/integrated programs than when they attended either a secular program or a faith-based/segmented program. At six months, 88 percent reported at least some staff contacts, and at twelve months 80 percent did so. These were higher percentages than the actively religious persons experienced in any other program type. This is one instance where our expected pattern materialized. It seems that clients who were themselves religiously committed and staff members of integrally religious programs, who would tend to be highly religious themselves, experienced a commonality that facilitated continuing ties, even after a program had ended.

Regarding race or ethnicity, the clearest pattern was that of faith-based/integrated programs' ability to maintain contacts with black clients. After six months, fifteen of sixteen black clients of faith-based/integrated programs (94 percent) reported at least some contacts with their programs' staffs, and after twelve months an impressive ten of eleven (91 percent) did so. These are better numbers than those for any other program type with any other racial or ethnic group, although the nonprofit/secular programs also did well with their black clients (at twelve months, eighteen of twenty clients, or 90 percent, reported some contacts). It may be that the faith-based/integrated and nonprofit/secular programs tended to have deeper roots into the black community than did the other program types, thereby explaining their success. In fact, a majority of both the nonprofit/secular and the faith-based/integrated black clients came from two predominantly black agencies located in south central Los Angeles. (See the descriptions in chapter 2 of the Together-We-Win and Community Skills Center programs.) The ability of their staffs in maintaining contacts with their clients after their programs had ended is an indication that small, community-based programs may—as is often claimed—be more effective in building their clients' social capital than are larger, less community-oriented programs, especially when dealing with racial minorities.

Social Capital: Contact with Other Program Participants

Another potential source of social capital consists of the contacts made among fellow participants in a welfare-to-work program. Welfare recipients might find in their fellow participants new friends or support networks that could help them both in concrete ways—such as with child care or job leads—and psychologically, such as being persons they could talk to after a bad day or to obtain advice. Fellow program participants could be sources of both bonding and bridging social capital. Thus we asked at both six and twelve months not only concerning continuing contacts with program staff but concerning other participants in the programs.

Table 4.14 shows that at six months 21 percent of the respondents reported having many contacts with fellow participants, and another 49 percent reported having some contacts. By twelve months those figures had shrunk somewhat, but 66 percent still reported either many or some contacts. Clearly the contacts that participants in welfare-to-work programs make with their fellow participants are a source of social capital for them. At six months the faith-based/integrated programs were the most effective by this standard. Some 84 percent of their clients reported having many or some contacts with their fellow participants. As with contacts with staff members, they were not able to sustain this over a twelve-month period, however. By twelve months only 10 percent reported many contacts (compared to 29 percent at six months). Nevertheless, a total of 67 percent—still an impressive number and higher than all but one of the other program types—reported at least some contacts with fellow participants in their faith-based/integrated programs. The participants in government programs reported the highest levels of contacts at twelve months, due to their being able to maintain the contacts that they had at six months. Government program clients had a very strong 29 percent who reported many contacts with fellow participants (compared to virtually the same number, 28 percent, at six months), and there was another 45 percent who reported some contacts (compared to 43 percent at six months). In short, both the faith-based/integrated and the government programs were more effective than the other program types in enabling their clients to develop contacts with their fellow participants, an important source of social capital. The religious nature of the faith-based programs, with their emphasis on attitudes, life skills, and other soft skills, combined with their small size would naturally tend to lead their clients to develop close contacts with each other. It is harder to explain why the government programs also did so well. At the least their effectiveness by this measure is added evidence that the old stereotype of government social welfare programs as being bureaucratic

Table 4.14

Respondent Contacts with Fellow Participants since Leaving Program, by Program Type

Program Type	At Six Months					At Twelve Months				
	Many Contacts	A Few Contacts	No Contacts	N	Total %	Many Contacts	A Few Contacts	No Contacts	N	Total %
	%					%				
Government	28	43	29	76	100	29	45	25	75	99
For-Profit	21	56	23	87	100	14	49	38	72	101
Nonprofit/secular	16	48	36	58	100	12	54	34	61	100
Faith-based/segmented	6	40	54	35	100	0	52	48	27	100
Faith-based/integrated	29	55	16	38	100	10	57	33	30	100
All respondents	21	49	30	294	100	16	50	34	265	100

and marked by an uncaring atmosphere does not hold for welfare-to-work programs in Los Angeles County.

It is helpful to ask whether or not the respondents' own level of religious involvement was related to their ability to maintain contacts with their fellow participants. Those who are religiously active might be the ones with the social skills and the desire to be of help to others that would result in their reaching out and making connections with other program participants. Table 4.15 reveals that overall there was a tendency for those with a high level of religious involvement to report more contacts with other participants in their programs than did those with a low level of religious involvement. Those with many or a few contacts with other program participants grew, at six months, from 61 percent for those who were not active religiously to 75 percent for those who were highly religiously active. At twelve months those with at least some contacts grew from 61 percent for those who were not religiously involved to 69 percent for those who were highly religiously involved. In fact, for every program type the percentage of their clients who reported many or a few contacts with fellow participants was higher for those with high religious involvement than for those with low religious involvement. This also holds true with only two exceptions for those with a moderate level of religious involvement. Personal, organic religion seemed to be a factor in enabling program participants to develop and maintain contact with fellow participants.

One might suppose that religiously active clients in faith-based programs would respond positively to the religious atmosphere of their programs by establishing more contacts with their fellow participants than would the religiously inactive clients in the same programs. Table 4.15 shows that the religiously involved clients in fact did better in developing and maintaining contacts with their fellow participants than did the religiously uninvolved clients in the case of both the faith-based/integrated and faith-based/segmented programs at both six and twelve months. But we have already seen that this was true of the religiously active participants in all five program types. Plus, the differences between the religiously active and inactive respondents were not consistently greater for clients in faith-based programs than for those in secular programs.

We also asked whether or not religiously active clients of faith-based programs did better at developing and maintaining contacts with their

Table 4.15

Respondent Contacts with Fellow Participants, by Level of Religious Involvement and Program Type

| | At Six Months | | | | | | At Twelve Months | | | | | |
| | High Religious Involvement[a] | | Moderate Religious Involvement[a] | | Low Religious Involvement[a] | | High Religious Involvement[b] | | Moderate Religious Involvement[b] | | Low Religious Involvement[b] | |
Program Type	Percent with Many or a Few Contacts	N	Percent with Many or a Few Contacts	N	Percent with Many or a Few Contacts	N	Percent with Many or a Few Contacts	N	Percent with Many or a Few Contacts	N	Percent with Many or a Few Contacts	N
Government	82	22	83	12	60	40	75	20	93	15	68	28
For-profit	82	33	74	23	74	31	59	17	65	23	57	21
Nonprofit/secular	71	28	64	11	50	18	78	23	53	17	63	16
Faith-based/segmented	47	19	57	7	33	9	54	13	56	9	50	4
Faith-based/integrated	88	24	83	6	75	8	70	10	73	11	50	8
All respondents	75	126	73	59	61	106	69	83	68	75	61	77

[a] As reported at the baseline, with the level of religious involvement measured the same way as in table 4.3.

[b] A combination of religious involvement at the baseline and at twelve months, determined by the same means used in table 4.4.

fellow participants than did religiously active clients of secular programs. The faith-based programs might be successful in stimulating their religiously active participants to reach out to and establish contacts with their fellow participants to a greater degree than would the secular programs. Table 4.15, however, shows no consistent pattern of the highly religious clients in faith-based programs doing better in maintaining contacts with fellow participants than did the highly religious clients in secular programs. At six months the highly religious clients at faith-based/integrated programs showed some tendency in this direction, with 88 percent reporting some contact with their fellow participants, a higher percentage than what we found for highly religious respondents in any other program type. But by twelve months this comparative advantage had disappeared. Highly religious respondents at both government and nonprofit/secular programs reported higher levels of contacts with fellow respondents than did highly religious respondents who had taken part in faith-based/integrated programs. And highly religious faith-based/segmented clients tended in fact to do worse at developing contacts with fellow participants than did the highly religious clients of the secular programs. As we have found elsewhere, it appears that what the clients brought to the programs in terms of religious involvement and commitments was more important in affecting the likelihood of developing and maintaining contacts with fellow participants than did the religious or secular nature of the program they were in.

In terms of race and ethnicity there were few differences. Whether a respondent was white, black, or Latino did not affect the likelihood of him or her developing contacts with fellow program participants. Black respondents who attended faith-based/integrated or nonprofit/secular programs did especially well at six months in terms of this form of social capital, but had lost this advantage at twelve months. The one exception was Latino clients attending government programs, who did especially well at both six and twelve months (79 percent at six months and 77 percent at twelve months reported having many or a few continuing contacts with fellow program participants). With this one exception, race and ethnicity seemed not to affect to any great extent how our respondents fared in developing and maintaining contacts with their fellow participants, and this was true no matter what type of program they were in.

Social Capital: Religious Involvement

A key aspect of social capital is a person's involvement within his or her community, and a significant form of involvement in one's community is participation in a religious congregation. In many lower income communities, churches, temples, mosques, and other religious bodies are the only institutions that thrive. To the extent that citizens are going to be engaged in such communities, it is most likely to take the form of participation in a religious congregation. Therefore, a final way in which we sought to evaluate how effective programs were at increasing the social capital of their clients was to analyze clients' religious involvement, as measured by church attendance, before and after they had participated in their programs. This form of social capital is likely to be bonding, rather than bridging, in nature.

Table 4.16 reports church attendance at the baseline and at twelve months. (Also see table 2.6 in chapter 2.)[6] It is not surprising to learn that almost two-thirds of the clients in faith-based/segmented (63 percent) and more than half of those in faith-based/integrated programs (57 percent) reported attending church once a week or more at the baseline. In comparison, 52 percent of the nonprofit/secular clients, 36 percent of for-profit clients, and 33 percent of the government program clients reported they attended church once a week or more. Not surprisingly the respondents in faith-based programs reported very high levels of church attendance, but those who were in secular programs—and especially those in nonprofit/secular programs—also reported rather high levels of weekly church attendance. These results suggest that there probably is an even larger market for religiously based welfare-to-work programs than religious agencies can currently provide, especially given our earlier finding that a majority of our respondents in faith-based programs reacted positively to the religious elements in their programs.

In order to assess the impact the different types of programs had on their clients' level of church involvement, we asked the same church-attendance question of the respondents at twelve months. The results, as reported in table 4.16, are mixed. Clients from government agencies were the most likely to have increased their weekly church attendance from the baseline to the twelve-month interviews, from 33 percent to 45 percent. In fact, identical percentages of clients from government-run and faith-based/integrated programs reported weekly church at-

Table 4.16

Church Attendance at Baseline and at Twelve Months, by Program Type,
Twelve-Month Respondents

Program Type	Once a Week or More at Baseline	Once a Week or More at 12 Months	A Few Times a Month at Baseline	A Few Times a Month at 12 Months	A Few Times a Year or Never at Baseline	A Few Times a Year or Never at 12 Months
Government	33%	45%	18%	20%	50%	35%
	(N = 73)	(N = 65)	(N = 73)	(N = 65)	(N = 73)	(N = 65)
For-profit	36%	38%	24%	34%	40%	28%
	(N = 72)	(N = 61)	(N = 72)	(N = 61)	(N = 72)	(N = 61)
Nonprofit/	52%	54%	17%	20%	32%	27%
secular	(N = 60)	(N = 56)	(N = 60)	(N = 56)	(N = 60)	(N = 56)
Faith-based/	63%	58%	22%	27%	15%	15%
segmented	(N = 27)	(N = 26)	(N = 27)	(N = 26)	(N = 27)	(N = 26)
Faith-based/	57%	45%	17%	35%	27%	21%
integrated	(N = 30)	(N = 29)	(N = 30)	(N = 29)	(N = 30)	(N = 29)
All respondents	44%	46%	20%	26%	37%	27%
	(N = 262)	(N = 237)	(N = 262)	(N = 237)	(N = 262)	(N = 237)

tendance in the twelve-month interviews. Clients from both types of faith-based programs, on the other hand, actually showed a decline in the percentage of respondents who reported that they attended church once a week or more (from 63 percent to 58 percent for faith-based/ segmented and from 57 percent to 45 percent for faith-based/integrated programs). Most of the faith-based/integrated clients who no longer were attending church at least once a week apparently were still attending a few times a month, because there was a doubling from the baseline to twelve months of the faith-based/integrated clients who reported attending church a few times a month and a slight decline in the number who reported attending seldom or never.

Table 4.17 demonstrates some of these conclusions more clearly by highlighting the percentage of clients from each of the program types who had become more religiously active at the twelve-month interview (as compared to the baseline) and the percentage who maintained the same level of religious activity from the baseline and at twelve months. Its percentages are based on individual respondents and the shifts in their reported church attendance from the baseline questionnaires to

Table 4.17

Changes in Religious Involvement, by Program Type, Twelve-Month Respondents

Program Type	Percent Religiously Involved at the Baseline That Were Still Religiously Involved at 12 Months[a]		Percent Religiously Uninvolved at the Baseline That Were Religiously Involved at 12 Months[a]	
	%	N	%	N
Government	94	35	25	28
For-profit	93	42	26	19
Nonprofit/secular	92	39	29	17
Faith-based/segmented	100	22	0	4
Faith-based/integrated	86	21	63	8
All respondents	93	159	29	76

[a] Respondents who reported they attended church at least a few times a month were considered religiously involved and those who reported they attended church a few times a year or never were considered religiously uninvolved.

the twelve-month telephone interviews. All of the program types did extremely well in terms of persons who were already religiously involved staying involved, although 14 percent of the faith-based/integrated program clients who were religiously involved at the baseline were no longer so at twelve months. Although the numbers are very small, and thus one can draw only highly tentative conclusions from them, the faith-based/integrated programs seemed to be doing especially well at encouraging their clients who were not involved in a church to become involved. Of their eight clients who were not involved at the baseline, five had become involved at the twelve-month mark.

In short, one can conclude that in terms of church involvement as a form of social capital, the programs did not differ greatly. All of their clients who were active in a church at the baseline tended to stay active, and the clients of all the program types who were not active tended not to become active. What is somewhat surprising is that 25 to 30 percent of the clients of secular programs who were not active in a church at the baseline reported being active twelve months later. It may be that simply getting out of the house and becoming active by participating in a welfare-to-work program, thereby meeting the other participants and staff, served as a stimulus to getting involved in other ways, with church involvement a ready-at-hand form of involvement in high poverty communities. Although one is dealing with only eight clients and thus any observations must be extremely tentative, it may be that the explicitly religious atmosphere of the faith-based/integrated programs reinforced and strengthened this tendency.

In regard to race and ethnicity, the black respondents who were religiously active at the baseline were the most likely to remain active (96 percent did so, versus 92 percent for the Latino and 90 percent for the white respondents), and those who were religiously inactive at the baseline were the most likely to become active (37 percent versus 32 percent for the Latino and 18 percent for the white respondents). When we examined the different program types, one or more types did not prove to be more effective at maintaining or increasing the religious involvement of certain racial or ethnic groups.

Summary

Ongoing contacts with program staff were clearly a source—even if a limited source—of social capital for the clients of the welfare-to-work programs we studied. This was the case because, while a majority of the respondents reported some contact with program staff, even at the twelve-month survey, only a minority reported many contacts with program staff. Given the large number of clients that go through most of the programs studied and the fact that their numbers would accumulate over time, this is understandable. The faith-based/integrated programs seemed to be more effective than the other four types of programs on this score. They may have been helped by their small size and thus fewer clients with whom to work, although their numbers of staff members were also small.

Those who were themselves religiously active were slightly more successful than those who were not religiously active in developing and maintaining contacts with program staff, and they tended to do especially well when they were in faith-based/integrated programs. Somewhat surprisingly, we found that the faith-based/integrated respondents who were religiously inactive tended to do better at maintaining contacts with staff then did religiously inactive respondents at secular programs. This is one of several findings pointing to the fact that faith-based/integrated programs can work effectively with nonreligious clients. The effectiveness of faith-based/integrated programs in strengthening their clients' social capital by way of staff contacts is also demonstrated by their being particularly successful in doing so with their black clients.

Ongoing contacts with fellow participants in their welfare-to-work programs were a second source of social capital we were able to document. Our findings here are similar to the ones regarding contacts with program staff. A strong majority of the respondents reported some contacts with fellow participants at both the six-month and the twelve-month surveys. Clearly fellow participants were a source of social capital but, again, a limited source. Only a minority of respondents reported many contacts. Here it was the government-run programs that were the most effective by this measure. The faith-based/integrated programs were the most effective type of program among respondents who themselves were religiously active at six months. But somewhat surprisingly they were also the most effective among those who were not religiously active. This comparative advantage was lost by twelve months, however. At twelve months the government programs proved to be the most effective, even among the highly religious respondents. Overall, the religiously involved respondents tended to maintain more contacts with their fellow participants than did the noninvolved respondents. Latino clients did especially well at developing and maintaining contacts with other participants at government programs.

The third form of social capital we explored was that of involvement in a religious congregation. We found that almost all the respondents who were religiously involved at the baseline were still religiously involved twelve months later. Somewhat unexpectedly, clients of almost all the program types who were not religiously involved at the baseline increased their religious involvement after twelve months. This was especially true of the faith-based/integrated programs.

What then can one say in regard to the program types and their effectiveness in building social capital? Three broad generalizations are in order. One is that the welfare-to-work programs as a whole were successful in building the social capital of their clients. No program type was a clear failure. The second generalization is that the faith-based/integrated programs by a number of measures tended to be more effective in building social capital than were the other four program types, and by several measures the nonprofit/secular and faith-based/segmented programs were the weakest. The third generalization is that respondents marked by personal, organic religion tended to be more successful in building social capital than were the less religious respondents.

Observations

There are four key conclusions we can draw from our findings regarding enabling outcomes. First, the clients of all five program types experienced gains in terms of enabling outcomes. In that sense all five types of programs were effective. The faith-based/segmented and nonprofit/secular programs proved to be the weakest in terms of enabling outcomes, but even they were not failures. Their clients showed evidence of making gains in terms of enabling outcomes.

Second, generally the faith-based/integrated programs did better than the other program types on all three enabling outcome measures used in this chapter, especially in terms of program completion and social capital. The government and for-profit programs also did well on our program completion and social capital measures, and they did especially well on our optimism measure. What may be most surprising here is the relative effectiveness of the government and for-profit programs. They have often been charged with being uncaring, overly bureaucratic, or both. Yet they did better than nonprofit/secular and faith-based/segmented programs in enabling outcomes, which by their nature tend to involve attitudes and personalized contacts. The effectiveness of the faith-based/integrated programs is less surprising, as such programs are often assumed to be marked by their small size, localized character, and individualized attention. But we were—if not surprised—impressed by this finding due to two factors. One was the often struggling nature and spartan facilities of the faith-based/integrated programs. They came nowhere near matching the for-profit and government programs in finances, facilities, and staffing, yet they outperformed their outwardly more impressive counterparts on most enabling outcome measures. Also, as mentioned earlier and as we will see in the next chapter, the faith-based/integrated clients did not do all that well in intermediate and ultimate outcomes. Nevertheless, they raised their clients' levels of optimism, enabled their clients to complete their programs, and increased the social capital of their clients. This may suggest that the enabling outcomes on which we focused are in fact not as "enabling" as we had believed. But it does demonstrate the power of faith-based/integrated programs to make advances in the lives of their clients, even when concrete economic advancements are not widely the case.

The third conclusion supported by the findings reported in this chapter is that religiously involved persons—those who were marked by organic religion—tended to be more successful in achieving enabling outcomes than were those who were nonreligious. This was not unexpected, because, as noted in chapter 1, there is a growing literature demonstrating that religiously involved persons tend to be marked by a host of more positive social and health characteristics than are nonreligious persons.

A final conclusion relates to the third one. Religiously active persons usually did not do better in faith-based programs than did the religiously inactive persons in them, nor did religiously active persons do better in faith-based programs than in secular programs. This surprised us. We thought common sense would indicate that—compared both to nonreligious persons in a faith-based program and to religious persons in a secular program—a person with a strong, active religious faith would prosper more fully in a faith-based program. But this usually was not the case with our enabling outcome measures. These findings were in part caused by religious persons doing better in secular programs than we had expected and nonreligious persons doing better in faith-based programs than we had expected. This suggests that there may be a significant role for faith-based programs, including integrally religious programs, in providing social service even to nonreligious persons. Their effectiveness does not seem to be limited to persons who are personally religious themselves. Perhaps the religious elements in a faith-based/integrated program would actually be newer and fresher for the nonreligious participants and thus would have as great or even a greater impact on them than they would have on the religious participants, who may have "heard it all before." This would only hold true, however, as long as the integrally faith-based programs presented their religious elements in a supportive and understanding manner, not in a heavy-handed or judgmental way, and as long as the clients were fully informed of the religious nature of the programs before taking part in them. As noted earlier, our research indicates that these two conditions are normally met by the faith-based/integrated programs we studied, but their importance should not be overlooked. All this leaves the crucial question of the intermediate and ultimate outcomes of our welfare-to-work programs. It is to these we turn in the next chapter.

5

INTERMEDIATE AND ULTIMATE OUTCOMES

"It was a pretty good program. They helped me a lot with transportation. As far as personal issues, they really helped out a lot. As far as employment, that didn't work out too well." This comment by a client in one of our government welfare-to-work programs illustrates the fact that generally positive reactions to a welfare-to-work program and assistance in achieving enabling outcomes—such as overcoming transportation and personal problems—do not necessarily lead to the desired goal of employment. Clients typically face a host of potential obstacles to employment that usually make it difficult for a particular program to empower persons to move immediately all the way to economic self-sufficiency, which is the desired ultimate outcome of welfare-to-work programs. There are not simply two extremes: no employment with total welfare dependency and full-time employment at sufficiently high wages that economic self-sufficiency results. Part-time employment and employment at wages so low that some forms of assistance are still needed can be combined to cause a wide range of intermediate outcomes between these two extremes. Thus both the ultimate outcome of economic self-sufficiency and intermediate, or partial, outcomes—which in chapter 1 we defined as movement or steps toward the ultimate outcome of economic self-sufficiency—need to be considered in assessing the effectiveness of welfare-to-work programs.

In this chapter we first consider three types of intermediate outcomes: employment of any type, full-time employment, and employment at higher than the minimum wage level. Next, we consider the ultimate outcome of replacing welfare dependence with full-time, self-supporting employment. As with our consideration of enabling outcomes, we will consider in what ways these outcomes varied by the type of program in which our respondents participated and how these

outcomes interacted with the respondents' own levels of religious involvement and race or ethnicity.

Full- and Part-Time Employment

We consider here the first two intermediate outcomes together: how
many of our respondents were employed and how many were employed
full-time versus part-time. We found that six months after the baseline data had been gathered half of the respondents were employed
and half were not. The for-profit programs fared the best, with 60 percent of their clients reporting either full- or part-time employment, and
the nonprofit/secular programs fared the worst, with only 36 percent
of their clients reporting employment. Twelve months after the baseline data were gathered 57 percent of the respondents reported they
were employed, a slight gain over the six-month number. The for-profit
programs again fared the best, with 75 percent of their clients reporting employment, and the nonprofit/secular programs again fared the
worst, with only 41 percent reporting employment.

Tables 5.1 and 5.2 are more revealing, however, because they take into
account the employment status of the respondents at the time the baseline data were gathered. Table 5.1 reveals for each type of program the
percentages of respondents who were not employed at the beginning of
the study and at six months were employed full-time, part-time, or not
at all. Table 5.2 does the same for our respondents at twelve months.
Here and throughout this study we considered full-time employment as
thirty hours or more of work a week. The tables also show the percentages of respondents who were employed at the beginning of the study
and were still employed at six and twelve months.

The tables demonstrate, first, how difficult it is for persons who are
unemployed to find employment. A majority of all the respondents who
were not employed at the baseline were still unemployed six and twelve
months later. Of those who did find jobs, about 30 percent had only
part-time jobs. In addition, about 25 percent of those who had been employed at the baseline were no longer employed six or twelve months
later.

Among the comments the respondents made concerning the programs in which they took part one can find many examples of the challenges they face in finding jobs. Child care often came up. A participant

in a nonprofit/secular program stated, "The most difficult aspect of job search is the issue of child care. It is the biggest problem for single parents, and one that [could] use more help from the government or private industry." Another person from the same program explained, "Hopefully you can open more places for people who need child care, so that it can make it easier for people to go and look for work." Many felt the programs they were in did not do enough in terms of help with finding jobs. One participant in a for-profit program complained: "[Name of the program] don't really help you looking for a job. As far as helping you out in job searching. It seems to me they don't really care." The client of a government program said, in response to a question asking how the program could have been improved, "If they would have talked with the employers personally. They gave us job leads and we went out on our own. I think it would have helped a lot by the director calling the employers and speaking with them." The client of a faith-based/segmented program stated, when asked what he/she did not like about the program: "More job opportunities and/or more help getting actual job. Not just school and training. I want to work but am having a very hard time finding a job."

Second, the tables reveal that among the five program types, the for-profit programs ranked first in enabling persons who were unemployed at the baseline to find employment. At six months, 53 percent of their clients who had been unemployed at the baseline were working full-time and another 7 percent were working part-time, and at twelve months 59 percent were working full-time and another 17 percent were working part-time. These are impressive numbers. The faith-based/integrated programs fared the worst in enabling their clients who had been unemployed at the baseline to find employment. Almost 80 percent of their clients who were unemployed at the baseline were still unemployed at six months, and at twelve months this figure had dropped to only 75 percent. Seventy-three percent of the faith-based/segmented clients who were unemployed at the baseline were still without employment six months later, but this had been reduced to 56 percent by twelve months, better than any other type of program except for the for-profit programs. However, most of this improvement came from their clients' finding part-time, not full-time employment. They were the least effective of the five program types in their clients finding full-time employment. The clients of the government and nonprofit/secular programs

Table 5.1

Employment at Baseline and at Six Months, by Program Type

Program Type	Percent of Respondents **Not** Employed at Baseline and Employed Full-Time at Six Months	Percent of Respondents **Not** Employed at Baseline and Employed Part-Time at Six Months	Percent of Respondents **Not** Employed at Baseline and Still **Not** Employed at Six Months	Totals for Respondents **Not** Employed at Baseline		Percent of Respondents Employed at Baseline and Still Employed at Six Months	
				N	%	N	%
Government	20	13	67	55	100	40	77
For-profit	53	7	40	55	100	36	61
Nonprofit/secular	17	15	69	54	101	10	70
Faith-based/segmented	14	14	73	22	101	14	86
Faith-based/integrated	17	4	79	24	100	14	93
All respondents	27	11	62	210	100	114	75

$\chi^2(8) = 28.39, p < .001$ $\qquad\qquad$ $\chi^2(4) = 7.11, p = .13$

Table 5.2

Employment at Baseline and at Twelve Months, by Program Type

Program Type	Percent of Respondents Not Employed at Baseline and Employed Full-Time at Twelve Months	Percent of Respondents Not Employed at Baseline and Employed Part-Time at Twelve Months	Percent of Respondents Not Employed at Baseline and Still Not Employed at Twelve Months	Totals for Respondents Not Employed at Baseline		Percent of Respondents Employed at Baseline and Still Employed at Twelve Months	
				N	%	N	%
Government	23	14	63	43	100	31	81
For-profit	59	17	24	41	100	30	73
Nonprofit/secular	29	8	63	49	100	10	60
Faith-based/segmented	13	31	56	16	100	11	82
Faith-based/integrated	15	10	75	20	100	10	80
All respondents	31	14	54	169	99	92	76

$\chi^2(8) = 28.84, p < .001$

$\chi^2(4) = 2.18, p = .70$

did only slightly better than the faith-based clients, with 60 to 70 percent of their clients who were unemployed at the baseline still unemployed at six and twelve months.

There is a surprising reversal, however, when one looks at the clients who were already employed at the baseline and were able to maintain their employment. At six months the faith-based/integrated clients fared the best with over 90 percent of their clients who were employed at the baseline maintaining an employed status; and the faith-based/segmented clients also did very well, with 86 percent maintaining employment. The for-profit programs did the worst, with only 61 percent of their clients who had been employed at the baseline remaining employed. In fact, clients from the for-profit programs who were employed at the baseline did not do any better at six months than their clients who were unemployed at the baseline (60 percent for those who were unemployed versus 61 percent for those who were employed). At twelve months the faith-based/integrated clients who had been employed at the baseline had dropped somewhat in maintaining employment, and the government and for-profit clients had improved somewhat. The two types of faith-based programs still had higher percentages of their clients employed (80 percent and 82 percent, respectively) than the for-profit and nonprofit/secular programs, but the differences among the five program types were not large.

The most likely explanation for these findings lies in the differing natures of the welfare-to-work services offered by the various types of programs and the faith-based programs' clients' positive enabling outcomes noted in the previous chapter. As seen in chapter 2, the government and for-profit programs included in our study tended to emphasize training and education in hard skills—marketable vocational skills—while the faith-based programs tended to emphasize soft skills—those of attitudes and perspectives on work and oneself. This was confirmed by the responses given to several open-ended questions by our respondents, as analyzed in chapter 3. Also, we earlier reported that the faith-based programs, and especially the faith-based/integrated programs, tended to be more successful than the other program types in creating social capital and in achieving positive assessments by their clients. Thus it may be that the for-profit clients were better equipped with the job-related skills they needed to go out into the job market and compete successfully for jobs than were the faith-based clients. However, the clients in faith-based/integrated programs who were already employed—who already had the knowledge or skills to land a job—gained the emotional support that carried them through the bad days and helped them to persevere in the jobs they had. Those who had taken part in other types of programs—programs that were evaluated less positively in terms of staff empathy and were less successful in increasing the social capital of their clients—may lack the emotional support and social capital that would get them through the tough days on the job. Since job retention is considered by many in the field to be a bigger challenge than simply finding employment, the success of the faith-based programs in helping their clients to maintain employment is a notable achievement.

We also performed a direct logistic regression analysis to assess which variables were statistically significant in predicting the work status of respondents at six and twelve months. This is a statistical technique that measures the independent impact that each of a number of variables has on the outcome one is seeking to explain. In this case, we are seeking to explain the employment status of our respondents. This status could be affected not only by the type of program in which they had taken part, but also by such factors as race, number of dependent children, gender, education level, and so forth. Direct logistic regression analysis enables us to answer the question of what impact each of these factors, or variables, had on the employment status of our respondents, if all of the other variables are held constant. Thus, for example, it answers the question of what was the independent impact on employment of having taken part in a for-profit welfare-to-work program if other variables, such as education, race, and gender, are the same.

The demographic variables we used were gender, race, marital status, and the number of children under the age of eighteen living at home with the respondent. Other variables used were the type of welfare-to-work program in which the respondents participated, their baseline employment status, and the number of work-related skills that they possessed. The skills we included in the work-related skills variable were having a high school diploma, an ability to read English well, and an ability to speak English well. In analyzing the effect of the type of program a respondent was in, we used participation in a government program as our reference category, that is, our base of comparison.

Table 5.3 reports the results for finding employment, whether full- or part-time. A positive coefficient indicates that there was a positive relationship between that variable and finding employment, with all of the other variables held constant. Similarly, a negative coefficient indicates there was a negative relationship between that variable and finding employment, again with all of the other variables held constant. Of course, many of these positive or negative coefficients could be purely the result of chance variations and not indicative of an actual relationship. Thus we have noted those coefficients that are statistically significant, that is, the ones that are very unlikely to have come about purely by chance. If there was a 10 percent or less chance that a coefficient could have come about purely by chance, we considered it statistically significant and noted it with a single asterisk; if there was a 5 percent or less chance that a coefficient could have come about purely by chance, we have noted it with a double asterisk.

With that as background, table 5.3 demonstrates that, at six months, being female and being unemployed at the baseline significantly decreased one's chances of finding employment, even with all the other variables held constant. Being unmarried significantly increased the chances that one found a job. At twelve months, being unemployed at the baseline continued to decrease significantly one's chances of having found employment, and being unmarried continued to increase significantly one's chances of having found employment.

Concerning the five program types, at twelve months, clients in the faith-based/segmented programs were more likely to find employment than were the clients in government-run programs, and their advantage over clients who had taken part in government-run programs was statistically significant. That was the only statistically significant relationship between full- or part-time employment and attending a certain type of program. At both six and twelve months, the clients of the for-profit programs were also more likely to have found employment than were the clients of the government-run programs, but the differences did not achieve statistical significance.

What do these findings say in regard to our central question of whether or not certain types of programs were more effective in terms of the intermediate outcome of their clients' being successful in finding employment? We can say that, compared to the government programs, the faith-based/segmented programs were more effective at twelve months, when the gender, race, baseline employment status, work-related skills (including education), marital status, and number

Table 5.3

Determinants of Either Full- or Part-Time Employment at Six and at Twelve Months

Predictor Variable	Full- or Part-Time Employment at 6 Months	Full- or Part-Time Employment at 12 Months
Gender		
Female	−.64*	−.03
Male (reference category)	—	—
Race		
Black	−.23	−1.30**
Latino	.17	.34
Other Race	−.01	−.41
White (reference category)	—	—
Employment status at baseline		
Unemployed	−1.59**	−1.09**
Employed (reference category)	—	—
Number of work-related skills[a]	−.05	.02
Marital status		
Unmarried	.83**	.97**
Married (reference category)	—	—
Number of children	.07	.10
Type of welfare-to-work program		
For-profit	.48	.47
Nonprofit/secular	−.12	−.52
Faith-based/segmented	.28	1.22*
Faith-based/integrated	.03	−.54
Government (reference category)	—	—
N	327	265
Nagelkirche R Square	.21	.15

Note: Numbers from each column are the logistic regression coefficients.

*$p < .10$. **$p < .05$.

[a] Number of work-related skills is a scale of 0–3 based on the sum of having a high school education, being able to read English, and being able to speak English.

of dependent children were all held constant. The for-profit programs may also have been more effective. The effectiveness of the faith-based/segmented programs by this measure is especially remarkable both because it came at twelve months, which would appear to indicate a longer lasting impact, and because these programs were typically without the sophistication and accoutrements that marked the better-financed government programs.

Table 5.3, however, includes any type of employment, whether full-time or part-time. Although finding even part-time employment is an important intermediate outcome, achieving full-time employment is a further step along the welfare-to-work continuum. Therefore we also performed a direct logistic regression analysis to assess which variables were statistically significant in predicting full-time employment. As before, we considered full-time employment as thirty hours of work a week or more. The results are reported in table 5.4. At six months we found that being female and being unemployed at the baseline significantly decreased one's chances of finding full-time employment, and being unmarried significantly increased one's chances of doing so. These were the same findings as in table 5.3, which considered both full- and part-time employment. At twelve months, being female or unemployed at the baseline continued to decrease one's chances of finding full-time employment, but the differences were no longer statistically significant. Being unmarried continued to increase one's chances of full-time employment at a statistically significant level.

The remarkable effectiveness of the for-profit programs in terms of their clients' finding full-time employment is clear. At both six and twelve months their clients were doing significantly better than were the clients who had been in government programs in finding full-time employment, even with the same key background characteristics mentioned earlier held constant. Being in either type of faith-based program increased one's chances of finding full-time employment when compared to being in a government-run program, but the differences were not great enough to reach statistical significance. The fact that faith-based/segmented clients were not doing significantly better in finding full-time employment reflects the findings seen earlier in table 5.2, which showed many faith-based/segmented clients finding jobs, but most of these being part-time jobs.

These findings help demonstrate the effectiveness of the for-profit programs in enabling their clients to find employment, and especially in the crucial step of finding full-time employment. Even when one holds constant gender, race, baseline employment status, work-related skills (including education), marital status, and the number of dependent children, the for-profit program clients still did significantly better than the government-program clients in finding full-time employment. This was true at both six and twelve months. Both types of faith-based

Table 5.4

Determinants of Full-Time Employment at Six and at Twelve Months

Predictor Variable	Full-Time Employment at 6 Months	Full-Time Employment at 12 Months
Gender		
Female	−.95**	−.40
Male (reference category)	—	—
Race		
Black	−.55	−.48
Latino	.10	.30
Other race	−.28	−.08
White (reference category)	—	—
Employment status at baseline		
Unemployed	−.67**	−.38
Employed (reference category)	—	—
Number of work-related skills[a]	.16	.04
Marital status		
Unmarried	.89**	1.00**
Married (reference category)	—	—
Number of children	.03	.12
Type of welfare-to-work program		
For-profit	1.13**	1.14**
Nonprofit/secular	.03	.23
Faith-based/segmented	.56	.66
Faith-based/integrated	.58	.12
Government (reference category)	—	—
N	327	265
Nagelkirche R Square	.16	.15

Note: Numbers from each column are the logistic regression coefficients.

*$p < .10$. ** $p < .05$.

[a] Number of work-related skills is a scale of 0–3 based on the sum of having a high school education, being able to read English, and being able to speak English.

programs had positive coefficient scores when compared to the government programs, indicating that when key relevant characteristics of their clients were taken into account, they were doing better at finding full-time employment than were the government clients. However, the differences may have come about by chance and not by the actual greater effectiveness of the faith-based programs. The advantage that the faith-based/integrated-program clients had over the government-program clients at twelve months was particularly small.

Table 5.5

Percentages of Respondents Who Were Employed at Six or Twelve Months, by Program Type and Religious Involvement (respondents who were unemployed at the baseline only)

Program Type	At Six Months						At Twelve Months					
	High Religious Involvement[a]		Moderate Religious Involvement[a]		Low Religious Involvement[a]		High Religious Involvement[b]		Moderate Religious Involvement[b]		Low Religious Involvement[b]	
	%	N	%	N	%	N	%	N	%	N	%	N
Government	44	18	29	7	27	30	42	12	17	6	35	17
For-profit	47	17	63	16	68	22	75	8	69	16	100	10
Nonprofit/secular	32	31	14	7	38	16	25	20	50	12	54	13
Faith-based[c]	27	26	25	8	17	12	38	16	39	13	17	6
All Respondents	36	92	40	38	39	80	39	56	49	47	52	46

[a] The level of religious involvement was measured the same way as it was in table 4.3.

[b] The level of religious involvement was measured the same way as it was in table 4.4.

[c] Included clients from faith-based/segmented and faith-based/integrated combined, as the number of respondents was very small. The results did not tend to differ greatly between the faith-based/segmented and faith-based/integrated respondents, however. See note 1.

In response to an open-ended question of what they liked about their program, clients of for-profit programs frequently referred to having found employment. One said, "Right away when I finished my intern job I was able to get a job quick. My teacher, ——, was always helpful." Another respondent in a different for-profit program also made reference to its use of internships: "Just pretty much that the program is, you know, somewhat helpful. It helped me get into an internship to where I got hired." Other for-profit clients were even more succinct in referring to jobs obtained. One said "Enabled me to get a good job," and another said, "Getting a job immediately!" Comments from clients of the faith-based programs, even when they referred to jobs obtained, often also included other supports or help. Typical is the comment from a respondent from a faith-based/segmented program: "They helped me with child care; they helped me find a job; they helped with tires on my car; they provided food."

We also considered the relationship between employment and the religious involvement of the clients of the five types of programs we studied. First, it is clear that being religiously involved, as measured by church attendance, was not related to success at finding employment. At six months, of those who attended church once a week or more and who had been unemployed at the baseline, 36 percent had found a job (either full- or part-time) and 64 percent had not, while of those who went to church only a few times a year or never, 39 percent had found a job and 61 percent had not. (See table 5.5.) At twelve months, persons who were not religiously involved actually were doing somewhat better at finding employment. Both the religiously involved and uninvolved who found employment did not vary in terms of finding full-time versus part-time jobs.

This, however, leaves the issue of the interplay between the religious involvement of the clients and the faith-based or secular nature of the welfare-to-work programs they attended. There are two questions here. One is whether or not the religiously active clients of a faith-based program were more likely to find a job than were the religiously inactive clients of a faith-based program. It is reasonable to suspect that clients who are themselves religiously involved might relate better to a faith-based program than would the nonreligious clients, and thus experience greater success with it. A second question is whether or not religiously active persons who participated in a faith-based program were more likely to find a job than were religiously active persons who participated in a secular program. If clients who are religiously involved in fact relate better to a faith-based program, they might do better at such a program. Unfortunately, we are dealing here with very small numbers, but some interesting and suggestive patterns emerge.

In regard to the first of these questions, table 5.5 takes the respondents who had been unemployed at the baseline and shows the percentages of them who had found jobs six and twelve months later (either full- or part-time), divided into categories by the program type they attended and their own level of religious involvement. Of the respondents who had been unemployed at the baseline, had attended a faith-based program, and were religiously active, 27 percent were employed at six months and 38 percent were employed at twelve months, while of the respondents who had been unemployed at the baseline, had attended a faith-based program, and were not religiously active, only 17 percent had found a job at both six and at twelve months.[1] These figures indicate that the religiously inactive clients were doing less well at the faith-based programs than were the religiously active in terms of finding jobs. As we had expected—and in contrast to most of the patterns we found in regard to enabling outcomes—the religiously active persons were doing better by this outcome measure than were the religiously inactive persons at faith-based programs. Meanwhile, there was no consistent pattern in terms of the nonprofit/secular programs' clients doing better at finding employment, depending on whether they were religiously active or inactive.

Table 5.5, however, also shows—in answer to our second question posed earlier—that the religiously involved clients who had been unemployed at the baseline did not consistently do better in terms of finding jobs at the faith-based programs than at the secular programs. For example, at twelve months, 75 percent of the religiously active clients of for-profit programs who had been unemployed at the baseline had found a job, compared to only 38 percent of the religiously active clients of faith-based programs. This no doubt reflects the fact that the for-profit programs generally did better by the employment measure, not that they were especially effective in working with religiously involved clients. This is supported by the fact that the for-profit nonreligiously involved clients did even better than did the religiously involved clients. Also, the religiously active faith-based clients did better at finding jobs at twelve months than the religiously active nonprofit/secular clients and about as well as the religiously active government program clients.

In summary, we found that our respondents' level of religious involvement or activity—as measured by church attendance—did not in itself lead to greater success in finding employment. Nor did we find that those respondents who were highly involved religiously were more likely to find employment if they attended a faith-based program instead of a secular program. We did, however, find that clients of a faith-based program who were religiously involved were more likely to find employment than were their uninvolved fellow participants. The first of these findings—that our respondents' level of religious involvement was not related to success in finding jobs—is surprising in light of the fact that in the case of almost all of our enabling outcomes the highly and moderately religiously active respondents had better outcomes than the religiously inactive respondents.

It must be borne in mind, however, that we were dealing here with some very small numbers. Thus our findings here should be seen as illustrative of what may be the case rather than clear evidence of tendencies. Nevertheless, here as elsewhere in this book, we present even our highly tentative findings in the hope that they will stimulate additional research, research that may or may not confirm our findings.

Our logistic regression analyses took race into account, but it is also informative to look briefly at how obtaining employment was related to the race or ethnicity of the respondents taking part in the various program types. Table 5.6 demonstrates, first, that whites and Latinos experienced much more success at finding jobs (either full- or part-time) than did blacks. Of those respondents who were unemployed at the baseline, 42 percent of the whites and 44 percent of the Latinos had found a job at six months, and 27 percent of the blacks had done so. Similarly, at twelve months, 61 percent of the whites and Latinos who had been unemployed at the baseline had found a job, but only 18 percent of the blacks had done so. Whether this is due to continuing discrimination, the availability of fewer jobs in predominately black neighborhoods, blacks facing more barriers to employment success, or other factors, we do not know. But the fact that our black respondents were experiencing less success at finding employment than were the whites or Latinos is all too clear.

In terms of the different program types, if one disregards the cells in which there are fewer than ten respondents, one can conclude that

Table 5.6

Percentages of Respondents Who Were Employed at Six or Twelve Months, by Program Type and Race/Ethnicity (respondents who were unemployed at the baseline only)

	At Six Months						At Twelve Months					
	White		Black		Latino		White		Black		Latino	
Program Type	%	N	%	N	%	N	%	N	%	N	%	N
Government	29	7	39	23	30	23	75	4	39	18	32	19
For-profit	73	11	50	2	57	37	86	7	50	2	79	29
Nonprofit/secular	0	1	16	19	40	30	0	1	0	17	55	29
Faith-Based[a]	14	7	21	24	36	11	33	6	11	18	78	9
All respondents	42	26	27	68	44	101	61	18	18	55	61	86

[a] Included clients from faith-based/segmented and faith-based/integrated combined, since the number of respondents was very small. See note 1.

the government programs tended to do better than the other program types among the black respondents—almost 40 percent had found jobs at both six and twelve months. The for-profit programs did well among both white and Latino clients. At twelve months an impressive 79 percent of their Latino clients had found jobs. The faith-based programs also did well among their Latino clients—better than the government programs and, at twelve months, as well as the for-profit programs. The nonprofit/secular programs also did well with their Latino clients, but clearly not as well as the for-profit and faith-based programs. Here we again see the effectiveness of the for-profit programs in enabling their clients to find jobs. Their chief weakness in terms of race was that they had so few black clients that they were not having much of an impact in the predominantly black neighborhoods.[2] Also noteworthy is the comparative weakness among blacks of the nonprofit/secular and faith-based programs, program types that have sometimes been looked to for help among minority clients.

Wage Levels

In addition to part-time or full-time employment, a third measure of intermediate welfare-to-work program outcomes we utilized is the wage level of the persons who were employed. It is often possible for welfare recipients to find minimum wage jobs, but such jobs usually leave persons still mired in poverty and dependent on some forms of public assistance. Thus a crucial part of moving persons from welfare dependence to the ultimate outcome of economic self-sufficiency is to help them obtain jobs that enable them to move above minimum wage levels. We judged that it is especially important to note the percentages of respondents earning ten dollars or more an hour, because this would seem to be the minimum required wage level to eliminate the need for welfare and to lift a person out of poverty. We made this judgment on the basis that our respondents had an average of 1.6 children under eighteen years of age and living at home. Because most of our respondents were single, the typical household in our study consisted of three persons. In 2002 the poverty threshold for a family of three persons, with two children under eighteen years of age, was $14,494, according to the U.S. Census Bureau.[3] Someone working an average of thirty hours a week for fifty weeks at ten dollars an hour would earn fifteen thousand dollars. Especially given the higher cost of living in Los Angeles compared to the national average, we concluded that anyone earning less than ten dollars an hour would have a very difficult time achieving economic self-sufficiency. Thus we concluded that a key intermediate outcome is enabling program participants to move from the very low wages of seven dollars or less an hour (essentially the minimum wage),[4] to seven to nine dollars an hour, and then to ten dollars or more an hour.

Table 5.7 shows the wage levels of employed respondents at six and twelve months. It demonstrates, first, how difficult it is for persons in poverty to reach the ten dollar an hour level. Overall, only 28 percent of the respondents who were working were earning at least ten dollars an hour at six months, although this had increased to 37 percent at twelve months. More encouraging is the fact that higher percentages of clients of all but one of the program types were earning ten dollars an hour at twelve months than at six months. This seems to indicate that the welfare-to-work programs were having a long-term, positive effect. Even though the differences in table 5.7 did not reach statistical significance, it is nevertheless noteworthy that only the nonprofit/secular clients were not doing better at twelve months than they were at six months. The faith-based/integrated programs did best at having clients in the "$10 or more" category: 39 percent at six months and a very high

Table 5.7

Hourly Wages of Employed Respondents, by Program Type

	At Six Months					At Twelve Months				
Program Type	Less Than $7	$7 to $9	$10 or More	N	Total %	Less Than $7	$7 to $9	$10 or More	N	Total %
	%					%				
Government	29	47	25	49	101	17	46	37	41	100
For-profit	7	63	30	54	100	4	59	38	53	101
Nonprofit/secular	13	58	29	24	100	20	52	28	25	100
Faith-based/segmented[a]	28	56	17	18	101	13	56	31	16	100
Faith-based/integrated[a]	17	44	39	18	100	15	23	62	13	100
All respondents	18	55	28	163	101	12	51	37	148	100

$\chi^2(8) = 11.38$, $p = .18$ $\chi^2(8) = 10.91$, $p = .21$

[a] We kept the faith-based/segmented and faith-based/integrated clients separate in this table in spite of the small numbers because they showed somewhat different patterns.

62 percent at twelve months. The for-profit programs were notable for the very small number of their employed clients who were mired in the "less than $7" an hour level: only 7 percent at six months and an even lower 4 percent at twelve months.

What these figures do not take into account are the changes in the wage levels of the clients who were already employed at the time they were in the various welfare-to-work programs. Table 5.8 gives, for each of the five program types, the percentages of their clients who at six months and at twelve months were experiencing lower, the same, and higher wages. At six months the government and for-profit programs showed especially positive outcomes. More than one-third of the for-profit clients and 27 percent of the government clients experienced increased wages, and more than one-half were able to maintain their earlier wage levels. At twelve months the government and for-profit programs' clients were able to maintain, and even increase, their six-month gains. Fifty-two percent of government clients and 45 percent of for-profit clients experienced wage increases over those at the baseline twelve months earlier. Very few of their clients who were working at both the baseline and at six or twelve months saw a decrease in their wages. One reason the for-profit and government programs did as well as they did was that many of their clients who were working both at the baseline and at twelve months had been earning only seven dollars or less at the baseline. Our data show that it is easier for persons to move from the "less than $7" category to the "$7 to $9" category than from the "$7 to $9" category to the "$10 or more" category. The faith-based clients fared the worst in moving to higher wage levels at both six and twelve months. As we will discuss more fully later, some of these patterns may be explained by the skills training emphasis of the government and for-profit programs and the de-emphasis of skills training by the faith-based programs. It may be that the development of marketable skills is necessary for persons to move up the wage scale.

Thus far we have only considered those respondents who were already employed at the baseline, and how their wages changed. Another measure considers those who were unemployed at the baseline and found employment. Were they overwhelmingly mired in minimum wage jobs, or were some able to achieve higher wages? Did the various types of programs differ at all in enabling their clients who were unemployed to advance to jobs paying more than the minimum wage? Table

Table 5.8

Net Changes in Wages at Six and at Twelve Months Compared with Baseline Wages, by Program Type (only respondents who were employed at both the baseline and at six and twelve months)

| | At Six Months | | | | | At Twelve Months | | | | |
Program Type	Wages Increased	Wages Stayed the Same	Wages Decreased	N	Total %	Wages Increased	Wages Stayed the Same	Wages Decreased	N	Total %
		%					%			
Government	27	57	17	30	101	52	44	4	25	100
For-profit	35	55	10	20	100	45	50	5	20	100
Nonprofit/secular	14	71	14	7	100	17	83	0	6	100
Faith-based[a]	4	87	9	23	100	13	86	0	8	100
All respondents	21	66	13	80	100	36	59	5	66	99

[a] Included clients from faith-based/segmented and faith-based/integrated combined, because the number of respondents was very small. The results did not tend to differ greatly between the faith-based/segmented and faith-based/integrated respondents, however. See note 1.

5.9 provides the answers to these questions. It shows, first of all, that a majority of the respondents who were unemployed at the baseline and had found jobs were being paid at more than the seven dollar an hour level. This was true of 82 percent of them at six months, and 86 percent of them at twelve months. However, only a minority (22 percent at six months and 29 percent at twelve months) had managed to advance to the desired wage level of ten dollars or more an hour. Yet even these figures are impressive, given the fact that we are only considering those persons who had no jobs at all at the baseline.

Table 5.9 also shows the wage levels of the clients of the different types of program who had obtained employment. Clearly the for-profit programs again proved themselves most effective. Particularly impressive is the fact that at both six and twelve months only 3 percent of their clients were stuck in jobs that paid them less than seven dollars an hour. By twelve months, almost 40 percent had managed to obtain a job paying ten dollars or more an hour. These persons were well on their way to being economically self-supporting. As noted before, this may be due to the for-profits' heavy emphasis on hard-skills training, or it may be due to certain strengths of efficiency and flexibility often attributed to the for-profit sector.

At six months, the faith-based programs fared the worst, with 46 percent of their clients who had managed to find employment at the inadequate seven dollars or less level. But their clients had made significant progress by twelve months. They had the next to the fewest clients at the lowest wage level and the next to the highest percentage in the desirable ten dollar or more level. This may indicate that it may take time for the faith-based programs—with their emphasis on soft-skills training and their success at creating social capital—to see positive wage results for their efforts. Without the skills training of the for-profit programs, their clients may have a harder time finding initial well-paying jobs, but in time their stronger attitudinal skills and support networks may reduce the advantage those with greater job skills training initially have. But there were so few faith-based clients who had been unemployed at the baseline and had obtained employment at six or at twelve months (eleven clients at six months and twelve at twelve months) that one must be careful in assigning weight to these findings. They are no more than suggestive of what may be the case.

Table 5.9

Hourly Wages of Employed Respondents, by Program Type
(only those respondents who were unemployed at the baseline)

	At Six Months					At Twelve Months				
Program Type	Less Than $7	$7 to $9	$10 or More	N	Total %	Less Than $7	$7 to $9	$10 or More	N	Total %
	%					%				
Government	28	50	22	18	100	19	56	25	16	100
For-profit	3	72	25	32	100	3	58	39	31	100
Nonprofit/secular	18	65	18	17	101	28	61	11	18	100
Faith-based[a]	46	36	18	11	100	17	50	33	12	100
All respondents	18	60	22	78	100	14	57	29	77	100

[a] Included clients from faith-based/segmented and faith-based/integrated combined, because the number of respondents was very small. The results did not tend to differ greatly between the faith-based/segmented and faith-based/integrated respondents, however. See note 1.

Table 5.10

Percentage of Respondents at Twelve Months Earning Ten Dollars or More an Hour, by Program Type and Race/Ethnicity

Program Type	White		Black		Latino	
	%	N	%	N	%	N
Government	57	7	25	12	32	19
For-profit	42	12	33	3	37	35
Nonprofit/secular	—	0	100	1	24	21
Faith-based[a]	50	6	50	6	47	15
All respondents	48	25	36	22	34	90

[a] Included clients from faith-based/segmented and faith-based/integrated combined, because the number of respondents was very small. See note 1.

There was no relationship between involvement in a religious congregation, as measured by church attendance, and wages earned by those who were employed. Of those who were employed at twelve months, 38 percent of the highly religiously active earned ten dollars or more an hour, and 33 percent of those who were low in religious activity did so. Neither did we find notable differences among the wages earned by the clients of the different program types when we controlled for religious involvement.

In regard to race or ethnicity, table 5.10 shows that a higher percentage of whites who were employed at twelve months (48 percent) earned ten dollars or more an hour than did blacks or Latinos (36 percent and 34 percent, respectively). This is additional evidence that the minority respondents were experiencing a harder time moving toward economic self-sufficiency than were the white respondents. Although the number of respondents was very small, the faith-based clients showed the greatest equality in wages, with about 50 percent of whites, blacks, and Latinos all earning ten dollars or more an hour. The clients of the other program types experienced greater disparities in wages, depending on race or ethnicity.

Economic Self-Sufficiency

The ultimate outcome of welfare-to-work programs—if they are to live up to their name—is to empower persons to obtain gainful work of sufficient hours and wages that they no longer need or qualify for welfare assistance. This section presents our findings in terms of the comparative effectiveness of the programs we studied in enabling their clients to make this tremendously difficult transition.

The first question to ask is whether or not the five types of programs differed in the extent to which their clients were able to leave the welfare rolls. The respondents were asked in the baseline questionnaire and in the six- and twelve-month telephone surveys whether or not they were receiving any assistance under any one or more of a laundry list of welfare programs. One of the programs we inquired about was the CalWORKs program, which is the California version of the TANF program. In the following analyses we focus on whether or not the respondents were receiving CalWORKs/TANF benefits, rather than other forms of welfare assistance such as food stamps or Medicaid. We did so because it is the major cash support program in California and is the program persons usually have in mind when they refer to "being on welfare." In addition, more than 90 percent of the respondents who were receiving TANF benefits were in fact also receiving food stamps and MediCal (California's version of Medicaid).

Table 5.11 reports the percentages of respondents for each program type who were receiving TANF/CalWORKs benefits at six months and at twelve months, divided by whether or not they were receiving them at the baseline. On the surface, the figures in T5.11 are somewhat encouraging. At six months, 28 percent of the persons who were receiving TANF benefits at the baseline were no longer doing so, and at twelve months this had improved to 44 percent. Also, very few of those who were not receiving TANF benefits at the baseline were doing so at either six or twelve months.

The differences among the five program types regarding clients leaving TANF were statistically significant. The for-profit programs had the highest percentages of clients leaving the TANF rolls, with 53 percent of their clients who had been receiving TANF benefits at the baseline no longer doing so at six months, and at twelve months a highly impressive 73 percent had managed to move off the TANF rolls. The faith-based/segmented programs were not far behind the for-profit programs in assisting those on TANF to move off it. The faith-based/integrated programs fared the worst. At both six and twelve months, they had the lowest percentages of clients moving off TANF (10 percent and 21 percent, respectively). The government programs barely did better; only 17 percent

Table 5.1.1

Percentage of Respondents Receiving TANF at Six and at Twelve Months, by Program Type and Whether or Not Receiving TANF at Baseline

Program Type	Percent of Respondents Receiving TANF at Baseline and Not Receiving It at Six Months		Percent of Respondents Not Receiving TANF at Baseline and Not Receiving It at Six Months		Percent of Respondents Receiving TANF at Baseline and Not Receiving It at Twelve Months		Percent of Respondents Not Receiving TANF at Baseline and Not Receiving It at Twelve Months	
	%	N	%	N	%	N	%	N
Government	17	52	95	40	23	40	91	32
For-profit	53	30	95	58	73	26	98	43
Nonprofit/secular	30	30	89	35	52	29	94	32
Faith-based/segmented	42	12	95	20	63	8	100	16
Faith-based/integrated	10	21	81	16	21	14	93	15
All respondents	28	145	92	169	44	117	95	138
	$\chi^2(4) = 17.12, p < .01$		$\chi^2(4) = 4.57, p = .33$		$\chi^2(4) = 21.17, p < .001$		$\chi^2(4) = 2.93, p < .57$	

of their clients who were on TANF at the baseline managed to leave it at six months, and 23 percent were able to leave it at twelve months.

In terms of respondents who were not receiving TANF assistance at the baseline and who avoided having to receive TANF assistance six and twelve months later, there were no significant differences among the five program types. All were effective by this measure, with 80 to 100 percent of their clients who were not receiving TANF at the baseline still not receiving it six and twelve months later.

One must treat all of these numbers, however, with a certain amount of caution because we cannot be certain why these persons were no longer receiving TANF benefits. Of the forty-one persons who had been receiving TANF benefits at the baseline and were not doing so at six months, only 54 percent reported that they were employed full-time (the others were either not working at all or working fewer than thirty hours a week). Similarly, of the fifty-one respondents who had been receiving TANF at the baseline and were not doing so at twelve months, only 56 percent were working full-time. In other words, about 45 percent of those who had been receiving TANF at the baseline and were no longer doing so at six or twelve months presumably left TANF not because they were economically self-supporting, but because of other causes. These causes could range from losing eligibility due to noncompliance with certain regulations to becoming married to a wage earner.

Therefore we assumed persons had left the TANF program for reasons other than economic self-support if they were employed only part-time or if they were earning less than ten dollars an hour. As explained earlier, wages less than ten dollars an hour would tend to leave our respondents still mired in poverty or, at best, on the borderline of poverty and most likely in need of some form of welfare assistance, if only food stamps. Thus we felt we could ascribe the achievement of the ultimate outcome of a successful transition from welfare dependent to economic self-sufficiency only in the case of respondents who had been receiving TANF at the baseline, were no longer doing so six or twelve months later, and were employed full-time at ten dollars or more an hour.

As seen in table 5.11, we found that at six months 28 percent, or 41, of the 145 respondents who were receiving TANF benefits at the baseline were no longer receiving them. Of the 41 who were not receiving TANF, 13 were not employed and 28 (68 percent) were employed. Thus only 28 of our respondents had actually transitioned from welfare to work. Of these 28, only 12 were employed full-time at ten dollars or more an hour. They were the ones, by our measures, that had successfully moved from welfare dependence to self-supporting employment. When one looks at the programs out of which these 12 came, the comparative effectiveness of the for-profit programs again becomes clear. Eight out of the 12 who had successfully transitioned from welfare to full-time employment at good wages (67 percent) had been clients of a for-profit program. The other 4 successful respondents were scattered among the other program types.

At twelve months the patterns were similar. There were 51 respondents who had been receiving TANF at the baseline and were no longer receiving it. Of these 51, 36 (71 percent) reported that they were working, and 15 (29 percent) reported that they were not. Of the 36 respondents who were working, only 14 (39 percent) were working full-time at ten dollars or more an hour. They were the ones, by our measures, that had successfully moved from welfare dependence to self-supporting employment. As at six months, the for-profit clients were experiencing the greatest success. Of the 14 respondents who had moved from welfare to self-supporting employment, 10 (71 percent) had participated in a for-profit program. The other 4 successful respondents were again scattered among the other program types.

These numbers are, of course, extremely small, and our level of confidence in them must be equally small. We are dealing here only with those respondents who had been receiving TANF benefits at the baseline, were no longer doing so six and twelve months later, and were gainfully employed at an economically self-supporting wage level. Yet we thought it helpful to present these numbers as an indication of what may be the case and to illustrate the sort of additional research we believe is necessary with a much larger pool of participants.

Our findings here are strengthened by the direct logistic regression analysis by which we assessed which variables were statistically significant in predicting the TANF status of respondents at six and twelve months (see table 5.12).[5] We used the same methodology that we did earlier in regard to employment (see tables 5.3 and 5.4). Not unexpectedly, the best predictor of whether or not a person would be receiving TANF at six or twelve months was whether or not they were receiving it at the baseline. Being female or black also significantly decreased one's chances of leaving the TANF rolls at both six and twelve months.

Among the five program types, participants in a for-profit program were significantly more likely to leave TANF than were participants in a government-run program (our reference category). This once again supports the conclusion that for-profit programs were particularly effective at moving people off welfare. When controlling for race, gender, TANF status at the baseline, work-related skills (including education), marital status, and the number of dependent children, taking part in a for-profit welfare-to-work program significantly increased the chances of a respondent being off TANF six and twelve months later. This finding strengthens the likelihood that our earlier finding that most of the respondents who had moved off TANF and were employed full-time at good wages had been for-profit clients was not merely a chance pattern. At twelve months the faith-based/segmented clients also had a statistically significant greater chance of leaving the TANF rolls than the government program clients. The only other positive correlation that was statistically significant in table 5.12 was the total skills measure. At six months—but not at twelve months—persons with more of the skills we measured (a high school diploma, the ability to speak English, and the ability to read English well) had a statistically better chance of moving off welfare. Curiously, at six months, participating in a faith-based/integrated program actually decreased a respondent's chances of being off TANF. By twelve months, however, participation in a faith-based/integrated program is correlated neither negatively nor positively with a respondent's TANF status.

We also explored the interplay between the religious involvement of the respondents and their ability to achieve the ultimate outcome of leaving TANF and finding self-supporting employment. Table 5.13 shows that those who were highly involved religiously were more likely to be off TANF and employed full-time at ten dollars or more an hour than were those who were low in religious involvement. Twenty-two percent of the highly religious respondents had achieved this success, but only 13 percent of those low in religious involvement had done so. And an even lower 8 percent of those who were low or moderate in religious involvement combined had done so. Less than half of the highly religious respondents who had been on TANF at the baseline were still on it at twelve months—something that was not true of either the moderately religious or nonreligious respondents. In other words, we found

Table 5.12

Determinants of TANF Status at Six and at Twelve Months

Predictor Variable	Off TANF at 6 Months	Off TANF at 12 Months
Gender		
Female	−1.36**	−1.86**
Male (reference category)	—	—
Race		
Black	−1.06*	−1.19*
Latino	−.70	−.78
Other race	−.75	−.80
White (reference category)	—	—
TANF status		
On TANF	−3.34**	−3.77**
Off TANF (reference category)	—	—
Number of work-related skills[a]	.43*	−.18
Marital status		
Unmarried	−.06	−.02
Married (reference category)	—	—
Number of children	−.13	.02
Type of welfare-to-work program		
For-profit	1.12**	2.24**
Nonprofit/secular	.18	1.03
Faith-based/segmented	.69	1.47*
Faith-based/integrated	−1.14*	.02
Government (reference category)	—	—
N	327	265
Nagelkirche R Square	.59	.58

Note: Numbers from each column are the logistic regression coefficient.

*$p < .10$. **$p < .05$.

[a] Number of work-related skills is a scale of 0–3 based on the sum of having a high school education, being able to read English, and being able to speak English.

that personal, organic religion was related to persons' success in replacing welfare dependence with gainful, self-supporting employment.

We did not try to determine whether the different program types did better among either the more or less religiously active. Because we were dealing here only with persons who had been on TANF at the baseline and had successfully left it for employment, the numbers were so small that further dividing them by our five program types would have been meaningless.

Table 5.13

The TANF and Economically Self-Supporting Status of Respondents Who Had Been
Receiving TANF at the Baseline and at Twelve Months, by Religious Involvement

TANF √ Self-Supporting Status	High Religious Involvement[a]		Moderate Religious Involvement[a]		Low Religious Involvement[a]	
	%	N	%	N	%	N
Still on TANF	47	15	62	21	55	22
Off TANF, not self-supporting	31	10	35	12	33	13
Off TANF, self-supporting[b]	22	7	3	1	13	5
Total	100	32	100	34	101	40

[a] The level of religious involvement was measured the same way as it was in table 4.4.

[b] We considered those who were employed full-time and earning ten dollars or more an hour as being economically self-supporting.

We did explore the relationship between successfully leaving TANF for self-supporting employment and race or ethnicity. As table 5.14 makes clear, the white respondents were the most successful in leaving TANF and achieving self-supporting status, and blacks were the least successful, with Latinos falling somewhere in between. Twenty-four percent of the whites achieved this level of success, but only 6 percent of blacks and 14 percent of Latinos did so. Perhaps most discouraging, almost 70 percent of the blacks who were receiving TANF assistance at the baseline where still doing so twelve months later, in spite of having taken part in a welfare-to-work program. This finding is in line with other evidence we have found that makes clear that for whatever reasons black welfare recipients face an especially difficult challenge in transitioning to economic self-sufficiency.

Summary and Observations

Table 5.15 summarizes the relative effectiveness of the five types of programs in terms of our intermediate and ultimate outcome measures. Overall, the for-profit programs had the best outcomes. Compared to the other types of programs, more of their clients had moved from unemployment to employment, had achieved full-time employment, had

Table 5.14

The TANF and Economically Self-Supporting Status of Respondents Who Had Been
Receiving TANF at the Baseline and at Twelve Months, by Race/Ethnicity

TANF √	White		Black		Latino	
Self-Supporting Status	%	N	%	N	%	N
On TANF	41	7	69	24	55	32
Off TANF, not self-supporting	35	6	26	9	31	18
Off TANF, self-supporting[a]	24	4	6	2	14	8
Total	100	17	101	35	100	58

[a] We considered those who were employed full-time and earning ten dollars or more an hour as being economically self-supporting.

increased their wages to ten dollars or more an hour (whether employed or unemployed at the baseline), and had left TANF and achieved economic self-sufficiency. The for-profit programs did not do as well in helping those already employed at the baseline to maintain their employment or in enabling their clients who were not on TANF at the baseline to remain off TANF, but even here they did about as well as the other types of programs. For the most part, there was no consistent pattern among the four other types of programs doing either comparatively better or worse. The government programs did better in terms of clients who increased their wages, the nonprofit/secular programs did better in terms of their clients who found employment in finding full-time employment, and the clients of both types of faith-based programs did better in helping those already employed to maintain their employment status.

The success of the for-profit programs is clear, but its causes must remain speculative. This success is particularly surprising given the fact that some other studies have found that for-profit health programs did less well than their nonprofit counterparts. One study of nursing homes and mentally handicapped facilities in the United States found that church-related nonprofit facilities provided more labor inputs (full-time registered nurses, dieticians, part-time nurses' aides, and maintenance workers) per one hundred beds than did private firms. The study also demonstrated that the level of customer satisfaction with the nonprofit

Table 5.15

Summary Assessments of Employment, Wage, and Welfare Outcomes, by Program Type[a]

Program Type	Those Unemployed at Baseline Finding Employment	Wages of Those Unemployed at Baseline Who Found Employment	Those Finding Employment Finding Full-Time Employment	Those Employed at Baseline Maintaining Employment	Those Employed at Baseline Increasing Their Wages	Those Not on TANF at Baseline Remaining off TANF	Those on TANF at Baseline off TANF and Employed Full-Time at $10 or More an Hour
Government	About average	About average	About average	About average	Better than average	About average	About average
For-profit	Better than average	Better than average	Better than average	About average	Better than average	About average	Better than average
Nonprofit/ secular	About average	Worse than average	Better than average	Worse than average	Worse than average	About average	About average
Faith-based/ segmented	About average	About average[b]	Worse than average	Better than average	Worse than average	About average	About average
Faith-based/ integrated	Worse than average	About average[b]	About average	Better than average	Worse than average	About average	Worse than average

[a] Based on the authors' judgments, taking into account both the six- and twelve-month data, but giving somewhat more weight to the twelve-month data.

[b] Due to the small numbers involved, the faith-based/segmented and faith-based/integrated were not considered separately on this measure.

facilities was considerably higher than with the for-profit firms.[6] A study that compared patients who received treatment at for-profit and non-profit hemodialysis centers for end-stage kidney disease determined that the sessions were longer—and therefore more helpful—and the mortality rates were lower at the nonprofit centers.[7] Counterbalancing these studies, however, is the study of for-profit and nonprofit HMOs discussed in chapter 1. It found that, in terms of providing public benefits, the nonprofit HMOs did not consistently outperform the for-profit HMOs. In fact, by one measure the for-profit HMOs actually outperformed the nonprofit HMOs.

What, then, might explain the relative success of for-profits in our study? As we have noted at various points, it may relate to the direct emphasis on job-skills training, although this tended to be true of the government programs also, and they did not do nearly as well as the for-profit programs. As mentioned earlier, both of the for-profit programs had an internship element in their programs, which may have contributed to their success. Several comments made by their clients point in this direction. But it may also be—as the advocates of using for-profits to provide needed social service often have claimed—that the profit motive and the alleged greater flexibility of the for-profit sector are the explanations. While visiting these programs and talking to their staff members, it was very clear to us that they felt they were being watched and felt the pressure to produce if they were to continue to be a part of the Los Angeles welfare-to-work continuum of programs. Another factor in their success might be the very controversy surrounding the use of for-profits in delivering social welfare services. The use of for-profits in welfare-to-work programs was a fairly recent development and had been highly contentious in Los Angeles County. Moreover, academics are generally skeptical about the value of using for-profit firms to provide public goods.[8] All of this might have combined to increase the pressure on the programs to produce positive results. We came away suspecting that this last factor may have been the key factor that distinguished our for-profit programs from the for-profit nursing homes and other health care services that some other researchers have found to be less effective.

We should also note that we controlled for the most likely background and demographic characteristics of the clients that could have led to the greater success of the for-profit programs. We took into account race and ethnicity, education, gender, work skills, employment status, and other such measurable characteristics, and still the for-profit programs tended to come out ahead in intermediate and ultimate outcomes. Nevertheless, it is conceivable that there are other, less obvious characteristics of the for-profit clients that would explain their success. The client recruitment process and the elements of self-selection that were a part of it may have led the for-profit programs we studied to have a disproportionate number of more highly motivated clients or clients with other unobservable characteristics that made their success more likely. Whatever the correct explanation, one cannot deny that our data here, as elsewhere in our study, point to the effectiveness of the Los Angeles for-profit programs that we examined.

Clients who were themselves religiously active tended to do better in terms of the crucial ultimate outcome of leaving TANF and holding a full-time job at economically sustainable wages, but they did not do better in finding employment or in increasing their wages. Also, there was not a pattern of religiously active clients doing better at faith-based programs than their religiously inactive fellow participants. When the religiously active clients did well at a faith-based program, their non-religious fellow participants usually did equally well. An exception to this pattern, however, was in finding employment, with the religiously active in faith-based programs doing better than the religiously inactive in the same programs. In addition, religiously active respondents did not tend to experience more positive outcomes in faith-based programs than they did in secular programs.

Blacks seemed to face particularly difficult challenges in achieving positive intermediate and ultimate outcomes. By most of our measures they did worse than either the white or Latino clients. Meanwhile, the Latino clients tended to fall in between the extremes of the white and black clients.

Six observations on the intermediate and ultimate outcomes covered in this chapter are in order. First, it is clear that it is very difficult for persons to move from unemployment to gainful employment and from gainful employment to economic self-sufficiency. Overall, a majority of the respondents who were unemployed at the baseline were still unemployed a year later, and of those who were employed, many were employed only part-time. Less than a third had moved from unemployment to full-time employment. And most of those who had attained full-time employment were not earning enough to be truly self-supporting. All of our analyses support this observation. There was a strong, consistent, and statistically significant negative correlation between those who were unemployed at the baseline and those who found a job at six or twelve months. Clearly, there is no simple answer to the myriad problems associated with helping people to make the transition to the world of work. None of the five types of programs we studied, with their varying emphasis on soft- or hard-skills training, possess a magic solution. It is even more difficult for persons receiving welfare benefits to achieve the ultimate outcome of finding employment of sufficient hours and wages that they no longer need or qualify for welfare. Very few of our respondents, no matter what type of program they were in, managed to achieve this level of success in the one-year time period our study covered. Whether with more time they might experience more success we cannot say.

Our second observation notes the greater success of the for-profit programs, compared to the four other program types, in enabling their clients in all four outcome measures used in this chapter. Respondents from for-profit programs were the only ones that consistently showed a positive correlation between work and wage status and successfully leaving the TANF program. However one looks at the data, for-profit welfare-to-work programs are performing remarkably well in terms of all four of our intermediate and ultimate outcome measures. As noted earlier, our various analyses indicate that these positive results cannot be explained simply by the for-profit firms having a disproportionate number of clients who possessed background characteristics most frequently associated with employment success. After having noted this, however, we must also point out that most of the for-profit clients who were receiving TANF benefits at the baseline were still receiving them six and twelve months later or for some reason had dropped out of the TANF program even though they were not employed full-time at self-sustaining wages. Obviously, transitioning from welfare to work is no easy task.

A third observation entails the two types of faith-based programs. Some have claimed that faith-based social service programs are spectacularly more effective than secular programs in achieving positive results. As is often the case, our data indicate that reality is more complex than such claims. Our findings show that in Los Angeles the faith-based welfare-to-work programs, both segmented and integrated, did about as well as their government-run and nonprofit/secular counterparts. By some measures they did somewhat better; on others they did somewhat worse. The one measure for which we found the faith-based programs—and especially the faith-based/integrated programs—doing better than the other programs was in clients who were already employed at the baseline tending to be more successful in maintaining their employment than the clients in the other types of programs. In fact, given the very small size of the programs, typical lack of government funding, lean budgets, and usually barely adequate facilities, we were surprised to find that they did as well as the larger government and government-funded nonprofit/secular programs. Also, they were able to do so while emphasizing "soft" life skills training over "hard" vocational or job skills training, even though some claim that it is essential for welfare recipients to receive the latter if they are to improve their employment and wage situation.[9]

A fourth observation concerns the interplay between the religious practices of the clients themselves and their success in achieving positive outcomes in the various types of programs. We did not find a consistent pattern of the personally religious clients doing better at faith-based programs than they did at secular programs, or doing better than their less religious fellow participants. By some measures they did; by other measures they did not. We did find, however, that by most measures those who were personally religiously active tended to achieve more positive intermediate and ultimate outcomes than did those were not religiously active. Religion is a factor in welfare-to-work success, and this argues for it not being ignored in welfare-to-work efforts. In the following chapter we suggest how managers of welfare-to-work programs could take advantage of the religious nature of many of their clients.

A fifth observation concerns the impact of race or ethnicity on the clients' success. By most of our measures, white clients experienced the most success, Latino clients experienced the next most favorable outcomes, and black clients experienced the least positive outcomes. Whether this is due to societal factors—such as continuing racism and the flight of jobs from predominantly black neighborhoods—or due to other factors that are race-related, is hard for us to say. But it is clear that the differential success rates by race or ethnicity is one of the realities that welfare-to-work efforts need to take into account.

Our final comment is that although the majority of our respondents who were unemployed at the start of our study were still unemployed six and twelve months later, and although the majority of our respondents who were receiving TANF assistance at the start of our study were still doing so six and twelve months later, this should not be interpreted to mean that the welfare-to-work programs we studied were failures. Rather, we believe that these findings are an indication of the enormity of the task of enabling persons who are unemployed and receiving welfare to move from welfare to work. The fact that, as seen in earlier chapters, most of our respondents evaluated their welfare-to-work experiences positively, that many experienced growth in terms of enabling outcomes, and that many—even if not a majority—experienced positive intermediate outcomes in the forms of finding employment and winning higher wages, all point to the value of the programs that we studied here.

6

OBSERVATIONS AND RECOMMENDATIONS

A faith-based/integrated program client, when asked at the end of a telephone interview if she had any further comments or suggestions, replied, "I think the [name of the program] is a great program to go through. I have not found a job yet, but it is nice to know that I am comfortable at least looking for a job. I appreciate them; keep up the good work." This response helps illustrate the error in drawing simple conclusions concerning program effectiveness. Should such a client be judged to be a program success or failure? Should her program be considered effective or ineffective? She had not found a job, not even a part-time, minimum wage job. She had not realized the hoped for ultimate or intermediate outcomes. But she had more confidence in herself, and she had acquired key skills needed to go out and compete for employment. She had experienced positive enabling outcomes, as we have termed them. One could even argue that this was a more positive outcome than acquiring a minimum wage, no-benefits job that in any case might not last more than a few months. Such questions have led us to avoid throughout this book simple yes-no, success-failure conclusions. We will not depart from this practice in this final chapter.

First we summarize our key findings and conclusions and then suggest a number of recommendations based on them. The preceding chapters have presented a maze of specific findings; so many, in fact, that both we as researchers and our readers court the danger of being overwhelmed by an avalanche of specific findings with no apparent pattern to them. Thus a vital objective of this last chapter is to organize our key findings and to highlight whatever patterns or regularities we discover. We also seek here to draw out a number of recommendations for policymakers, human service managers, and researchers. We have grouped our recommendations into three categories: public policy recommendations, recommendations related to managing human service agencies, and recommendations relevant to the study of the effectiveness of human service programs.

Summary Conclusions

In our introduction we outlined three key questions we sought to explore by the research reported in this book: (1) whether or not certain types of welfare-to-work programs provide particular types of services in an especially effective manner, (2) whether or not different types of programs seem to provide services to different types of clients in a particularly effective manner, and (3) what further insights into effectiveness research were revealed by our research. In this section we summarize what we found in response to the first two of these questions, and in a later section we consider what we learned about effectiveness research.

What Programs Provided What Services in a Particularly Effective Manner?

In response to the first question, we initially summarize our respondents' own evaluations of their programs, followed by evidence of positive enabling outcomes and then by evidence of positive intermediate and ultimate outcomes. Table 6.1 summarizes our assessments of the relative effectiveness of the five program types in terms of client evaluations and enabling outcomes. In regard to our respondents' evaluations of their programs (the first two columns of the table), the clearest pattern was that of the clients of both types of faith-based programs and of nonprofit/secular programs rating their programs more highly in terms of staff empathy than did the clients of the for-profit and government programs. When we took instrumental evaluations into account, the for-profit programs continued to do poorly, and the nonprofit/secular programs continued to do well. The faith-based/integrated programs, however, went from doing well on the empathy measure to doing poorly on the instrumental measure. Overall, the nonprofit/secular programs did the best on these two client evaluation measures, and the for-profit programs did the worst. Overshadowing these differences, however, was the fact that our respondents generally evaluated their programs positively. Although not included in table 6.1, the clients of the faith-based programs were nearly unanimous in positively evaluating the

Table 6.1

Summary Assessments of Respondent Evaluations and Enabling Outcomes, by Program Type

Program Type[a]	Client Evaluations of Programs' Sense of Empathy	Client Evaluations of Programs' Instrumental Value	Increases in Levels of Client Optimism for the Future[b]	Success of Clients in Completing Their Programs	Social Capital: Client Contacts with Staff after Leaving Their Programs[b]	Social Capital: Client Contacts with Fellow Participants after Leaving Their Programs[b]	Social Capital: Increased Involvement in a Church
Government	Average	Better than average	Better than average	About average	About average	Better than average	About average
For-profit	Worse than average	Worse than average	Better than average	Better than average	About average	About average	About average
Nonprofit/secular	Better than average	Better than average	About average	Worse than average	About average	About average	About average
Faith-based/segmented	Better than average	About average	Worse than average	Worse than average	Worse than average	Worse than average	About average
Faith-based/integrated	Better than average	Worse than average	Better than average	Better than average	Better than average	About average	Better than average

[a] Based on the authors' judgments, taking into account the findings we presented in chapters 3 and 4.

[b] We took into account both the six- and twelve-month data, but gave somewhat more weight to the twelve-month data.

religious aspects of their programs. These findings indicate that, measured by client evaluations, the welfare-to-work programs we studied were working effectively. "Consumer satisfaction" was high. We believe that these findings contain some clear public policy implications that we will explore shortly.

In regard to enabling outcomes (columns 3 to 7 of table 6.1), we found that overall the faith-based/integrated programs fared the best. Compared to the average of the other four types of programs, they did better on four of the five enabling outcome measures we used and worse on none of them. The government programs also fared well; they did better than average on two of the five measures and worse than average on none of them. The faith-based/segmented programs fared the worst. They were worse than average on four of our five enabling outcome measures and better than average on none of them. The for-profit and non-profit/secular programs fell somewhere in the middle. The fact that the faith-based/integrated and faith-based/segmented programs fared very differently on the enabling outcomes measures further demonstrates that our distinction between integrated and segmented faith-based programs is an important one. That the government programs continued to fare as well as they did argues—as we have noted earlier—that the old stereotype of huge, uncaring, ineffective government bureaucracies is in need of some reworking, at least as it applies to welfare-to-work programs that have been contracted out to public community colleges and other localized government entities. Their success suggests that localized, decentralized government programs can be effective.

In regard to intermediate and ultimate outcomes, as noted in the previous chapter, the one type of program that we found was clearly more effective than the other programs was the for-profit programs. As table 5.15 summarized, the for-profit programs did better than the four other program types on five of the seven outcome measures and about average on the remaining two. Their unemployed clients did well in finding any type of employment, as well as in finding full-time employment and employment at wages of ten dollars or more an hour. Of those who were receiving TANF benefits at the baseline, a large majority of the for-profit clients were no longer doing so twelve months later. The two types of faith-based programs, the government-run programs, and the nonprofit/secular programs all did about equally well on these intermediate and ultimate outcome measures. Some did better on some measures; others did better on other measures. There was no consistent pattern of one doing worse or better.

The use of for-profit programs in antipoverty programs is often highly controversial and denigrated by many, but our findings indicate that they may very well have a positive, useful role to play in welfare-to-work efforts. Similarly, some have argued that faith-based antipoverty programs are too small and not sufficiently professional to run complex antipoverty programs. They may be able to run simple programs such as a food pantry or emergency overnight housing—so the argument goes—but they are too small and unsophisticated to run longer-term programs that must deal with clients facing multiple problems. Our findings indicate that many faith-based programs can do as effective a job in dealing with the complexities of welfare-to-work as the larger, better funded government and secular nonprofit programs.

In addition, these findings speak to the value of training in "hard," vocational skills versus training in "soft," life skills and attitudes. Because the government programs emphasized hard skills and the faith-based programs emphasized soft skills, and yet their intermediate and ultimate outcomes were about the same, our findings do not support the claim that only training in vocational or job skills will yield positive results. From hours poring over our findings, countless conversations with welfare-to-work providers and clients, and hours observing welfare-to-work programs, we came away with the strong impression that focusing on both types of skills is better than one approach or the other.

What impressed us as much as the relative differences and similarities in the intermediate and ultimate outcomes among the five program types was the difficulty the programs experienced in enabling persons who are unemployed and receiving welfare assistance to move to or even to move toward economic self-sufficiency. The challenges and pitfalls are many, the failures more numerous than the successes. A majority of our respondents who were unemployed at the baseline were still unemployed six and twelve months later; a majority of those who were receiving TANF assistance were still receiving it six and twelve months later. Only a handful of our respondents had combined leaving welfare with full-time employment at wages sufficient to ensure economic self-sufficiency.

Yet we are convinced these findings point, not to the failure of welfare-to-work programs, but simply to the challenges and difficulties confronting persons whose economic circumstances had sunk to such a point that they had to seek welfare assistance. To reenter the world of work, they typically need to deal with and overcome multiple barriers—barriers of both objective circumstances and subjective attitudes—in order to achieve success in an inevitably highly competitive job market. Given the challenges our respondents faced, we were impressed that some 45 percent of our respondents who were unemployed at the baseline had found employment twelve months later, and that 44 percent who were receiving TANF assistance at the baseline were not receiving it twelve months later. Many other respondents—such as the one we quote at the beginning of this chapter—had made gains in self-confidence and attitude that would greatly increase their chances of finding employment later on. These are not minor achievements. And among the respondents who had attended for-profit programs, even more progress had been made—a large majority who had been unemployed at the baseline were employed twelve months later, and a majority who had been receiving TANF assistance at the baseline were no longer doing so twelve months later. The seventeen welfare-to-work programs we studied in Los Angeles were not working perfectly, but they were working.

Were Certain Types of Programs Able to Provide Services to Certain Types of Clients in a Particularly Effective Manner?

We were unable to explore this question as fully as we would have liked or as thoroughly as we did the question of the comparative effectiveness of the five different program types. The problem we ran into was one of too few respondents who were included in our study. Thus whenever we divided our respondents not only by program types but also by characteristics such as religious involvement or race, the numbers were so small that our findings were no more than suggestive. Nevertheless, we reported these findings in order to give an indication of what may be the case and to point out what we believe are important questions for future researchers to ask.

Table 6.2 outlines our summaries of what we found in regard to four questions: Whether or not the religiously active clients were experiencing better outcomes than the religiously inactive clients, whether or not the religiously active clients were doing better at faith-based programs than at secular programs, whether or not the religiously active clients were doing better than religiously inactive clients at faith-based programs, and whether or not the outcomes our respondents experienced differed by race or ethnicity. In regard to the first question, we found that the religiously active respondents—that is, those marked by personal, organic religion as measured by reported church attendance—tended to do better by most of our outcome measures, no matter what type of program they participated in. In five of the six outcome measures where this was the case for the religiously active, it was equally the case for those who were highly involved in a church (attended church once a week or more) or were moderately involved (attended church a few times a month). In the case of only one outcome measure (that of leaving TANF and being employed full-time at ten dollars an hour or more) was it true of only the highly religious respondents. The three areas in which we found religious involvement by the clients did not make a difference were feeling increases in optimism for the future, finding employment, and attaining wages of ten dollars or more an hour. These areas are significant, but they were the exceptions—in six other outcome measures the religiously involved respondents experienced more success than the religiously uninvolved respondents. This finding matches that of many other researchers that we noted in chapter 1 who have documented the relationship between personal religious involvement and many positive social and health indications.

We usually did not find that the religiously active clients experienced greater success at faith-based programs than at secular programs. The two exceptions were in client evaluations of the sense of empathy toward them shown by program staff and client contacts with staff once the clients had completed the program. In both of these cases the faith-based/integrated clients who were religiously active reported more positive results than the religiously active clients in the other types of programs, including the faith-based/segmented programs.

There was a tendency—but no more than a tendency—for religiously active clients to experience more positive outcomes at faith-based programs than did the religiously inactive clients at the same programs. This was especially true of the faith-based/integrated clients. But on three of the seven outcome measures for which we had data, there were no differences between the outcomes for the religious and the nonreligious clients. This demonstrates that faith-based programs—and especially integrally faith-based programs—may be particularly suitable for those who are personally religious, but that the nonreligious also can do well at such programs. The differences were not as clear or as strong as we had anticipated.

We found some intriguing differences by race and ethnicity, with only one of our outcome measures showing no differences. By all three of our intermediate and ultimate outcome measures reported here (the last three items in table 6.2), whites did better than blacks, and on two of the three whites also did better than Latinos. This is an indication that race indeed does still matter in seeking employment. In terms of client evaluations and enabling outcomes, the results often varied by race or ethnicity and by the programs attended. The only discernable pattern, however, was that of blacks tending to have better experiences at nonprofit/secular and faith-based/integrated programs by several of our outcome measures. This may be an indication that blacks are more likely to thrive in programs that are localized and oriented toward the black experience.

Public Policy Recommendations

In the course of our research we met many persons who are outsiders to the America most of us know. They often were marginally educated, some had made bad choices in regard to drug use or having children outside of marriage, some suffered from health problems, some struggled with language or literacy problems, and almost all faced seemingly insurmountable problems blocking their entrance into the world of full-time, self-supporting work. But we also found them to be caring, sincere persons who wanted to overcome the challenges they faced, to better themselves, to care responsibly for their children, and to regain a sense of pride and accomplishment. Many expressed a desire to contribute to the broader communities of which they were a part. We quickly learned to respect and to care about what happened to those whom we were studying. Equally, we came to respect and care about those who were working in the various programs included in our study. They give of themselves day after day in jobs that often pay less than they could receive in other pursuits. They rejoice when their clients find jobs or achieve other gains; they despair when their clients fail to find jobs or go back to old self-defeating ways. Both the clients we interviewed and the staff of the programs we studied earned a large measure of our respect. It would be hard for us to overstate this observation.

Table 6.2

Summary Assessments of Respondents' Personal Religious Involvement and Race/Ethnicity as They Relate to Program Outcomes[a]

Outcome Measures	Religiously Active Clients Doing Better?	Religiously Active Clients Doing Better at Faith-Based Programs than at Secular Programs?	Religiously Active Clients Doing Better than Nonactive Clients at Faith-Based Programs?	Differences by Race and Ethnicity
Client evaluations of programs' sense of empathy	Highly and moderately active did better	Yes for FB/I clients, no for FB/S clients	Yes for FB/I clients, no for FB/S clients	Blacks did better, especially at NP/S
Client evaluations of programs' instrumental value	Highly and moderately active did slightly better	No	Yes for FB/I, no for FB/S	Blacks did better at NP/S and Latinos at Govt
Increases in levels of client optimism for the future	No	No	No	Whites did slightly better, especially at Govt and FB/I
Success of clients in completing their programs	Highly and moderately active did better	No	No	Whites did better, except Latinos did better at FP, blacks and Latinos did better at FB/I

Social capital: Client contacts with staff after leaving their programs[b]	Highly and moderately active did better	Yes for FB/I clients, no for FB/S clients	Yes for both FB/I and FB/S clients	Blacks did better at NP/S and FB/I
Social capital: Client contacts with fellow participants after leaving their programs[b]	Highly and moderately active did slightly better	No	Yes, especially for FB/I clients	No
Social capital: Increased involvement in a church	NA[c]	NA[c]	NA[c]	Blacks and Latinos did slightly better
Those unemployed at baseline finding employment	No	No	Yes for both FB/I and FB/S clients	Whites and Latinos did better than blacks
Wages of those unemployed at baselines who found employment	No	No	No	Whites did better than blacks and Latinos
Those on TANF at baseline off TANF and employed full-time at $10 or more an hour	Highly active did better	NA[d]	NA[d]	Whites did better than blacks and Latinos

Note: Our base of comparison for doing "better" was other clients of different level of religious involvement or of a different race or ethnicity. Govt refers to government programs, FP refers to for-profit programs, NP/S refers to nonprofit/secular programs, FB/S refers to faith-based/segmented programs, and FB/I refers to faith-based/integrated programs.

[a] Based on the authors' judgments, taking into account the findings we presented in chapters 3, 4, and 5.

[b] We took into account both the six- and twelve-month data, but gave somewhat more weight to the twelve-month data.

[c] In the case of church involvement it made no sense to run our data, because our measure of religiously active was church involvement.

[d] In the case of being off TANF, there were so few respondents that it was impossible to further divide them by religious activity.

Therefore we believe it essential for us to make a number of public policy recommendations based on our findings. From the beginning we did not view this research as a theoretical academic exercise, but as a means to help achieve more effective public policies that will help the all too many persons struggling against vast odds to find economic independence. We do so in the hope that our recommendations will lead to public policies that will make the work of the dedicated staff members of a host of welfare-to-work programs easier, leading many more welfare recipients to find gainful employment and, eventually, the economic self-sufficiency and sense of pride and accomplishment for which almost all of our respondents hope and dream.

Here we make five basic public policy recommendations that grow out of our findings. We are convinced that if followed they would result in many more persons being able to make that difficult, yet highly desirable transition from welfare dependence to economic self-sufficiency. Our recommendations deal solely with welfare-to-work efforts, because we do not want to claim more for our findings than is appropriate by generalizing to human service areas other than welfare-to-work. And yet they may have applications to other human service fields. Those who are more familiar with those fields than we are can make the proper applications and adjustments.

Our first recommendation is that *government should continue its own welfare-to-work programs and continue to fund for-profit, secular nonprofit, and both types of faith-based programs.* Some shifts in funding are called for—as we argue shortly—but our findings do not support any massive shift of resources that puts all or nearly all of society's welfare-to-work resources into only one or two types of programs. Our findings did not point to any one type of provider possessing a magic potion that leads to spectacularly positive results. All five types of providers had strengths and weaknesses.

Our findings do suggest, however, that two gradual, moderate shifts in government welfare-to-work funding are in order. One is to *increase funding to for-profit welfare-to-work providers.* This is our second public policy recommendation. For government to enter into financial partnerships with for-profit providers for basic social services, such as welfare-to-work programming, is controversial and historically has certainly been so in Los Angeles. But our data suggest that for-profit programs may be especially effective in the welfare-to-work realm. On almost all of our intermediate and ultimate outcome measures the for-profit clients experienced better outcomes than did the clients of the other four types of programs, often significantly so.

Yet a word of caution is in order. Only two for-profit programs were included in our study, and they did not outperform the other program types consistently or by huge margins. In fact, they did worse than the other program types by some of our measures. Thus we do not believe a sudden, massive shift of resources to for-profit programs is warranted. But we do believe our findings suggest that federal, state, and local governments should experiment more widely with financial partnerships with for-profit providers.

A second gradual, moderate shift in government funding suggested by our findings constitutes our third policy recommendation. It is to *engage in more funding of faith-based programs, and especially of faith-based/integrated programs.* We make this recommendation, not because the faith-based programs consistently outperformed the non-profit/secular and government programs in our study. They did so by some of our measures—and this is especially true of the faith-based/integrated programs—but by other measures they did no better and even did worse on several measures. However, in spite of very limited resources in terms of staff, facilities, and equipment, they performed about as well overall as their better-funded secular counterparts on most of our measures and even better on some measures. Our findings suggest that even modest amounts of government funding might lead to results that exceed that of the government-run and nonprofit/secular programs. Also, a sense of fairness would argue that faith-based providers that are providing a valuable public service—and doing so as well as the government and nonprofit/secular providers—should share more fully in public funding. On a number of our measures the faith-based/integrated providers appeared to be, if anything, more effective than the faith-based/segmented programs. Thus efforts to redistribute funds in the direction of faith-based providers should surely include the faith-based/integrated providers, if appropriate First Amendment concerns can be met.[1] Yet our findings do not support the conclusion that there should be a massive shift of funds toward faith-based providers. Again, a gradual, moderate shift of funds, which will allow for experimentation and analyses of outcomes, is what we are convinced is needed.

Ideally, our second and third policy recommendations, which involved increased funding of for-profit and faith-based programs, would be accomplished by increasing the overall funding of welfare-to-work programs, with most of the new money going to these two types of programs. This is what we prefer. If this proves politically impossible, however, we would favor shifting some of the funding now going to government-run and nonprofit/secular programs to for-profit and faith-based/integrated programs. The often better outcomes experienced by the for-profit clients and the usual equality of outcomes between the faith-based and the other three program types suggest that the current pattern of much greater funding of government-run and nonprofit/secular programs is hard to justify.

A fourth public policy recommendation is that *public policy should seek to encourage more collaborative efforts among a variety of welfare-to-work program types.* This recommendation is rooted in the concept of niche effectiveness, about which William Galston has written. He has raised the question of whether perhaps there is "such a niche or niches in the general area of social welfare and social service provision such that religious congregations and faith-based organizations are uniquely well suited to fill that niche or those niches."[2] Our findings tend to support the idea that certain types of programs may be especially effective in serving certain types of clients. Faith-based/integrated programs were especially effective in working with blacks as measured by program completion, maintaining contacts between staff and clients once the program had ended, and increasing involvement with a religious congregation. They also did better by some outcome measures in working with highly religious clients. All these conclusions are tentative at this point, but they certainly merit further exploration by way of pilot programs and additional research. The fact that the respondents who were themselves involved religiously tended to experience more positive outcomes by most of our outcome measures—when combined with the fact that the highly religious and even the nonreligious clients of faith-based programs tended to evaluate the religious aspects of their programs very positively—suggests that faith may have more potential in welfare-to-work efforts than previously thought. This also suggests that faith-based programs have a niche they could fill in the assortment of welfare-to-work programs now available to those working to move from welfare dependence to economic independence.

These observations form a backdrop for our recommendation for more collaborative welfare-to-work efforts. It is clear from our findings that no one type of welfare-to-work program does equally well at all aspects of helping persons to achieve economic independence or in working with all types of clients. The logical conclusion is that collaborative efforts may be more effective than reliance on any one type of program. Some program types may be best at working with certain clients in terms of race, religiosity, or other characteristics; others may work less well with those same clients. Under a collaborative effort, each program type would work with the type of clients with whom they have the best track record.

Our findings also indicate that some programs—such as government and for-profit programs—may be best at hard-skills training (job training or vocational skills) and enabling persons to find actual jobs, and other programs—such as faith-based/integrated—may be better at developing social capital in their clients and enabling them to maintain employment once they have found an initial job. Each of these program types has its niche. A collaborative effort would take this into account and allow different programs to provide clients with those services it does best. We believe public policy—by way of directed funding, pilot programs, and regulatory changes—should encourage collaborative efforts such as these.

We also think that such collaborative efforts would help to alleviate some of the concerns raised by those who oppose using for-profits to deliver social welfare services. Specifically, many point out that there is an intimate relationship between ownership type and organizational behavior. For-profit firms have to be profitable, which requires them to render services in a particular way and quite possibly to undersupply public goods that are not profitable. If program success is defined solely in terms of profitability, then nonprofits would be compelled to emulate the behavior of private firms and thereby lose sight of their social goals.[3]

In some respects, the results of our study confirm this particular point. As we have noted, for profits did particularly well at providing clients with hard skills and delivering the ultimate outcome of helping their clients to find work, but they fared less well than the faith-based/integrated programs in providing clients with enabling outcomes, such as building up their social capital and helping clients to keep a job once they had found one. If someone mistakenly concluded that the only measure of success that mattered in welfare-to-work programs was their delivery of hard skills, it is quite possible that both the secular and faith-based nonprofit programs would be under some pressure to conform to the model of private firms. Collaborative efforts such as we are recommending would help remove much of this pressure.

What we have tried to make clear, however, is that there should not be a single model of success applied to all welfare-to-work programs. There are various factors involved in helping persons make the transition from unemployment to the world of self-supporting work. Job training and vocational skills are clearly very important, but so too are creating social capital for persons mired in unemployment, changing clients' level of personal optimism, and providing them with the aptitudes necessary to keep a job once they have found one. In short, the different strengths of the program types can be recognized and they should complement one another.

Our fifth public policy recommendation is *for the creation of a pilot program that would be a specific instance of the collaborative efforts we put forward in our fourth recommendation.* We have worked it out in some detail, so that it is clear what we have in mind. We anticipate that at least it will illustrate the sort of innovative approaches to welfare-to-work to which we hope our findings will give birth. We recommend that several local or state governments or a department of the federal government develop a pilot program in several cities that would feature a collaborative venture between for-profit firms and faith-based and community organizations (FBCOs). The FBCOs would provide soft-skills training, mentoring services, and other supportive services; the for-profit firms would provide job-skills training and job search and placement services.

More specifically, under our proposal there would be a division of labor between the FBCOs and the for-profit firms, each doing what our findings indicate they do best. The clients selected for this pilot program would be provided with vouchers and a list of FBCOs in their city that had been authorized to receive the vouchers. The FBCOs would provide the following four services to the clients:

1. *Soft-skills training.* The FBCOs would work with the clients to develop work-appropriate values and attitudes, a healthy sense of

self-esteem or self-worth, attitudes of hopefulness or optimism, a sense of appropriate work-place dress, anger management skills, household budgeting skills, a sense of punctuality, resume writing skills, plans to deal with histories of drug or alcohol abuse or crime convictions when applying for a job, and other such value-related attitudes and behaviors.

2. *Goal setting and goal assessment.* The FBCOs would help the clients to set reasonable, realistic employment goals and help them chart out a career path to reach those goals.

3. *Planning for child care, transportation, and unexpected emergencies.* The FBCOs would help the clients to plan for appropriate child care and transportation options. They would not themselves be responsible for providing either, but would put the clients in touch with community resources, discuss the most appropriate child care options that they have, and consider how transportation needs can best be addressed. Also, because clients receiving welfare assistance often face unexpected emergencies, such as illnesses (in themselves or their children), utility cutoffs, and rent arrears, the FBCOs would work with clients on anticipating and solving such problems.

4. *Maintaining continuing client contact.* The FBCOs would maintain contact with their clients for at least one year once they have completed the initial training. Through staff members, volunteer mentors, and occasional group classes and discussions they would seek to encourage the clients and respond to emergencies or other needs. The clients' social capital would thereby be built up and maintained.

Initially, the FBCOs would provide this training and assistance on a full-time basis over approximately a four-week time period through classes, group discussions, role-playing, peer counseling, one-on-one counseling and mentoring, and other such activities.

Following the four weeks of training by the FBCOs, the program participants would go to a for-profit organization for training in job skills and job search and for placement services. Here the emphasis would be on marketable skills. Exactly what skills would be taught would vary by the local labor market, the desires of the clients, and what the for-profit firms are able to provide. These skills would largely be taught in traditional classroom settings. The length of time the clients would spend in these skills classes would vary by the nature of the skills being taught, but five to ten weeks would be the norm. The for-profit firms would be teaching very basic skills, not highly technical, high-level skills. Reimbursement to the for-profit companies could be via either vouchers or contracts. This training would not have to be given in separate classes, but pilot program clients could be integrated into other, ongoing classes. Following the skills classes, the for-profit firms would provide job placement and job search assistance.

The FBCOs would continue to work with their clients for one year after they begin their job skills classes. While attending the skills classes the clients would continue to meet for a half-day a week with their FCBO for support, discussion, and feedback. After the skills classes end and, hopefully, a job has been found, the FBCOs would meet with their clients weekly by way of mentors and/or staff assigned by each FCBO.

Ideally a large, respected, professionally run faith-based or community-based organization would serve as an intermediary organization between the government and the FBCOs participating in the voucher program. It would recruit and approve the FBCOs to take part in the program, monitor the FBCOs' program standards and performance, and meet governmental reporting requirements.

There are five new or special features of this proposed program, each one of which is rooted in our findings reported in this book. Each of these features and the rationale for them are discussed in the following list:

1. *A collaborative effort between faith-based and community-based programs and for-profit programs.* The most obvious feature of this proposal is a collaborative effort between FBCOs—which would provide soft-skills training, practical and emotional support, and a continuing presence—and for-profits, which would provide training in more concrete, instrumental job skills and help in job search and placement. One of the central findings of our study is that faith-based and other nonprofit organizations seem to excel in treating their clients in a caring, empathic manner. The more integrally religious programs seem to do well in three additional areas: maintaining contacts with their clients once their programs had ended, helping their clients who were already employed to

maintain their jobs, and raising their clients' sense of hope and optimism. Meanwhile, the for-profit firms seem to excel in job-skills training and enabling their clients to find employment. Combining the efforts of FBCOs in soft-skills training and follow-up with the efforts of for-profits in skills training would be playing to the strengths of these two types of entities. Together they may very well be more effective in helping those on welfare attain economic self-sufficiency than either one would do separately.

2. *The use of vouchers to cover the participation of clients in FBCO programs.* Using vouchers would remove First Amendment challenges and concerns and would allow the faith-based programs that are integrally religious to take part in the program. As noted earlier, our research shows that by several measures the integrally religious faith-based programs did better than the other types of programs. Thus taking steps to ensure that the more integrally religious faith-based organizations could take part in the programs would be crucial to its success.

3. *A locally known and respected organization to serve as an intermediary.* This intermediary would relate to and serve as a liaison between the sponsoring governmental agency and the local, small FBCOs. Prior research by one of us has found that many small faith-based and community-based organizations are fearful of partnering with government due to the paper work, unknown regulations, and fears of delayed payments.[4] The use of an intermediary organization that is locally known and respected would do much to allay these fears, thereby encouraging their participation. Also, the government would be relieved of the burden of dealing with a host of small organizations, many of which would not be used to dealing with government and its necessary processes.

4. *Initial soft-skills training and clients' continuing contact with mentors or staff from the FBCOs' programs.* The proposed program would begin with the FBCOs' soft-skills training, but also provide for a continuing relationship between FBCOs' staff or mentors. A number of researchers, as well as many employers, report that the biggest barriers to stable employment are ones of attitudes and self-defeating patterns of behavior, combined with an inability to deal with emergencies when they arise. These seem to be as great a barrier as a simple lack of job skills. Even to succeed in job-skills

training, persons need certain attitudes and patterns of behavior. Often clients need to alter lifelong or even generational attitudes and patterns of behavior. Thus it makes sense to begin with an emphasis on soft skills and realistic goal setting. It also makes sense to maintain contacts with FBCOs' staff, mentors, and fellow program participants during the skills training and subsequent employment. Many have argued that finding employment is much easier than maintaining employment. Thus the support and encouragement of ongoing contacts with the FBCO in whose program one took part and one's fellow participants in that program is crucial. One is building the social capital that most of us take for granted, but that welfare recipients often lack.

5. *The initial pilot programs should be limited to two or three large cities.* Piloting this program in large cities has the advantage of there being a large enough number of FBCOs that the clients would have real choices. Also, most large cities have well-established, locally respected faith-based or community-based organizations that could serve as intermediaries and for-profit firms already active in employment and training programs.

We are convinced that these five public policy recommendations would make a huge difference in the lives of many who are now struggling to escape poverty and dependence on welfare assistance. The recommendations no doubt are not a panacea, but they are rooted in our research findings and would, we are convinced, make a positive difference in the lives of many and, ultimately, in the well-being of society as a whole.

Recommendations for Program Managers

The findings reported in this book have within them implications for the way managers of welfare-to-work and other education and training programs structure and run their programs. In this section we develop what we believe are three crucial ways in which our findings suggest welfare-to-work programs managers could improve the effectiveness of their programs. They may also be relevant to the managers of other types of human service programs.

Our first recommendation for this group is that *program managers recognize, allow for, and make use of the important role religion plays in the lives of many of their clients.* Clearly, religion is important in the lives of a majority of the respondents included in our study. This is not unique to the Los Angles area. In fact, it is likely that this is even more fully the case in large areas of the nation, especially in the South and the Midwest. Managers must be careful how they go about recognizing and making use of this religions dimension in order not to violate church-state norms or the rights of the clients who are not religious. But there is no reason, for example, why purely optional, voluntary activities such as prayer sessions or a Bible study could not be incorporated into government-run, for-profit, and other secular programs. Hiring staff members who have a sympathetic understanding of where many of their clients are coming from religiously is another example of a step that could be taken, as long as one does not demand or favor staff members with certain religious convictions. Seeking staff members who have a sympathetic understanding of religion and a sensitivity to the role religion plays in the lives of many of their clients is different from seeking staff members who personally hold to certain religious beliefs. There may be additional, creative ways program managers can take into account the religiosity of most of their clients in order to improve the effectiveness of their programs.

A second recommendation is for program managers *to borrow successful techniques from other programs.* We think program managers should observe other programs, learn from them, and borrow from them. We observed some of this already being done, but we are convinced much more can and should be done in terms of programs learning and borrowing from each other. In doing so, program managers should not overlook the small faith-based and community-based programs in their area, even if they are small and not as "professional" as their own programs.

In the welfare-to-work programs we studied we found four techniques or practices that we believe are especially worthy of emulation: combining soft- and hard-skills training, fostering client contacts with staff and program participants after the formal program is over, developing mentoring components in programs, and incorporating internships into programs. We mention these four characteristics as examples of what we have in mind in part because they frequently came up in our respondents' answers to open-ended questions probing what they liked about their programs. These also seem to be related to the success that certain types of programs experienced. In the course of our research we often wondered when we observed a successful outcome of a certain program type if that success could best be attributed to that program being of that certain type, or if it could better be attributed to the fact that programs of that type tend to stress one or more of the previously mentioned characteristics. For example, for-profit programs were more successful in their clients' finding employment. Is that due to something inherent in the for-profit programs, or is it due to the fact that both of the for-profit programs we studied had internships as a part of their programs? Similarly, the faith-based programs excelled in their clients' perceiving their staff members as being highly empathic. Is this due to something inherent in faith-based programs, or is it due to the fact that the faith-based programs tend to stress soft-skills training more than the other program types? We suspect that if program managers would do more in terms of learning and borrowing from other programs, their programs could be strengthened. Then, for example, faith-based programs might offer more hard-skills training, and for-profit and government programs more soft-skills training. The for-profit and government programs might more often include a mentoring dimension in their programs or in other ways purposefully seek to build ongoing contacts between their clients and their staff or other program participants, as the faith-based providers now tend to do.

Our third recommendation to program managers is *to work more actively at developing collaborative relationships with other welfare-to-work programs*. This is a counterpart to one of the public policy recommendations we made. Collaborative efforts can be encouraged or even required by public policy; they can also be entered into voluntarily by program managers. We already saw much of this going on during our study and thus this is really not an innovation, but we believe what is already being done can and should be expanded. This goes back to our observation concerning niche effectiveness and the fact that our findings support the proposition that no one program type does everything well and others do everything poorly. All do some things well and other things not so well. When a particular program is not providing a certain service effectively, the usual answer is simply to redouble one's effort and do better. But often there is a history or a tradition that keeps the first agency from doing certain things well. Thus the appropriate answer will often be to form a cooperative relationship with another agency that supplements or complements what the first agency is not doing effectively. Here again it is important for the government, for-profit, and large secular nonprofit programs not to ignore the smaller community-based and faith-based programs just because they are small and perhaps not as "professional" as they are. Program managers of these large, secular agencies need to learn what their smaller, more grassroots counterparts have to offer and take advantage of it.

As with our public policy recommendations, we make these three recommendations for program managers in the hope that they will lead to improvements in the services offered those in the most need.

Recommendations for Researchers

Earlier we identified this as an exploratory, not a definitive, study. And so it is. We were breaking new ground in terms of studying the comparative effectiveness of different types of organizations engaged in providing social services. In particular, it was breaking new ground in our attempts to compare the effectiveness of two types of faith-based organizations and three types of secular organizations. In this section we make five recommendations to others who will engage in similar research in the future.

Our first recommendation is that future researchers *divide, as we did, faith-based programs into those that leave the religious elements largely implicit, or clearly separated from the human services they provide, from those programs that make certain religious elements explicit and integrate them into the services provided.* This proved to be a highly important distinction in our research. This study shows that all faith-based welfare-to-work programs are not the same. Although our two types of welfare-to-work programs were similar in some outcomes and in some other respects, they clearly differed in other outcomes and in other respects. The distinction is an important one, and one we believe future researchers into faith-based social service programs should maintain.

Our second recommendation is that future researchers into program outcome effectiveness *use the same three-way distinction of enabling, intermediate, and ultimate outcomes.* We found this distinction a very fruitful way to organize program outcomes. Doing so helped us to think through the most appropriate ways to measure these different types of outcomes. Also, we found in practice that some programs were more effective in some types of outcomes and less so in others. Based on our experience, we would recommend that future research use the same or similar categories.

We also recommend that future researchers studying social service program effectiveness *use a research design similar to the one we used.* This is our third recommendation. Our research design involved, it will be recalled, selecting a limited number of welfare-to-work programs that by several key characteristics were representative of the larger universe of Los Angeles County welfare-to-work programs. Then we used a panel study design, obtaining baseline data from individual clients taking part in those programs and next conducting telephone interviews with those same clients six and twelve months later. This design worked well and resulted in a wealth of highly relevant data. The responses from both the welfare-to-work programs and the individual clients were good, both in quantity and in quality. As discussed briefly in chapter 2 and developed more fully in appendix A, we have a basis on which to conclude that the responses to our mail questionnaire soliciting information from the Los Angeles welfare-to-work program resulted in a pool of programs similar to all welfare-to-work programs in Los Angeles. The information they gave us enabled us to select seventeen programs that were representative of the five program types into which we had divided our responding programs. The programs and their clients were almost invariably cooperative in the process of obtaining baseline data on the clients. The fact that these baseline data were collected in person by one of the researchers was no doubt helpful in this regard. The follow-up telephone interviews achieved high response rates. The thoughtful comments the respondents made to a number of open-ended questions revealed the seriousness with which they took the questions.

This research design had several advantages over other approaches we might have taken. First, it enabled us to relate individual respondents to changes in employment and welfare status over a twelve-month period. Aggregate data always have the problem of not revealing whether or not apparently stable numbers are perhaps masking movement of individual respondents that are canceling each other out. Official records or data often do not speak to the key questions one is posing. Also, one always wonders about the accuracy of officially reported information. Attempts to exaggerate one's successes and outright errors can all too easily creep in. Second, our approach enabled us to get beyond the mere question of program success or failure to begin to answer the question of why these successes or failures occurred. Third, our method was able to obtain information about "off-the-books" employment and wages. It has been suggested that there is a large underground economy within poor communities that—even when legal—is marked by informal arrangements and cash payments.

Our fourth recommendation is that future researchers *obtain a much larger number of respondents than we were able to do*. We felt that the biggest weakness of our study was the small number of respondents we had in our study by the time we completed our twelve-month interviews. This limited the analyses we could do and reduced the likelihood of finding statistically significant relationships. We felt it was very useful not only to ask which program types were especially effective in terms of which program outcomes but also to ask whether or not respondents with certain characteristics differed in the outcomes they experienced. We did not want to assume that. when it came to welfare-to-work programs, one size would fit all. That is why we looked at the more and the less religiously active clients separately and at the black, Latino, and white clients separately. This was helpful to do, as demonstrated by the differences by religious involvement or by race and ethnicity that we often discovered. But the value of these findings was greatly reduced by the fact that we were working with very small numbers by the time we had made these divisions. A larger number of initial respondents would allow more meaningful distinctions among different types of clients.

Our fifth recommendation is that future researchers *study the effectiveness of different types of human service programs in more areas than Los Angeles*. We were, of course, only dealing with welfare-to-work programs in urban Los Angeles County. A broader, national study would have either confirmed that the patterns we found in Los Angeles hold elsewhere or that they are quite different than those in other cities in other regions. There is no reason to believe that they are unique to the Los Angeles area, but one cannot be sure until this study is replicated elsewhere.

Our hope is twofold as we come to the end of our analysis of the comparative effectiveness of five different types of welfare-to-work programs: that we have shed new, helpful light on a vital question, and that ultimately this study will lead to more effective efforts at helping those among us who are now mired in poverty and welfare dependence. If that happens, many will one day experience fuller, more meaningful lives than they do now and will be able to contribute more fully to their families, communities, and the nation.

APPENDIX A
THE QUESTIONNAIRE SURVEY

This study was, first of all, based on the results of a questionnaire mailed to a comprehensive list of welfare-to-work programs in urban Los Angeles County. If the results of that initial survey were biased or incomplete, the findings of the rest of the study would be suspect. Thus in this appendix we present evidence that has convinced us that our original questionnaire survey of welfare-to-work programs yielded information from welfare-to-work programs that were representative of all Los Angeles welfare-to-work programs. There were two possible sources of bias or incompleteness in this first stage of our study: our original list of welfare-to-work programs to which we mailed our questionnaire could have been incomplete, and the welfare-to-work programs that responded to our questionnaire might not have been representative of the welfare-to-work programs as a whole. We consider here each of these potential problem areas in turn.

Identifying All of the Welfare-to-Work Programs in Los Angeles

Our first step was to develop a comprehensive list of all welfare-to-work programs in urban Los Angeles County to which we could mail our questionnaire. Any program offering welfare recipients one or more of the services listed in question 1 of the questionnaire was considered a welfare-to-work program. (See appendix B for a full copy of the questionnaire.) The initial goal was to identify all of the welfare-to-work programs operating in Los Angeles. Our associate researcher and we spent many hours working on compiling this list. A total of 469 welfare-to-work programs were thereby identified. One means we used both to check on the completeness of the initial list and to add any programs that may have been missed was to ask the questionnaire respondents to give the names and addresses "of three programs or organizations in your area that you know are providing similar services to those that your program provides or other programs that help persons on welfare to improve their economic circumstances." (See question 23 of the questionnaire.)

The returned questionnaires named a total of 163 programs or organizations in response to this question. Of these programs, 121 either were already on our list of welfare-to-work programs or had been eliminated earlier due to our determining that they do not offer the type of welfare-to-work services that were the focus of our study. This left 42 programs named by the responding organizations that were not on our original list of welfare-to-work programs. Questionnaires were also sent to these 42 programs, giving a total of 511 programs to which questionnaires were sent.

This means that 74 percent of the programs named in response to the question asking organizations for names of additional programs similar to their own either were already on our original list of welfare-to-work programs or were programs we had previously determined did not offer welfare-to-work services of the type we were studying. Of the remaining 26 percent, an unknown number no doubt did not provide welfare-to-work services of the type we were researching. Based on this, we concluded that our original list used for mailing out the questionnaires included the vast majority of all the welfare-to-work programs in Los Angeles. Also, of the programs or agencies that were named by two or more respondents, 98 percent were already on our list. This helps to confirm that our original mailing list included nearly all of the programs that were at all significant players in the welfare-to-work field in Los Angeles. If there was any bias in the list of welfare-to-work programs that we compiled, it was in the direction of missing a few very small, not-well-known programs. Since we mailed questionnaires to the 42 programs that were given by our respondents and who were not on our original list, many of the apparently very small, not-well-known programs that were originally missed were also ultimately included in our study.

The Representativeness of the Responding Welfare-to-Work Programs

This leaves the question of whether the welfare-to-work programs that completed our questionnaire were representative of our entire list, or whether a bias was perhaps introduced by those who did or did not respond. As noted earlier, we mailed out a total of 511 questionnaires. We received a total of 211 back, for a very good response rate of 41 percent. Of these, 11 (5 percent) stated that they were not providing at that time any of the welfare-to-work services listed in the questionnaire. This left exactly 200 completed, usable questionnaires.

Our general impression—based on uncounted hours becoming acquainted with Los Angeles' welfare-to-work structure and ferreting out welfare-to-work programs—is that the responding programs were at least roughly representative of all the welfare-to-work programs in Los Angeles. We tested this general impression by checking the zip codes of the responding questionnaires with those of all the programs on our list. Since zip codes, or geographic locations, tend to correspond to characteristics such as racial and ethnic makeup and socioeconomic status, we felt that if the responding programs were representative geographically of all programs receiving the questionnaire, our confidence in the representativeness of the respondents would be significantly increased.

We divided urban Los Angeles County into thirteen neighborhoods based on similar ethnicity and socioeconomic characteristics. (Each of the neighborhoods and the zip codes that made up each one are given in the following paragraph.) Next, we determined the percentage of programs that were on the original list of welfare-to-work programs that fell into each of these neighborhoods, and then determined the percentage of the responding programs that fell into each of these neighborhoods. Then we determined for each of the thirteen neighborhoods the differences between the percentage each neighborhood contributed to the mailing list and the percentage each contributed to the total number of responding programs. The differences ranged from a high of 10.1 percentage points to a low of only 0.2 percentage points, with the average difference proving to be only 3.3 percentage points. These small differences indicated to us that, based on neighborhood or geographic location, the programs that responded to the questionnaire were indeed closely reflective of the 511 programs on the mailing lists.

Following are the zip codes for each of the thirteen neighborhoods into which we divided urban Los Angeles County:

Neighborhood 1: 91311, 91344, 91344, 91306, 91303, 91335, 91406, 91367, 91371, 91411, 91326, 91330, 91324, 91325, 91307, 91364, 91356, 91316, 91436, and 91304.

Neighborhood 2: 91340, 91345, 91331, 91352, 91402, 91405, 91605, 91401, 91606, 91040, 91042, 91505, 91506, 91607, 91423, 91604, 91602, and 91601.

Neighborhood 3: 90042, 91504, 91502, 91208, 91204, 91205, 911101, 91103, 91104, 91105, 91106, 91107, 91780, 91010, 91011, 91214, 91020, 91001, 91501, 91201, 91207, 91202, 91203, 91206, 91024, 91006, 91007, 91775, 91108, 90041, 90065, 90031, 90039, and 91016.

Neighborhood 4: 90045, 90066, 90272, 90049, 90073, 90402, 90403, 90404, 90094, 90293, 90292, 90291, 90025, 90401, and 90405.

Neighborhood 5: 90027, 90064, 90035, 90077, 90210, 90046, 90019, 90068, 90024, 90212, 90211, 90069, 90067, 90036, 90028, and 90048.

Neighborhood 6: 90029, 90038, 90012, 90004, 90026, 90071, 90021, 90010, 90026, 90057, 90006, 90017, 90015, 90020, 90005, 90014, 90013, and 90031.

Neighborhood 7: 91770, 91732, 91733, 91755, 91803, 90063, 90023, 90022, 91030, 90032, 91801, 91776, 90033, 91754, 91755, and 91731.

Neighborhood 8: 91702, 91741, 91711, 91768, 91773, 91750, 91722, 91791, 91723, 91724, 91740, 91767, 91790, and 91706.

Neighborhood 9: 91746, 91748, 91744, 91789, 91792, 91765, 91766, 91745, 90601, 90602, 90603, 90604, 90605, 90606, 90608, 90638, 90670, 90650, 90701, and 90703.

Neighborhood 10: 90034, 90016, 90018, 90007, 90089, 90008, 90230, 90232, 90056, 90043, 90062, 90037, 90301, 90305, 90047, 90044, 90302, 90304, 90303, 90250, 90247, 90248, 90249, 90504, 90506, 90260, 90003, and 90061.

Neighborhood 11: 90011, 90040, 90058, 90640, 90660, 90001, 90255, 90201, 90270, 90240, 90280, 90002, 90241, 90242, 90262, 90059, 90278, 90222,

90220, 90221, 90503, 90710, 90254, 90717, 90732, 90274, 90275, 90732, 90723, and 90706.

Neighborhood 12: 90245, 90266, 90277, 90501, 90502, and 90505.

Neighborhood 13: 90713, 90715, 90716, 90747, 90745, 90810, 90744, 90731, 90804, 90805, 90806, 90807, 90808, 90822, 90814, 90712, 90803, 90813, 90815, and 90802.

APPENDIX B
THE SURVEY INSTRUMENTS

In this appendix we give the four survey instruments used in this study: the initial mailed questionnaire sent to all of the Los Angeles welfare-to-work programs; the initial, baseline questionnaire filled out by clients in the seventeen welfare-to-work programs selected for intensive study; the interview schedule used in the telephone interviews with program clients six months after they had filled out the baseline questionnaire; and the interview schedule used in the telephone interviews with clients twelve months after they had filled out the baseline questionnaire. In order to save space we have made a number of formatting changes and, in the case of the telephone interview schedules, have left out some screening and concluding questions, as well as instructions to those doing the interviewing.

The Initial Mailed Questionnaire

Following is the questionnaire sent to the 511 welfare-to-work programs included in our initial mailed questionnaire.

Questionnaire on Programs to Assist Persons Towards Economic Self-Sufficiency

Introduction: If the organization of which you are a part has more than one program, please answer the following questions in terms of your specific program, not in terms of the entire organization or agency.

Q1. Which of the following services are provided by your program? *Please circle as many as apply.*
1. Job search
2. Education/literary
3. Education/English as a second language
4. Education/GED preparation
5. Education/vocational training, work skills
6. Work preparedness (job interviewing skills, relating to coworkers, appropriate dress, etc.)
7. Life skills (self-esteem, budgeting, etc.)
8. Job placement
9. Job internships/apprenticeships
10. Client assessment
11. Mentoring
12. Other welfare-to-work type services. Please specify.

If your organization or agency does not offer any of the above services or other services that work to help persons move from welfare to economic self-sufficiency, please go to Q24.

Q2. Are the above services offered at only one site or at multiple sites?
    1. One site.
    2. Multiple sites. How many?

Q3. Do different groups of clients normally take part in the different services you offer, or do most clients take advantage of all of the above services?
    1. All/most clients receive the same services.
    2. Different groups of clients receive different services.

Q4. Approximately what percentage of the persons you serve are receiving assistance under TANF or other welfare assistance programs?

Q5. In what year did your program first start offering any of the above services?

Q6. What is the estimated total annual budget for the above services in the current fiscal year?

Q7. Do your current plans call for you to: *Circle only one.*
    1. Expand your services greatly in the next 5 years?
    2. Expand your services somewhat in the next 5 years?
    3. Keep your services at the same size they are now?
    4. Reduce the size of your program?

Q8. If you had the opportunity and resources to do so, would you prefer to: *Circle one.*
    1. Expand your services greatly? *Go to Q9.*
    2. Expand your services somewhat from what they are now? *Go to Q9.*
    3. Even if you could expand your services, you prefer to keep them the same size they are now. *Go to Q8a.*

Q8a. Why don't you wish to expand? *Circle as many as apply.*
    1. We are afraid we would lose our effectiveness.
    2. We are afraid we would lose touch with our community.
    3. We have no physical space where we are now to expand.
    4. All the needs in our community are already being met. No need to expand.
    5. With increased size would come increased headaches and problems.
    6. Other. Please specify.

Q9. Which statement best describes your program? *Circle one.*
    1. A public, government program. *Go to Q13.*
    2. A private, for-profit program. *Go to Q13.*
    3. A private, nonprofit program with no religious base or history. *Go to Q13.*
    4. A private, nonprofit program that at one time had a religious orientation, but today has evolved into a program that is largely secular in nature. *Go to Q12.*

5. A private, nonprofit program that continues to have a clear religious base and orientation. *Go to Q10.*

Q10. If your program has a continuing religious orientation, please indicate its relationship to its religious tradition.

1. It is sponsored and run by a religious congregation.

2. It is sponsored and run by a national denomination or a regional network of congregations.

3. It is sponsored by a religious congregation, but a separate entity has been created to run the program, such as a 501(c)(3).

4. It is sponsored by several local congregations, but is run by a separate entity.

5. It is sponsored by a national denomination or a regional network of congregations, but is run by a separate entity.

6. It is run by a separate entity that is largely supported by individuals, **not** sponsored by a religious congregation or network of congregations.

7. Other. specify.

Q11. If your program has a continuing religious orientation, please indicate which of the following practices characterize your program. *Circle as many as apply.*

1. Placing religious symbols or pictures in the facility where your program is held.

2. Opening or closing sessions with prayer.

3. Using religious values as a guiding motivation for staff in delivering services.

4. Having voluntary religious exercises, such as worship or Bible studies

5. Having required religious exercises, such as worship or Bible studies.

6. Using religious values or motivations to encourage clients to change attitudes or values.

7. Encouraging clients to make personal religious commitments.

8. Giving preference in hiring staff to persons in agreement with your religious orientation.

9. Hiring only staff in agreement with your religious orientation.

10. Giving preference in accepting clients to those in agreement with your religious orientation.

11. Other practices your program engages in that are motivated by your religious orientation. Please specify other practice(s).

Q12. If your program at one time had or continues to have a religious orientation, would you describe that orientation as: *Circle one.*

1. Jewish
2. Roman Catholic
3. Orthodox
4. Protestant denominational. Which denomination?
5. Protestant interdenominational, evangelical

6. Protestant interdenominational, Pentecostal
7. Protestant interdenominational, mainline or liberal
8. Muslim
9. Other. Please specify.

Q13. Which of the following types of government funds (national, state, or local) do you receive? *Circle as many as apply.*
  1. We receive no governmental funds of any kind. *Go to Q14.*
  2. We are a government agency, with all or almost all of our funds from the government. *Go to Q19.*
  3. Federal Department of Labor or HUD funds. *Go to Q15.*
  4. TANF funds. *Go to Q15.*
  5. State government funds. *Go to Q15.*
  6. Local government funds. *Go to Q15.*
  7. Funds for supportive services such as child care or transportation. *Go to Q15.*
  8. Grants of in-kind materials (food, supplies, etc.) *Go to Q15.*
  9. Other types of government funds. Please specify. *Go to Q15.*

Q14. If you receive no government funds, is this due to: *Circle one, then go to Q17.*
  1. A self-conscious policy not to seek government funds?
  2. Your having applied for government funds, but not being awarded any?
  3. Your having made inquiries about government funds, but deciding not to apply?
  4. That is just the way things have worked out.

Q15. Approximately what percentage of your program's total annual budget comes from government funds?

Q16. Which of the following have occurred in your program because you receive government funds? *Circle as many as apply.*
  1. Expanded the number of clients we are able to serve
  2. Hired staff with higher levels of education
  3. Hired staff with stronger qualifications and more experience
  4. Put more time and effort into paper work than should be necessary
  5. Improved our facilities to better serve our clients
  6. Cut down on our religious emphasis or practices
  7. Received fewer private gifts and volunteer hours than we otherwise would
  8. Became more "bureaucratic" and less flexible and creative
  9. Provided services more professionally and effectively
  10. Became less efficient
  11. Other. Please specify.

Q17. Have you had any of the following contacts with government? *Circle as many as apply.*
  1. Government offices have referred clients to us.

2. We have referred clients who had problems with which we could not deal to government offices.

3. We are licensed by a government agency.

4. We have undergone health or safety inspections by the government.

5. We have placed clients in jobs in government offices.

6. We have had informal consultations or exchanges of information with government offices.

7. Other contacts with government agencies or officials. Please specify.

8. We have had no contacts with government offices. *Go to Q19.*

Q18. Generally would you say your contacts with government officials and agencies have been:

1. Very satisfactory.
2. Usually satisfactory.
3. Neither satisfactory nor unsatisfactory.
4. Usually unsatisfactory.
5. Very unsatisfactory.

Q19. Do you attempt to follow the progress of clients after they have completed a program of services?

1. Yes. *Go to Q19b.*
2. No. *Go to Q20.*
3. Yes, for some program of services; No, for other programs of services. *Go to Q19a.*

Q19a. For which programs of services you offer do you attempt to follow the progress of clients who have completed the program of services?

Q19b. How successful are you in keeping track of clients who have completed a program of services?

1. Very successful, we know where most are.
2. Somewhat successful, we know where some are.
3. Not very successful, we only know where a few are.
4. Not at all successful, we don't know where any are.

Q19c. Of those you have been able to follow, how many are: *Circle one on each line.*

1. No better off. Most, Some, Few, None.
2. In an improved economic situation, but still receiving welfare assistance. Most, Some, Few, None.
3. No longer receiving welfare, but still under the poverty line. Most, Some, Few, None.
4. Off welfare and above the poverty line. Most, Some, Few, None.

Q20. Please give me some indication of the size of your program:

a. The approximate number of full-time, paid employees involved in providing services.

b. The approximate number of part-time, paid employees involved in providing services.

c. Of the paid employees (both full- and part-time), approximately how many have: *If none, write in 0.*
1. Less than a high school education?
2. A high school education?
3. Some college education?
4. A college degree?
5. A graduate degree such as a master's in social work?

d. Of the paid employees (both full- and part-time), approximately how many are former clients who are graduates of your program? *If none, please write 0.*

e. What is the approximate number of volunteers in any one month?

f. What was the approximate number of clients you served in the year 2000?

g. What was the approximate percent of the above clients who completed your program during 2000?

h. In 1996, were you offering the same services as you are today, or were you offering different services?
1. Much the same services as today.
2. Quite different services in 1996.
3. We were not in existence in 1996. Go to Q21.

i. In 1996, approximately how many clients did you serve?

Q21. Approximately what percentage of your *paid staff* are: *If none, please write 0.*
1. African American
2. Caucasian
3. Latino
4. Asian American
5. Native American
6. Other. Please specify.

Q22. Approximately what percentage of your clients are: *If none, please write 0.*
1. African American
2. Caucasian
3. Latino
4. Asian American
5. Native American
6. Other. Please specify.

Q23. Please give the names and addresses of three programs or organizations in your area that you know are providing similar services to those that your program provides or other programs that help persons on welfare to improve their economic circumstances.

Q24. I will not use the name of you or your organization or program in any publications, but the following information will tell me you have completed the questionnaire so I can remove your name from the follow-up list and to get back to you for any further information, if I should need to do so.
Name of your program.
Name of the organization sponsoring the program.

Your name.
Phone number where I can reach you.

Q25. Would you like a summary report of the findings from this study?
   1. Yes.
   2. No.

THANK YOU FOR YOUR HELP IN FILLING OUT THIS QUESTIONNAIRE.
If you need additional space to answer any questions or have any other comments about the topic of this questionnaire, please use the remaining pages.

The Initial Baseline Questionnaire

Following is the questionnaire completed by welfare-to-work program clients while they were participating in one of the seventeen welfare-to-work programs included in our study. It was administered in person by one of the researchers and was available in English and Spanish versions.

Pepperdine University
Study of Welfare-to-Work Programs

Q1. First, we would like to know something about yourself:
   a. Name
   b. Address
   c. Telephone number
   d. Since we will be calling you 6 months from now and again 12 months from now, who are two persons who will know how we can reach you in case you move or change your phone number?
   First person who will know how to reach you:
       His or her address; His or her phone number
   Second person who will know how to reach you
       His or her address; His or her phone number
   e. Your date of birth
   f. Your gender: *Please check one.*
       female;   male
   g. Are you: *Please check one.*
   Caucasian (White); African American (Black); Latino; Asian/Pacific Islander American; Native American; Other. Please specify:
   h. Are you: *Please check one.*
   Single; Married; Separated; Divorced; Widowed; Living with a partner

Q2. In terms of religion, are you: *Please check one.*
   Protestant; Catholic; Other Christian; Jewish; Muslim; Something else, Please specify:
   None

Q3. How often do you attend religious services? *Please check one.*
   More than once a week; Once a week; A few times a month; A few times a year; Never

Q4. How well do you read English? *Please check one.*
   I can read almost anything in English with ease; I can read almost anything in English, but it takes me more time than others; Reading English is difficult for me

Q5. What is the primary language spoken at home?

Q6. If your primary language is **NOT** English, how well do you speak English? *Please check one.*

I speak it almost as well as my native language; I speak it well enough to get by in most situations; I speak very little English

Q7. Next, we would like to know about your work experience.

    a. Are you presently employed? yes; no

    b. If you are presently working or have worked in the past, please tell us about the last three jobs you have had: *If you have never worked for pay, please go to the next question.*

Present or most recent job: How long did you have this job? Less than 1 month; 2–3 months; 4–6 months; 7+ months. About how many hours a week did you work: less than 10 hours a week; 10–19 hours a week; 20–29 hours a week; 30+ hours a week. Your pay per hour? Less than $7 an hour; $7–$9 an hour; $10–$14 an hour; $15+ an hour.

Previous job: How long did you have this job? Less than 1 month; 2–3 months; 4–6 months; 7+ months. About how many hours a week did you work: less than 10 hours a week; 10–19 hours a week; 20–29 hours a week; 30+ hours a week. Your pay per hour? Less than $7 an hour; $7–$9 an hour; $10–$14 an hour; $15+ an hour.

Q8. Are you now receiving any welfare assistance? *Please check as many as apply.*

Yes, TANF or CalWORKs assistance. For how long have you been receiving this assistance? less than 1 year; 1–2 years; more than 2 years.

Yes, food stamps. For how long have you been receiving this assistance? less than 1 year; 1–2 years; more than 2 years.

Yes, MediCal. For how long have you been receiving this assistance? less than 1 year; 1–2 years; more than 2 years.

Other type of welfare assistance. What is it? For how long have you been receiving this assistance? less than 1 year; 1–2 years; more than 2 years.

No, I am not now receiving any welfare assistance.

Q9. What is your total family income per month from all sources? (From welfare, wages earned, child support payments, etc.) *Please check one.* up to $400 a month; $400 to $999 a month; $1,000 to $1,500 a month; more than $1,500 a month

Q10. What was the last grade in school you completed? *Please check one.* Did not complete high school; Graduated from high school or have your GED; Some college education; Graduated from college

Q11. How many children do you have living with you who are:

    a. Under 3 years of age? *If none, put 0 down.*

    b. From 4 to 6 years of age? *If none, put 0 down.*

    c. From 7 to 11 years of age? *If none, put 0 down.*

    d. From 12 to 18 years of age? *If none, put 0 down.*

Q12. We have found that there are a number of barriers that have made it difficult for persons to find a good job. Which of the following are barriers that you face? *Please check as many as apply to you.*

I have children, and it is hard to find good, dependable child care.
I have trouble finding transportation to get me to and from work.
I have a past history of alcohol or drug abuse.
I have health problems that sometimes make it hard for me to come to work every day.
I was once convicted of a crime.

Q13. Following are several statements; for each one please indicate whether you agree strongly, agree, are uncertain, disagree, or disagree strongly with it:

    a. Sometimes I get so discouraged it is hard for me to keep going.
    b. No matter how hard I work I doubt I will ever have a really good job.
    c. I am confident one year from now I will be better off than I am now.

THANK YOU VERY MUCH FOR YOUR HELP IN FILLING OUT THIS QUESTIONNAIRE.

The Six-Month Telephone Survey of Clients

Following is the survey instrument we used for calling the welfare-to-work program clients who had completed the initial baseline questionnaire. Only the substantive questions are included here; some introductory, screening, and concluding questions have been eliminated. The interviews were conducted in English or Spanish, as appropriate.

B1. Are you presently employed? That is, are you presently working for pay? Yes; no; don't know; refused.

B1A. Have you had this job for: less than one month? 1–3 months? 4–6 months? Or 7 or more months? Don't know. Refused.

B1B. About how many hours a week do you work? less than 10 hours a week? 10–19 hours a week? 20–29 hours a week? 30 hours or more a week? Don't know. Refused.

B1C. About what is your pay per hour? less than $7 an hour? $7–$9 an hour? $10–$14 an hour? $15 or more an hour? Don't know. Refused.

B2. Are you now receiving any of the following forms of welfare assistance, either for yourself or for your children?

B2A. [Are you receiving] TANF, that is, Temporary Assistance for Needy Families? This is the same as CalWORKs. yes; no; don't know; refused.

B2B. [Are you receiving] food stamps? yes; no; don't know; refused.

B2C. [Are you receiving] MediCal? yes; no; don't know; refused.

B2D. Are you receiving any other type of welfare assistance? yes; no; don't know; refused. What is it? Specify:

B3. About what is your total family income from all sources per month? I'm thinking of all the money your family receives from welfare, wages earned, child support payments, and so forth. Is it: less than $400 a month? $400 to $999 a month? $1,000 to $1,500 a month? more than $1,500 a month? Don't know. Refused.

B4. How many children do you now have living with you? How old is the youngest child? How old is the next youngest child? How old is the next youngest child? [The interviewer asked this question for as many children as there were.]

B5. Do you have any children under 18 years of age who are not living with you? Number of children? How old is the youngest child? How old is the next youngest child? How old is the next youngest child? [The interviewer asked this question for as many children as there were.] Are you helping to support this child financially?

B6. Following are several statements; for each one please indicate whether you agree strongly, agree, are uncertain, disagree, or disagree strongly:

B6A. Sometimes I get so discouraged it is hard for me to keep going. Do you agree strongly, agree, are uncertain, disagree, or disagree strongly?

B6B. No matter how hard I work I doubt I will ever have a really good job. Do you agree strongly, agree, are uncertain, disagree, or disagree strongly?

B6C. I am confident one year from now I will be better off than I am now. Do you agree strongly, agree, are uncertain, disagree, or disagree strongly?

N1P. Now I would like to ask you a few questions about the ———— program at ———— that you were in several months ago.

N1. Were you able to complete the program/class, or did you leave it early?

N1AP. [If left early.] Why was it that you left? Could you tell me more about what was going on in your life then?

N1B. [If still in the program.] Can you tell me when you will complete this program?

N2. Now, I would like to ask you a few questions about the people who were teaching or running ————. I am going to read you some statements describing these people, and I would like you to tell me if the statement was always true, sometimes true, or never true.

N2A. The people running or teaching ———— were people who took an interest in me personally. Would you say that this statement was always true, sometimes true, or never true?

N2B. [The people running or teaching ————] were people knowledgeable about how to help me. Would you say that this statement was always true, sometimes true, or never true?

N2C. [The people running or teaching ————] were people who really cared about my problems. Would you say that this statement was always true, sometimes true, or never true?

N2D. [The people running or teaching ————] were people who understood me and the situation I was in. Would you say that this statement was always true, sometimes true, or never true?

N3. Was ———— helpful to you, somewhat helpful to you, or not at all helpful to you?

N3AP. What was it about the program that was helpful to you?

N3BP. Why do you think the program wasn't helpful? What in particular did you not like about it?

N3C. Was there any way that you think the program could have been improved?

N3CP. How do you think it could have been improved?

[At this point we had intended to ask several questions of those clients in a faith-based program about the faith-based nature of it. Due to some programming confusion, many were not asked these questions, and thus they were included in the twelve-month instrument instead, and we do not include those questions here.]

N6. Now I want to ask you a few questions about the contact you have had with the people who taught or helped to run ———. Since leaving the program, have you had many, few, or no contacts with the people who taught or ran the program?

N6A. How helpful do you think these contacts have been? Have these contacts always been helpful, sometimes been helpful, or have the contacts never been helpful at all?

N7. Now I would like to ask you about the contacts you might have had with the other people who were students or participants in ———.

Since leaving the program, how much contact have you had with the other participants or students? Have you had many contacts, a few, or no contacts with other participants or students?

N7A. How helpful do you think these contacts have been? Have these contacts always been helpful, sometimes been helpful, or have the contacts never been helpful at all?

N8. Finally, I have one other question. In terms of your marital status are you: Single? Married? Separated? Divorced? Widowed? or Living with a partner?

N9P. Are there any comments, ideas, or suggestions you want to share with the people at Pepperdine or the program you participated in? Both Pepperdine and the programs are anxious to hear from you and know your thoughts and feelings about your participation.

THANK YOU FOR TAKING PART IN THIS STUDY. YOUR ANSWERS WILL BE VERY HELPFUL TO US.

The Twelve-Month Telephone Survey of Clients

Following is the survey instrument we used at twelve months for calling the welfare-to-work program clients who had completed the initial baseline questionnaire and taken part in the six-month survey. As with the six-month interview schedule, only the substantive questions are included here; some introductory, screening, and concluding questions have been eliminated. The interviews were conducted in English or Spanish, as appropriate.

B1. Are you presently employed? That is, are you presently working for pay? Yes; no; don't know; refused.

B1A. Have you had this job for: less than one month? 1–3 months? 4–6 months? Or 7 or more months? Don't know. Refused.

B1B. About how many hours a week do you work? less than 10 hours a week? 10–19 hours a week? 20–29 hours a week? 30 hours or more a week? Don't know. Refused.

B1C. About what is your pay per hour? less than $7 an hour? $7–$9 an hour? $10–$14 an hour? $15 or more an hour? Don't know. Refused.

B2. Are you now receiving any of the following forms of welfare assistance, either for yourself or for your children?

B2A. [Are you receiving] TANF, that is, Temporary Assistance for Needy Families? This is the same as CalWORKs. yes; no; don't know; refused.

B2B. [Are you receiving] food stamps? yes; no; don't know; refused.

B2C. [Are you receiving] MediCal? yes; no; don't know; refused.

B2D. Are you receiving any other type of welfare assistance? yes; no; don't know; refused. What is it? Specify:

B3. About what is your total family income from all sources per month? I'm thinking of all the money your family receives from welfare, wages earned, child support payments, and so forth. Is it: less than $400 a month? $400 to $999 a month? $1,000 to $1,500 a month? more than $1,500 a month? Don't know. Refused.

B4. How many children do you now have living with you? How old is the youngest child? How old is the next youngest child? How old is the next youngest child? [The interviewer asked this question for as many children as there were.]

B5. Do you have any children under 18 years of age who are not living with you? How many children are not living with you? How old is the youngest child? How old is the next youngest child? How old is the next youngest child? [The interviewer asked this question for as many children as there were.] Are you helping to support this child financially? yes; no; don't know; refused.

B6. Following are several statements; for each one please indicate whether you agree strongly, agree, are uncertain, disagree, or disagree strongly:

B6A. Sometimes I get so discouraged it is hard for me to keep going. Do you agree strongly, agree, are uncertain, disagree, or disagree strongly?

B6B. No matter how hard I work I doubt I will ever have a really good job. Do you agree strongly, agree, are uncertain, disagree, or disagree strongly?

B6C. I am confident one year from now I will be better off than I am now. Do you agree strongly, agree, are uncertain, disagree, or disagree strongly?

N6. Now I want to ask you a few questions about the contact you have had with the people who taught or helped to run ———. Since leaving the program, have you had many, few, or no contacts with the people who taught or ran the program?

N6A. How helpful do you think these contacts have been? Have these contacts always been helpful, sometimes been helpful, or have the contacts never been helpful at all?

N7. Now I would like to ask you about the contacts you might have had with the other people who were students or participants in ———.

Since leaving the program, how much contact have you had with the other participants or students? Have you had many contacts, a few, or no contacts with other participants or students?

N7A. How helpful do you think these contacts have been? Have these contacts always been helpful, sometimes been helpful, or have the contacts never been helpful at all?

S1. [Asked only of those in a faith-based program.] Now I would like to ask you a few questions about ———, the program at ——— you were in a year ago. ———, the program you were in, is what has been called a faith-based or a religious program. Are you aware that this program was a faith-based program? yes; no; don't know; refused.

S1A. In deciding to take part in this program, did the fact that it had a religious or faith-based aspect to it: Make you more eager to take part in it? Make you less eager to take part in it? Have no effect on your desire to take part in it? Or didn't you know that it had religious or faith-based aspects to it when deciding to take part?

S1B. Can you remember some religious aspects to the program? yes; no; don't know; refused. What were they? Could you describe some for me?

S1C. Now, I am going to read you some statements concerning the religious aspects of ——— and how they made you feel. For each statement, please let me know if you felt it was always true, sometimes true, or never true.

S1C1. The religious aspects of ———— helped me in my efforts to improve myself and prepare to get a good job. Was this always true, sometimes true, or never true?

S1C2. I enjoyed the religious aspects of ————. Was this always true, sometimes true, or never true?

S1C3. The religious aspects of ———— were a waste of time. Was this always true, sometimes true, or never true?

S1C4. The religious aspects of ———— made me feel uncomfortable. Was this always true, sometimes true, or never true?

S2. Now I would like to ask you to recall when you were in the ———— program at ———— about a year ago. At the time a year ago when you were in the ———— program at —— about a year ago, were you employed at that time? That is, were you working for pay at that time? no; yes; don't know; refused.

S2A. About how many hours a week were you working? less than 10 hours a week? 10–19 hours a week? 20–29 hours a week? 30 hours or more a week? Don't know. Refused.

S2B. About what was your pay per hour? less than $7 an hour? $7–$9 an hour? $10–$14 an hour? $15 or more an hour? Don't know. Refused.

S3. Finally, I have one other question. In terms of your marital status are you: Single? Married? Separated? Divorced? Widowed? or Living with a partner?

NEW1. How would you describe your religious affiliation? Are you Protestant, Catholic, another Christian denomination, Jewish, Muslim, something else, or do you not have a religious affiliation?

NEW2. How often do you attend religious services these days? More than once a week; once a week; a few times a month; a few times a year; never; don't know; refused.

THANK YOU FOR TAKING PART IN THIS STUDY.

APPENDIX C
THE FAITH-BASED/SEGMENTED VERSUS FAITH-BASED/INTEGRATED DISTINCTION

The twenty-eight welfare-to-work programs that stated they had a continuing religious orientation were sorted into those with an integrated approach (in which religious elements tend to be explicit and woven into the delivery of services) and those with a segmented approach (in which religious elements tend to be implicit and kept separate from the delivery of services).

This distinction is based on the responses to question 11 in the initial questionnaire that we mailed to the Los Angeles welfare-to-work programs. (See appendix B.) We first assigned the responding programs 1 to 5 points for each religious practice in which they reported engaging. The practices that tended to be separate and distinct from the welfare-to-work services being provided were assigned fewer points, and those that tended to bring religious elements into the services provided were assigned more points. We then divided the programs into integrated and segmented based on the total number of points received. Following are the points that were assigned for each religious practice in which the responding programs indicated they engaged:

- Placing religious symbols or pictures in the facility where your program is held   2
- Opening or closing sessions with prayer   3
- Using religious values as a guiding motivation for staff in delivering services   1
- Having voluntary religious exercises, such as worship or Bible studies   3
- Having required religious exercises, such as worship or Bible studies   5
- Using religious values or motivations to encourage clients to change attitudes or values   5
- Encouraging clients to make personal religious commitments   5
- Giving preference in hiring staff to persons in agreement with your religious orientation   3
- Hiring only staff in agreement with your religious orientation   5
- Giving preference in accepting clients to those in agreement with your religious orientation   4
- Other practices your program engages in that are motivated by your religious orientation   1

Total possible points   **37**

The scores ranged from 0 to 33. The mean score was 10.1 and the median score was 8. Those programs scoring 12 or higher were classified as faith-based/integrated and those scoring 11 or lower were classified as faith-based/ segmented. We chose 12 as the score a program had to attain in order to be classified as integrated because if we had chosen either the mean or median, a program could have qualified for the integrated category simply by engaging in only two of the practices that we had scored as 5s. Setting the cutoff point slightly higher ensured that a program had to engage in at least three of the listed practices in order to be placed in the integrated category.

NOTES

Introduction

1. See Martha Minow, *Partners, Not Rivals: Privatization and the Public Good* (Boston: Beacon Press, 2002), 3.

2. See Peter Dobkin Hall, "Faith, Practice, and Civic Engagement: A Historical Case Study" (paper presented at the 2003 ARNOVA National Conference, Denver, Colorado); Michael Lipsky and Stephen Rathgab Smith, *Nonprofits for Hire* (Cambridge, MA: Harvard University Press, 1993), 47–50; and Stephen V. Monsma, *When Sacred and Secular Mix: Religious Nonprofit Organizations and Public Money* (Lanham, MD: Rowman & Littlefield, 1996), 4–7.

3. Mark Carl Rom, "From Welfare State to Opportunity, Inc.: Public-Private Partnerships in Welfare Reform," in *Public-Private Policy Partnerships*, ed. Pauline Vaillancourt Rosenau (Cambridge, MA: MIT Press, 2000), 166.

4. For an excellent summary of charitable choice (Section 104 of PRWORA) from a supportive perspective, see *A Guide to Charitable Choice: The Rules of Section 104 of the 1996 Federal Welfare Law Governing State Cooperation with Faith-based Social-Service Providers* (Washington, DC: Center for Public Justice and Christian Legal Society's Center for Law and Religious Freedom, 1997).

5. They were the Welfare-to-Work Act (1997), the Community Services Block Grant Program (1998), and the Substance Abuse and Mental Health Service Administration drug treatment program (2000).

6. Anne Farris, Richard P. Nathan, and David J. Wright, *The Expanding Administrative Presidency: George W. Bush and the Faith-based Initiative* (Albany, NY: Roundtable on Religion and Social Welfare Policy, 2004), 5.

7. Ibid., 1.

8. "Grants to Faith-based Organizations, Fiscal Year 2005," March 9, 2006. Available at www.whitehouse.gov/government/fbci/final_report_2005.pdf (accessed March 20, 2006).

9. Quoted in Farris, Nathan, and Wright, *Expanding Administrative Presidency*, 4.

10. "Speech at the AME Convention," July 6, 2004, www.beliefnet.com/story/149/story-14928_1.html (accessed March 27, 2006).

11. Jim Towey, "Next Steps for the President's Faith-Based Initiative" (speech given as a part of the Heritage Foundation Lectures, No. 752 [July 10, 2002]).

12. For especially helpful accounts of the Ten Point Coalition and the resulting "Boston Miracle," see Jenny Berrien, Omar McRoberts, and Christopher Winship, "Religion and the Boston Miracle: The Effect of Black Ministry on Youth Violence," in *Who Will Provide? The Changing Role of Religion in American Social Welfare*, ed. Mary Jo Bane, Brent Coffin, and Ronald Thiemann (Boulder, CO: Westview, 2000), 266–85, and Sasha Polakow-Suransky, "Boston's Ten Point Coalition: A Faith-based Approach to Fighting Crime in the Inner City," *The Responsive Community* 13 (2003):

49–59. The latter essay suggests that the dramatic decrease in Boston homicides was due to a combination of the Ten Point Coalition and other initiatives.

13. Byron R. Johnson, *Objective Hope: Assessing the Effectiveness of Faith-based Organizations: A Review of the Literature* (Philadelphia: Center for Research on Religion and Urban Civil Society, University of Pennsylvania, 2002), 20.

14. Ibid., 17.

15. Partha Deb and Dana Jones, "Does Faith Work? A Preliminary Comparison of Labor Market Outcomes of Job Training Programs," in *Charitable Choice: First Results from Three States,* ed. Sheila Suess Kennedy and Wolfgang Bielefeld (Indianapolis: Center for Urban Policy and the Environment, School of Public and Environmental Affairs, Indiana University-Purdue University Indianapolis, 2003), 57.

16. Rom, "From Welfare State to Opportunity," 173.

17. Melissa M. Stone and Susan Cutcher-Gersenfeld, "Challenges of Measuring Performance in Nonprofit Organizations," in *Measuring the Impact of the Nonprofit Sector,* ed. Patrice Flynn and Virginia A. Hodgkinson (New York: Kluwer Academic/ Plenum, 2001), 39.

Chapter 1

1. Daniel P. Forbes, "Measuring the Unmeasurable: Empirical Studies of Nonprofit Organization Effectiveness from 1977 to 1997," *Nonprofit and Voluntary Sector Quarterly* 27 (1998): 183.

2. Robert Wuthnow, Conrad Hackett, and Becky Yang Hsu, "The Effectiveness and Trustworthiness of Faith-based and Other Service Organizations: A Study of Recipients' Perceptions" (paper given at the Roundtable on Religion and Social Welfare Policy Research Conference, Washington, DC, March 2003), 2.

3. For a good defense of the multidimensional nature of the concept of effectiveness, see Robert D. Herman and David O. Renz, "Theses on Nonprofit Organizational Effectiveness," *Nonprofit and Voluntary Sector Quarterly* 28 (1999): 110–13.

4. Paul DiMaggio, "Measuring the Impact of the Nonprofit Sector on Society Is Probably Impossible but Possibly Useful," in *Measuring the Impact of the Nonprofit Sector,* ed. Flynn and Hodgkinson, 269.

5. Here and throughout the book we preserve the anonymity of the seventeen programs that took part in our study. We did so due to the sensitive nature of the data we gathered and report here and—even more importantly—in order to protect the confidentiality of the programs' participants who took part in our study.

6. Deb and Jones, "Does Faith Work?" 58.

7. Elaine Morley, Elisa Vinson, and Harry P. Hatry, *Outcome Measurement in Nonprofit Organizations: Current Practices and Recommendations* (Washington, DC: Independent Sector and Urban Institute, 2001), 27.

8. Martha Taylor Greenway, "The Emerging Status of Outcome Measurement in the Nonprofit Human Service Sector," in *Measuring the Impact of the Nonprofit Sector,* ed. Flynn and Hodgkinson, 217.

9. DiMaggio, "Measuring the Impact of the Nonprofit Sector," 252.

10. For a brief but helpful discussion of outputs versus outcomes, see Greenway, "Emerging Status of Outcome Measurement," 218.

11. Morley, Vinson, and Hatry, *Outcome Measurement in Nonprofit Organizations,* 11.

12. Greenway, "Emerging Status of Outcome Measurement," 218 (italics removed).

13. Ibid., 225.

14. "Report #2: Touching Lives and Communities," U.S. Department of Labor, Office of the Secretary, Center for Faith-based and Community Initiatives (May 5, 2003), 4–5.

15. See Robert D. Putnam, *Bowling Along: The Collapse and Revival of American Community* (New York: Simon & Schuster, 2000), 22–24. Also see Robert Wuthnow, *Saving America? Faith-based Services and the Future of Civil Society* (Princeton, NJ: Princeton University Press, 2004), 79–84.

16. We do not attempt to cite sources for the various arguments presented here, but they will sound very familiar to anyone acquainted with this debate. They have been made by many persons in many places.

17. See Stephen V. Monsma, *Putting Faith in Partnerships: Welfare-to-Work in Four Cities* (Ann Arbor: University of Michigan Press, 2004), 105–9.

18. See ibid., which found that 96 percent of the large, secular nonprofit welfare-to-work programs received government funding and that they received an average of 76 percent of their budgets from government sources (pp. 138 and 140).

19. See Mark Chaves, "Debunking Charitable Choice," *Stanford Social Innovations Review* 1 (2003): 28–36.

20. See Stone and Cutcher-Gershenfeld, "Challenges of Measuring Performance in Nonprofit Organizations," 44–48.

21. Ibid., 40–43.

22. Patrick Burns, Mark Drayse, Daniel Flaming, and Brent Haydamack, *Prisoners of Hope: Welfare to Work in Los Angeles* (Los Angeles: Economic Roundtable, 2003).

23. Johnson, *Objective Hope,* 7.

24. Ibid., 8.

25. Ibid.

26. Ibid., 13.

27. Ibid., 15.

28. Ibid., 18.

29. Ibid., 19.

30. James S. Coleman, Thomas Hoffer, and Sally Kilgore, *High School Achievement: Public, Catholic, and Private Schools Compared* (New York: Basic Books, 1982), 144.

31. James S. Coleman and Thomas Hoffer, *Public and Private High Schools* (New York: Basic Books, 1987), 213.

32. Paul E. Peterson and William G. Howell, "Voucher Programs and the Effect of Ethnicity on Test Scores," in *Bridging the Achievement Gap,* ed. John E. Chubb and Tom Loveless (Washington, DC: Brookings, 2002), 48. Also see William G. Howell and Paul E. Peterson, *The Education Gap: Vouchers and Urban Schools* (Washington, DC: Brookings, 2002).

33. Peterson and Howell, "Voucher Programs," 53.

34. See Howell and Peterson, *Education Gap,* 36.

35. Aaron Bicknese, "The Teen Challenge Drug Treatment Program in Comparative Perspective" (Ph.D. diss., Northwestern University, 1999).

36. Ibid., 150.

37. Ibid., 172.

38. Ibid., 171–72.

39. Ibid., 163–71.

40. Byron R. Johnson, *The InnerChange Freedom Initiative: A Preliminary Evalu-*

ation of a Faith-based Prison Program (Philadelphia: Center for Research on Religion and Urban Civil Society, University of Pennsylvania, 2003).

41. Ibid., 15.
42. Ibid., 17 and 19.
43. Ibid., 17.
44. See Wuthnow, *Saving America?*, 192–213.
45. Ibid., 207.
46. Ibid., 212.
47. Deb and Jones, "Does Faith Work?," 57–64.
48. The larger study was conducted by a group of researchers at the Center for Urban Policy and the Environment at Indiana University-Purdue University Indianapolis. See Kennedy and Bielefeld, *Charitable Choice*. A book-length report on this study, including a section on the effectiveness study we summarize here, is forthcoming. See Sheila Suess Kennedy and Wolfgang Bielefeld, *Charitable Choice at Work: Evaluating Faith-Based Job Programs in the States* (Washington, DC: Georgetown University Press, 2006).
49. Deb and Jones, "Does Faith Work?" 62.
50. Ibid., 63.
51. Laura Littlepage, Rachel Thelin, Wolfgang Bielefeld, and Brian Sedaca, "Do Faith-based Organizations Transform Their Clients?" in *Faith-based Social Service Provision under Charitable Choice: A Study of Implementation in Three States, Final Results* (Indianapolis: Center for Urban Policy and the Environment, Indiana University-Purdue University Indianapolis, 2003), 62–74.
52. Ibid., 65.
53. Ibid., 67 and 71.
54. Ibid., 68
55. Ibid., 71.
56. Mark Ragan, "Faith-based vs. Secular: Using Administrative Data to Compare the Performance of Faith-affiliated and Other Social Service Providers" (The Roundtable on Religion and Social Welfare Policy, December 2004). Available at www.religionandsocialpolicy.org/docs/research/Benchmarking_report_12-23-04.pdf (accessed March 20, 2006).
57. Ibid., 15.
58. Ibid.
59. Ibid., from the executive summary.
60. Ibid., 25.
61. See ibid., 28.
62. Mark Schlesinger, Mitchell Shannon, and Bradford Gray, "Measuring Community Benefits Provided by Nonprofit and For-Profit HMOs," *Inquiry: Excellus Health Plan* 40 (Summer 2003), 114–31.
63. See Burton A. Weisbrod, "The Nonprofit Mission and Its Financing," in *To Profit or Not to Profit: The Commercial Transformation of the Nonprofit Sector,* ed. Burton A. Weisbrod (Cambridge: Cambridge University Press, 1998), 1–22.
64. Schlesinger, Shannon, and Gray, "Measuring Community Benefits," 127.

Chapter 2

1. Burns, Drayse, Flaming, and Haydamack, *Prisoners of Hope*, 8.
2. Here and throughout this report we use the term *clients* to refer to persons who were taking part in the welfare-to-work programs being studied. Some have

objected to the use of this term on the basis that it implies a passive role for those active in the programs. We found the actual programs studied using a variety of terms: customers, clients, students, participants, and recipients. We decided to use the term *client* for the sake of convenience and because we do not believe the dictionary definition of the term implies passivity. The unabridged *Merriam-Webster Dictionary* gives as the second definition of client "a person who engages the professional advice or services of another." It is in this sense we use this word in our book.

3. The first three stages of the research were part of a wider national study of welfare-to-work programs in Chicago, Dallas, and Philadelphia, as well as Los Angeles. The research being reported here took this earlier study's first three stages further in the case of Los Angeles in order to explore the question of the comparative effectiveness of different types of programs. For reports on the earlier study, see Monsma, *Putting Faith in Partnerships*, and Stephen V. Monsma, *Working Faith: Welfare-to-Work in Four Cities*, (Philadelphia: Center for Research in Religion and Urban Civil Society, the University of Pennsylvania, 2002). Including only urban Los Angeles County meant the northern Santa Clarita and Lancaster-Palmdale and the western Malibu/Agoura areas were excluded. The zip codes that were excluded from our study were 93563, 91342, 91321, 91381, 91355, 91354, 91351, 91350, 93510, 93550, 93543, 93553, 93544, 93591, 93535, 93552, 93534, 93551, 93536, 93532, 91384, 93243, 90265, 90290, 91302, and 91301.

4. See the Working Group on Human Needs and Faith-based and Community Initiatives, *Finding Common Ground: 29 Recommendations of the Working Group on Human Needs and Faith-based and Community Initiatives* (Washington, DC: Search for Common Ground, 2002), 34–37.

5. Virginia Hodgkinson and Murray Weitzman, *Giving and Volunteering in the United States: 1992 Edition* (Washington, DC: Independent Sector, 1992), 25. Cited in David Horton Smith, "The Rest of the Nonprofit Sector: Grassroots Associations as the Dark Matter Ignored in Prevailing 'Flat Earth' Maps of the Sector," *Nonprofit and Voluntary Sector Quarterly* 26 (1997): 115.

6. Our associate researcher was Carolyn Mounts. Ms. Mounts is a M.S.W. graduate of the University of Southern California and has extensive experience in field research, especially with faith-based organizations, in the Los Angeles area. She worked full-time on this current study at the crucial initial list-preparation and data-collection stages.

7. The interviews were conducted by a firm skilled in this sort of telephone survey, ORC Macro. It did a superb job in tracking and interviewing the program clients.

8. On the soft versus hard skills distinction, see Philip Moss and Chris Tilly, *Stories Employers Tell: Race, Skill, and Hiring in America* (New York: Russell Sage Foundation, 2001), 44.

9. This is a pattern that other researchers have found. See Monsma, *Putting Faith in Partnerships*, 102–5; Wolfgang Bielefeld, Laura Littlepage, and Rachel Thelin, "Organizational Analysis: The Influence of Faith on IMPACT Service Providers," in *Charitable Choice*, ed. Kennedy and Bielefeld, 76; William H. Lockhart, "Getting Saved from Poverty: Religion in Poverty-to-Work Programs" (doctoral diss., Department of Sociology, University of Virginia, 2001); and Malcolm L. Goggin and Deborah A. Orth, "How Faith-based and Secular Organizations Tackle Housing for the Homeless" (The Roundtable on Religion and Social Welfare Policy, The Rockefeller Institute of Government, October 2002).

10. The data for the CalWORKs population in Los Angeles come from *Monitor-*

ing the Implementation of CalWORKs: Welfare Reform and Welfare Service Provision in Los Angeles County, 1998 (Los Angeles County Department of Public Social Services). Document can be found at www.ladpss.org/dpss/urd/evaluating_calworks_rpt1.cfm (accessed June 6, 2005).

11. See, for example, Kathryn Edin, Kathleen Mullan Harris, and Gary D. Sandefur, Welfare to Work: Opportunities and Pitfalls (Washington, DC: American Sociological Association, 1998), 23. Also see Daniel Flaming, Patricia Kwon, and Patrick Burns, Running Out of Time: Voices of Parents Struggling to Move from Welfare to Work (Los Angeles: Economic Roundtable, 2002).

12. This compares to a 1999 study of welfare recipients in California that found 39 percent with less than a high school education. See Hans P. Johnson and Sonya M. Tafoya, The Basic Skills of Welfare Recipients: Implications for Reform (San Francisco: Public Policy Institute of California, 1999), 30.

13. See Thomas McCurdy, David C. Mancuso, and Margaret O'Brien-Strain, Does California's Welfare Policy Explain the Slower Decline of Its Caseload? (San Francisco: Public Policy Institute of California, 2002).

14. Burns et al., Prisoners of Hope, 17.

15. Ibid., 20.

Chapter 3

1. A notable and valuable exception is Robert Wuthnow's study of client evaluations of social service agencies from which they had sought help. See Wuthnow, Saving America? chap. 6.

2. We also would have included gender, but with some 85 percent of our respondents being female and only 15 percent male, there would have been too few male respondents to generate valid comparisons.

3. As we pointed out earlier, the number of respondents in some of the cells in this and some of the other tables dealing with race and ethnicity or religiosity is very small. When that is the case, we claim only that our findings are interesting and suggestive. We would not attempt to claim that they are conclusive.

4. See, for example, Kennedy and Bielefeld, Charitable Choice; Monsma, Putting Faith in Partnerships, Amy L. Sherman and John Green, Fruitful Collaborations: A Survey of Government-Funded Faith-based Programs in 15 States (Charlottesville, VA: Hudson Institute, 2002), and Wuthnow, Saving America?

5. We had intended to ask these questions in the six-month survey, but due to a programming error they were asked of only some of the six-month respondents who had been in a faith-based program.

6. Survey research has often demonstrated this to be the case. See, for example, a survey done by Greenberg, Quinlan, Rosner Research, Inc. for the Religion and Ethics News Weekly, April 5, 2004, www.pbs.org/wnet/religionandethics/week733/release.html (accessed March 21, 2006).

7. The third question included in this analysis was the same as the second question included in the analysis presented in table 3.10. What we did was to classify the answers to this question as being positive, negative, or neutral in nature. The positive responses we included in the table 3.10 analysis of open-ended positive responses, and the negative responses we included in the table 3.11 analysis of open-ended negative responses. The neutral comments were not included in either analysis.

Chapter 4

1. Several researchers have found a pattern of explicitly faith-based groups presenting their religious elements in a caring, healing manner, not in a judgmental manner. See Monsma, *Putting Faith in Partnerships*, 115–19; Lockhart, "Getting Saved from Poverty," 27; and Goggin and Orth, "How Faith-Based and Secular Organizations Tackle Housing for the Homeless," 45.

2. First we planned to combine the faith-based/segmented and faith-based/integrated respondents, as the numbers of respondents from these program types are especially small. But then we found that in a number of measures the respondents from these two different types of faith-based programs differed markedly, and thus concluded it would be better to continue to analyze the respondents from the two types of faith-based programs separately. As we warned earlier, any observed patterns with such small numbers in many of the cells must be treated with extreme caution. When dealing with tables with very small numbers in many of the cells, we did not run tests of significance, because statistically significant patterns would clearly not be found in such cases. Nevertheless, we judged it would be better to present what patterns we found rather than not presenting our findings at all or masking what differences there are between the faith-based/segmented and faith-based/integrated clients. At a minimum, doing so will help indicate the questions that future research should explore.

3. It should be noted that of the sixty respondents who had left their programs before completing them and had given a reason for not completing them, 6 (or 10 percent) indicated that they left their programs because they had found jobs. This small number, however, does not materially affect our findings.

4. See, for example, Mark R. Warren, *Dry Bones Rattling: Community Building to Revitalize American Democracy* (Princeton, NJ: Princeton University Press, 2001); and Sidney Verba, Kay Lehman Schlozman, and Henry E. Brady, *Voice and Equality: Civic Participation in American Politics* (Cambridge, MA: Harvard University Press, 1995).

5. One might hypothesize that this could be due to our using somewhat different measures of religious involvement at six months and at twelve months. As noted in table 4.13, at six months we used church attendance as reported at the baseline, and at twelve months—in an attempt to have as current church attendance numbers as possible—we used a combination of reported church attendance at the baseline and at twelve months. But when we used the baseline church attendance numbers at both six and twelve months, we still found the reported staff contacts were higher among the religiously inactive at twelve than at six months.

6. The numbers in table 2.6 are slightly different from those in table 4.16 because table 2.6 included all the respondents in our six-month survey, and table 4.16 included only the respondents in our twelve-month survey.

Chapter 5

1. Here and elsewhere when we had very small numbers in some of the cells of our tables, we faced the question of whether or not to combine the two faith-based programs in order to reduce the number of cells with only a handful of respondents in them. The argument in favor of doing so lies in the fact that when the number

of respondents in a cell is in the single digits any findings approach meaninglessness. On the other hand, we have demonstrated at many points in this book that the faith-based/segmented and faith-based/integrated programs are different and often experience different outcomes. The compromise we reached was usually to combine the two types of faith-based programs when the numbers in the cells are very small and there is no clear pattern of the two program types tending to differ in outcomes. When the respondents from the two faith-based program types showed distinct patterns we either note this fact or present our findings for the two faith-based programs separately even when the numbers are very small.

2. This may be due in part to a political compromise that was reached on the Los Angeles County Board of Supervisors, which restricted for-profit welfare-related programs to the districts of supervisors who were supportive of the county working with for-profit firms. Because a particularly effective supervisor represents much of the predominantly black south central Los Angeles area was opposed to using for-profit firms, this had the effect of for-profit firms largely working in areas other than the predominantly black south central area of Los Angeles.

3. See www.census.gov/hhes/poverty/threshld/thresh02.

4. At the time of our survey, the California minimum wage was $6.75 an hour, which was higher than the federal minimum wage and took precedence.

5. Our logistic regression analyses took into account whether or not a respondent was or was not receiving TANF assistance at six and twelve months. We did not, however, attempt to take into account the employment and wage status of the respondents who were not receiving TANF as we did earlier.

6. See Burton A. Weisbrod and Mark Schlesinger, "Ownership and Regulation in Markets with Asymmetric Information: Theory and Empirical Applications to the Nursing Home Industry," in *The Economics of Nonprofit Institutions: Studies in Structure and Policy*, ed. Susan Rose-Ackerman (New York: Oxford University Press, 1986): 133–51.

7. See R. J. Devereaux, Holger J. Schünemann, Nikila Ravindran, Mohi Bhandari, Amit X. Garg, Peter T.-L. Choi, Brydon J. B. Grant et al., "Comparison of Mortality between Private For-Profit and Private Not-for-Profit Hemodialysis Centers," *Journal of the American Medical Association* 288, no.19 (2002): 2449–57.

8. See, for example, Weisbrod, *To Profit or Not to Profit.*

9. For a study that emphasizes the importance of vocational education and training in order for welfare recipients to obtain employment, see Johnson and Tafoya, *Basic Skills of Welfare Recipients*, esp. 45–47. Also see Burns, Drayse, Flaming, and Haydamack, *Prisoners of Hope.* Based on a study of welfare-to-work efforts in Los Angeles County, the authors conclude in this study that education and training (i.e., hard-skills training) is essential for wage increases.

Chapter 6

1. Stephen Monsma has argued elsewhere that this can be accomplished under the terms of "charitable choice" provisions as contained in the 1996 Personal Responsibility and Work Incentive Reconciliation Act (Welfare Reform). See our description of charitable choice in chapter 1. Also see Monsma, *Putting Faith in Partnerships.*

2. William Galston, "The Role of Faith-based Organizations in the Social Welfare System" (The Roundtable on Religion and Social Welfare Policy Breakout Session: Faith-Based Service Niches, 2003 Spring Research Forum, March 6, 2003), 3.

3. See Burton A. Weisbrod, "The Pitfalls of Profit," *Stanford Social Innovation Review* 2 (Winter 2004): 40–48; Howard A. Tuckman, "Competition, Commercialization, and the Evolution of Nonprofit Organizational Structures," in *To Profit or Not to Profit*, ed. Weisbrod, 25–46.

4. Monsma, *Putting Faith in Partnerships.*

INDEX

Alcoholics Anonymous (AA), 28–29
Association of Gospel Rescue Missions, 3
attitudes
    as barriers to employment, 64–66,
        181–82
    behavioral changes and, 16
    hope and optimism, increases in,
        94–102

Bay City College, 48–49
Bicknese, Aaron, 28–30
bonding capital, 16, 107. *See also* social
    capital
Boston, Massachusetts, Ten Point
    Coalition, 3
bridging capital, 16–17, 107–8. *See also*
    social capital
Brown, Jeffrey, 3
Bush, George W., 2, 29

California
    minimum wage in, 218n.4
    welfare-to-work programs in Los
        Angeles (*see* Los Angeles County
        welfare-to-work programs)
California Work Opportunity and Re-
    sponsibility to Kids program (Cal-
    WORKs), 49–50, 53–54, 56–57, 150
CalWORKs. *See* California Work
    Opportunity and Responsibility to
    Kids program
Catholic Charities, 3, 52
Catholic schools, 26–28
Center for Adult Education, 49–50
Centers for Medicare and Medicaid
    Services, 34
charitable choice, 1–2, 32, 218n.1
child care, 61, 128–29
children, dependent
    chances of escaping from welfare
        dependency and number of, 154–55

employment prospects and number
    of, 134–37
clients of selected programs
    attitudinal barriers to employment
        faced by, 64–66, 181–82
    church attendance of, 58–59 (*see also*
        religious involvement)
    obtaining data from, 44–48, 200–208
    program evaluations by, 67–68, 165–67
    program evaluations by: instrumental
        value, 76–80
    program evaluations by: religious
        elements of faith-based programs,
        80–86
    program evaluations by: staff empathy,
        69–76
    program evaluations by: variation in
        program emphases and responses,
        86–91
    representativeness and differences
        across program types, 55–66
    skills and life-situation barriers to
        employment faced by, 59–64
    types of and program types, variations
        in good matchups between, 76,
        86–92, 169–73
"client," use of the term, 214–15n.2
Clinton, Bill, 2
Coleman, James, 27
collaboration
    proposed pilot program utilizing,
        178–82
    recommendation of, 176–78
    recommendation for program
        managers to utilize, 184–85
Colson, Charles, 29
Community and Senior Services of Los
    Angeles County, 48
Community Skills Center, 54, 63, 114
comparative effectiveness research
    challenges of, 7–13, 37

comparative effectiveness research
(cont.)
conceptualizing effectiveness, 7–8,
13–18
data for, difficulties associated with, 8
human service organizations/
programs, previous efforts
regarding, 21–37
measuring effectiveness, 8–9, 12, 17–18
program clientele, comparison
problems due to variation in, 9–12
program outcomes, categories of, 14–17
recommendations for, 185–88
theory, lack of, 12
types of human service programs,
arguments regarding, 18–21
welfare-to-work programs' effectiveness, conceptualization of, 17–18
welfare-to-work programs in Los
Angeles County (*see* Los Angeles
County welfare-to-work programs)
completion of programs, 102–7
cost-benefit analysis, 7–8, 14
Cutcher-Gershenfeld, Susan, 21

Deb, Partha, 32
DiMaggio, Paul, 8, 12
DPSS. *See* Public Social Services, Los
Angeles County Department of

Eastern One-Stop, 51, 63
economic self-sufficiency, 149–56, 168
education, faith-based *vs.* public, studies
of the effectiveness of, 26–28
effectiveness
agency/organizational and program,
distinction between, 13–14
defining, 7–8, 13–18
of faith-based organizations, beliefs
regarding, 3–4 (*see also* faith-based
nonprofit organizations/programs)
of human service organizations/
programs, previous studies of,
21–37
research studies of (*see* comparative
effectiveness research)
of welfare-to-work programs (*see*
welfare-to-work programs)

Ellis Center, 52
empathy of staff in welfare-to-work
programs, 69–76
employment, finding of full- and part-
time, 128–42
enabling outcomes
church attendance before and after
leaving a program, 120–24
contact with fellow participants after
leaving a program, 114–19, 124
contact with program staff after
leaving a program, 108–14, 123
from different program types,
comparison of, 93–94, 125–26
hope/optimism, increases in, 94–102
measurement of, 46–47
program completion, 102–7
reported in a previous study, 33
social capital, creation of, 107–24
summary conclusions regarding, 166–67
types of for welfare-to-work program
clients, 15–17
ethnicity. *See* race/ethnicity

faith-based and community
organizations (FBCOs), 178–82
faith-based nonprofit organizations/
programs
arguments regarding effectiveness of,
20–21
attitudinal optimism, success in
promoting, 95–102
beliefs regarding effectiveness of, 3–4
client contact with fellow participants
after leaving, 115–19, 124
client contact with staff after leaving,
108–14, 123
client's church attendance before and
after participating in, 120–23
completion of, 103–7
economic self-sufficiency,
effectiveness in helping clients to
achieve, 150–55
effectiveness of, summary conclusions
regarding, 165–71
effectiveness of employment/job
training programs, previous studies
of, 32–33

effectiveness of *vs.* secular organizations/programs, previous studies regarding, 22–33
emphases of, 86–91
employment, effectiveness in helping clients to find, 129–42
enabling outcomes, conclusions regarding, 125–26
government, fears of partnering with, 181
instrumental value of, 76–80
integrated *vs.* faith-saturated, distinction between, 41
integrated *vs.* segmented, distinction between, 40–41, 185, 209–10, 217–18n.1, 217n.2
integrated welfare-to-work programs in Los Angeles County provided by, 53–55
intermediate and ultimate outcomes from, effectiveness regarding, 157–58, 161–62
percentage of all welfare-to-work programs in Los Angeles County provided by, 41–43
public policy recommendations regarding, 174–82
public-private partnerships, increasing participation in, 1–3
religious elements of, 80–86
religiously active clients and, 169–71
research studies of the effectiveness of (*see* comparative effectiveness research)
segmented welfare-to-work programs in Los Angeles County provided by, 52–53
staff empathy in, 69–71, 75
wages, effectiveness in helping clients to find jobs with adequate, 143–49
welfare-to-work programs in Los Angeles County, employees and volunteers in, 42–44
faith-saturated programs, 41
FBCOs. *See* faith-based and community organizations
First Amendment, 175, 181
Forbes, Daniel, 7

for-profit welfare-to-work programs
attitudinal optimism, success in promoting, 95–97, 102
client contact with fellow participants after leaving, 115–18
client contact with staff after leaving, 109–14
client's church attendance before and after participating in, 120–23
completion of, 103–7
controversy surrounding, 159, 177
economic self-sufficiency, effectiveness in helping clients to achieve, 150–55
effectiveness of, arguments regarding, 19–20
effectiveness of, summary conclusions regarding, 165–71
effectiveness of *vs.* nonprofit programs, previous studies regarding, 33–37
emphases of, 86–91
employment, effectiveness in helping clients to find, 128–42
enabling outcomes from, conclusions regarding, 125–26
instrumental value of, 76–79
intermediate and ultimate outcomes from, effectiveness regarding, 156–61
in Los Angeles County, 50–51, 218n.2 (*see also* clients of selected programs; Los Angeles County welfare-to-work programs)
percentage of all welfare-to-work programs in Los Angeles County provided by, 41–43
public policy recommendations regarding, 174–81
recommendations for program managers, 182–85
staff empathy in, 69–71, 75
wages, effectiveness in helping clients to find jobs with adequate, 144–49

Galston, William, 176
gender
chances of escaping from welfare dependency and, 153–55

gender (cont.)
difficulties of including in the
analysis, 216n.2
employment prospects and, 134–37
Gore, Al, 2
government welfare-to-work programs
attitudinal optimism, success in
promoting, 95–97, 102
client contact with fellow participants
after leaving, 115–18, 124
client contact with staff after leaving,
108–14
client's church attendance before and
after participating in, 120–23
completion of, 103–7
economic self-sufficiency,
effectiveness in helping clients to
achieve, 150–55
effectiveness of, arguments regarding,
18–19
effectiveness of, summary conclusions
regarding, 165–71
emphases of, 86–91
employment, effectiveness in helping
clients to find, 129–42
enabling outcomes from, conclusions
regarding, 125–26
instrumental value of, 76–79
intermediate and ultimate outcomes
from, effectiveness regarding,
157–58, 162
in Los Angeles County, 48–50 (see also
clients of selected programs; Los
Angeles County welfare-to-work
programs)
percentage of all welfare-to-work programs in Los Angeles County, 41–43
public policy recommendations
regarding, 174–77
recommendations for program
managers, 182–85
staff empathy in Los Angeles County,
69–71, 74–75
wages, effectiveness in helping clients
to find jobs with adequate, 144–49
Greenway, Martha, 12, 14

'at for Humanity, 3
ond, Ray, 3

Health and Human Services, U.S.
Department of (HHS), 2, 34
health maintenance organizations
(HMOs), 35–36, 159
HHS. See Health and Human Services,
U.S. Department of
HMOs. See health maintenance
organizations
Hodgkinson, Virginia, 43
Housing and Urban Development, U.S.
Department of (HUD), 2
Howell, William, 68
HUD. See Housing and Urban
Development, U.S. Department of

IFI. See InnerChange Freedom Initiative
InnerChange Freedom Initiative (IFI),
29–30
intentional religion, 23
intermediate outcomes
consideration of, 127
effectiveness of programs regarding,
summary observations of, 156–63
full- and part-time employment,
128–42
measurement of, 46
summary conclusions regarding, 167–69
wage levels, 142–49
of welfare-to-work programs,
conceptualization of, 14–15

job retention, 132–33
Johnson, Byron, 3–4, 22–26, 29–30, 71
Jones, Dana, 32

Kerry, John, 2

Labor, U.S. Department of, 51–52
life-situation barriers to employment,
60–64
Lockheed Martin IMS, 1, 19
Los Angeles County welfare-to-work
programs
anonymity of programs selected for intensive study, preservation of, 212n.5
basic information regarding, use of questionnaires to obtain, 39–40, 189–99
classification of, 40–44
clients and programs, variation in and

impact of different combinations of characteristics, 76, 86–92, 169–73
clients of programs selected for intensive study (*see* clients of selected programs)
different programs for different clients, need for, 91–92
economic conditions during the study period, 47–48
effectiveness of, conceptualization of, 17–18
effectiveness of, summary conclusions regarding, 165–71
employees and volunteers in, 42–44
evaluation of by clients (*see* clients of selected programs)
faith-based/integrated programs selected for intensive study, 53–55
faith-based/segmented programs selected for intensive study, 52–53
for-profit programs selected for intensive study, 50–51
government programs selected for intensive study, 48–50
identification of all, 39, 189–90
identification of programs for intensive study, 44
nonprofit/secular programs selected for intensive study, 51–52
providers, local contractors as, 19
representativeness of the programs selected for intensive study, 56, 190–92
research design, 39–48, 186–87
staff empathy in, 69–76
studying the effectiveness of, 4–5, 12–13, 38 (*see also* comparative effectiveness research)
variation in program emphases, 86–91
"work first" approaches, 22
See also welfare-to-work programs
Los Angeles Unified School District, 49–53
Love and Life Center, 53
Lutheran Services in America (LSA), 3–4

marital status
chances of escaping from welfare dependency and, 154–55
employment prospects and, 134–37

Maximus, 1, 19
minimum wage in California, 218n.4
Minow, Martha, 1
Monsma, Stephen, 218n.1
Mounts, Carolyn, 215n.6

New Beginnings Center, 52
New Hope Services, 54–55
New Skills Center, 53–54
niche effectiveness, 176, 184
nonprofit organizations/programs
effectiveness of faith-based *vs.* secular, previous studies regarding, 22–33
effectiveness of *vs.* for-profit firms, previous studies regarding, 33–37
faith-based (*see* faith-based nonprofit organizations/programs)
measuring the impact of efforts by, difficulties of, 12
research studies of the effectiveness of (*see* comparative effectiveness research)
secular (*see* secular nonprofit welfare-to-work programs)

Olsen Center, 53
Opportunity-for-All, 51
optimism, attitudinal, 94–102
ORC Macro, 215n.7
organic religion, 22–23
Our Father's House, 52–53
outcomes
categories of, 14–17, 185–86 (*see also* enabling outcomes; intermediate outcomes; ultimate outcomes)
definition of program, 14
measurement of, 46–48
summary conclusions regarding, 165–71

People-at-Work, 50
Personal Responsibility and Work Opportunity Reconciliation Act of 1996 (PRWORA), charitable choice provision, 1–2, 32, 218n.1
Peterson, Paul, 68
pilot program, proposal for, 178–82
poverty threshold, 143
Prison Fellowship, 29

profit
    efficiency and, 19
    for-profit welfare-to-work programs
        (see for-profit welfare-to-work
        programs)
    program managers, recommendations
        for, 182–85
PRWORA. See Personal Responsibility
    and Work Opportunity
    Reconciliation Act of 1996
public policy recommendations, 171,
    174–82
public–private partnerships, 1–3
Public Social Services, Los Angeles
    County Department of (DPSS),
    49–51, 53
Putnam, Robert, 16

race/ethnicity
    attitudinal optimism and, 101–2
    chances of escaping from welfare
        dependency and, 153–57
    client contact with fellow participants
        after leaving a program, impact on,
        119, 124
    client contact with program staff after
        leaving a program, impact on, 114
    client evaluations of program
        instrumental value and, 79
    client evaluations of programs and,
        68, 91
    client evaluations of program staff
        empathy and, 73–74
    client's church attendance before
        and after leaving a program, impact
        on, 123
    decision to participate in a faith-based
        program and, 81–82, 84–85
    employment prospects and, 134–37,
        141–42
    intermediate and ultimate outcomes,
        impact on achieving, 160, 162, 171
    program completion, impact on, 106
    religious involvement, program
        outcomes, and, 172–73
    wages, impact on efforts to find jobs
        with adequate, 149
    n, Mark, 34–35
        a assignment model, 9–11

religion
    faith-based schools, effectiveness of,
        26–28
    in faith-based welfare-to-work pro-
        grams, client evaluations of, 80–86
    organic and intentional, distinction
        between, 22–23
    See also faith-based nonprofit
        organizations/programs
religious involvement
    attitudinal optimism, impact on
        improvements in, 98–101
    client contact with fellow participants
        after leaving a program, impact on,
        117–19, 124
    client contact with program staff after
        leaving a program, impact on, 110,
        112–14, 123
    client evaluations of program
        instrumental value and, 78–80
    client evaluations of programs and,
        68, 91
    client evaluations of program staff
        empathy and, 71–73
    client's church attendance, 58–59,
        120–24
    decision to participate in a faith-based
        program, impact on, 81, 84
    desirable social characteristics and,
        23–24
    effectiveness of in human services
        programs, 24–26
    employment, impact on efforts to find,
        138–41
    intermediate and ultimate outcomes,
        impact on achieving, 160, 162
    program completion, impact on,
        103–6
    program type and effectiveness related
        to client, 169–71
    recommendation that program
        managers make use of, 183
    wages, impact on efforts to find jobs
        with adequate, 149
    welfare dependency and, chances of
        escaping from, 154–56
Responsible Fathers, 48, 55
Rivers, Eugene, 3
Rom, Mark Carl, 4

Salvation Army, 3–4
schools, faith-based vs. public, 26–28
secular nonprofit welfare-to-work
  programs
  attitudinal optimism, success at
    promoting, 95–97, 102
  client contact with fellow participants
    after leaving, 115–19
  client contact with staff after leaving,
    109–14
  client's church attendance before and
    after participating in, 120–23
  completion of, 103–6
  economic self-sufficiency,
    effectiveness in helping clients to
    achieve, 150–55
  effectiveness of, arguments regarding,
    20–21
  effectiveness of, summary conclusions
    regarding, 165–71
  emphases of, 86–91
  employment, effectiveness in helping
    clients to find, 128–42
  enabling outcomes, conclusions
    regarding, 125–26
  government funding of, 213n.18
  instrumental value of, 77–79
  intermediate and ultimate outcomes,
    effectiveness in helping clients to
    achieve, 157–59, 162
  in Los Angeles County, 51–52 (see also
    clients of selected programs; Los
    Angeles County welfare-to-work
    programs)
  public policy recommendations
    regarding, 174–76
  recommendations for program
    managers, 182–85
  staff empathy in, 69–71, 75
  wages, effectiveness in helping
    clients to find jobs with adequate,
    143–49
skills
  barriers to employment, lack of as,
    59–64
  chances of escaping from welfare
    dependency and, 154–55
  hard vs. soft and client evaluation of
    programs, 86–92

hard vs. soft and effectiveness of
  programs, 132–33, 168
proposed pilot program combining
  training in hard- and soft-, 178–82
social capital
  bridging and bonding distinguished,
    16–17, 107
  church attendance before and after
    leaving the program, 120–24
  contact with fellow participants after
    leaving the program, 124
  contact with program staff after
    leaving the program, 108–14, 123
  creation of by welfare-to-work
    programs, 107–24
  enabling outcome, as a type of, 16–17
Stone, Melissa, 21
Suburban Community College, 49

TANF. See Temporary Assistance for
  Needy Families
Teen Challenge, 26, 28–30
Temporary Assistance for Needy
  Families (TANF), 38, 52, 97, 150–57,
  160–61. See also California Work
  Opportunity and Responsibility to
  Kids program (CalWORKs)
Ten Point Coalition, 3
Together-We-Win, 51–52, 114
Towey, Jim, 3

ultimate outcomes
  consideration of, 127
  economic self-sufficiency, 149–56
  effectiveness of programs regarding,
    summary observations of, 156–63
  measurement of, 46
  summary conclusions regarding, 167–69
  of welfare-to-work programs,
    conceptualization of, 14–15
unemployment
  impact on client's efforts to find
    employment, 128–29, 134–37, 160–
    61, 168
  impact on client's wages in subsequent
    employment, 145, 147–48
  rate in Los Angeles during the study
    period, 47–48
United Jewish Communities, 3

vocational skills, 15–16
vouchers, 178, 181

wages, 142–49
Weitzman, Murray, 43
welfare reform. *See* Personal Responsibility and Work Opportunity Reconciliation Act of 1996
welfare-to-work programs
  collaborative, encouragement of, 176–82
  definition of, 39
  difficulties of evaluating, 164
  in Los Angeles County (*see* Los Angeles County welfare-to-work programs)
  outcomes of, categories of, 14–17 (*see also* outcomes)
  program managers, recommendations for, 182–85
  public policy recommendations regarding, 171, 174–82
  study of effectiveness of, 4–5, 12–13 (*see also* comparative effectiveness research)
Western College, 50–51
White House Office of Faith-Based and Community Initiatives, 2
Work Investment Act, 51
Wuthnow, Robert, 7, 31, 216n.1